PRENTICE HALL INTERNATIONAL

Language Teaching Methodology Series

Applied Linguistics

General Editor: Christopher N. Candlin

ESP Today: A Practitioner's Guide

Other titles in this series include:

ESP Today:
A Practitioner's Guide

PAULINE C. ROBINSON

Centre for Applied Language Studies
University of Reading

ENGLISH LANGUAGE TEACHING

Prentice Hall

New York London Toronto Sydney Tokyo Singapore

First published 1991 by
Prentice Hall International (UK) Ltd
66 Wood Lane End, Hemel Hempstead
Hertfordshire HP2 4RG
A division of
Simon & Schuster International Group

Typeset in 10/12pt Times
by MHL Typesetting Ltd, Coventry

Printed and bound in Great Britain
by Dotesios Limited, Trowbridge

Library of Congress Cataloging-in-Publication Data

Robinson, Pauline C.
  ESP today: a practitioner's guide/Pauline C. Robinson.
    p.   cm.—(Language teaching methodology series) (English
  language teaching)
    "First published 1991 by Prentice Hall International (UK) Ltd.
  Hemel Hempstead, Hertfordshire"—T.p. verso.
    Includes bibliographical references and index.
    ISBN 0-13-284084-7
    1. English language—Study and teaching—Foreign speakers.
I. Title. II. Series. III. Series: English language teaching.
PE1128.A2R584 1991
                                                   91-30-192
                                                        CIP

British Library Cataloguing in Publication Data

Robinson, Pauline
  ESP today: a practitioner's guide.
  I. Title
  428

  ISBN 0-13-284084-7

---

1 2 3 4 5 94 93 92 91

This book is dedicated to all the CALS MA TEFL students who have participated in the ESP option

Contents

Preface

I suspect that there will not be many teachers of ESP who missed the opportunity to buy Pauline Robinson's original book on the topic, which was published in 1980. For many, it will be a classic on their shelves, offering in one place at that time unmatched coverage of the publications and research of a rapidly developing field.

This new contribution to the Language Teaching Methodology Series is not, however, merely an updating of the record in the last ten years, useful though that would have been. Pauline Robinson's purpose is much broader; effectively to address three issues and challenges that have arisen within the field, examining critically not only what is the content of ESP but also what are its characteristic processes of teaching and learning, secondly, to indicate and reference the breadth of ESP as a major discipline in English Language Teaching, and thirdly, to emphasise the importance of the research and practice of ESP for the general language teacher.

As the book amply illustrates, there are a variety of issues and challenges to explore. She identifies some of them very clearly: the highlighting of the surface features of special purpose language on underlying rhetorical structures — what we might call a focus on *text*; the contrasts between a focus on the 'ends-needs' and the 'means-needs' of the learner — what we might call a focus on *task*; the location of ESP teaching in the language classroom or in the work- or study-place — the focus on *place*; and the ESP teacher seen as service provider or as collaborator with the specialist subject-matter teacher or workplace supervisor — the focus on *role*.

ESP Today achieves these first two purposes; it offers explanatory reference but it also presents challanges for seminar discussion within professional in-service development. Pauline Robinson has very expertly organised her material so that, as the issues are explored, readers come to know the major research and materials publications which illustrate the issues in question. Cumulatively, readers obtain an account of available resources but they are also confronted with curriculum design and delivery problems which need local debate. In a way, the book offers a new genre for language teachers, both compendium and in-service course, and I hope that it will find a ready readership.

There is more to the book, however, than its focus on ESP. Her third purpose addresses the issue of ESP not only as a specialist discipline but also as part of the larger world of language teaching and learning. In its purposefulness and in its characteristic learner-centredness, ESP serves to highlight and problematise more generally current issues in the language curriculum. In this sense, *ESP Today* is a book for all teachers of language not just the specialist cadre of ESP teachers. Indeed, about fifteen years ago now I asked why the requirements of ESP ought not to be requirements of language teaching and learning in general. The question still holds true as ESP serves to set in relief issues that concern us all. We are all special purpose teachers and special purpose learners.

Professor Christopher N. Candlin
General Editor
National Centre for English Language Teaching & Research
Macquarie University
Sydney

Acknowledgements

A number of people have helped me with this book, which has been a great deal longer in the making than I anticipated or would have wished. First of all, I would like to thank David Haines and Chris Candlin for their great patience and tolerance. I would like to thank Chris, additionally, for all his many useful suggestions and invaluable references. Several people kindly gave me their time, advice and materials: Moya Brennan, Caroline Clapham, Betty Lou Dubois, Ann Johns and John Swales. My colleagues Margaret Matthews, Gill Sturtridge, Alan Tonkyn, John Trzeciak and Ron White read parts of the manuscript, making many excellent suggestions for revisions and additions. I would also like to acknowledge the courteous help and advice of the staff, in particular Dorothy Farrell, at the ESP Reference Collection at the Language Studies Unit, the University of Aston in Birmingham. Additionally, I must thank Helen Hathaway, librarian at the Centre for Applied Language Studies, University of Reading, for her help in finding many of the things I needed.

Finally, I would like to thank the British Council for involving me in a number of ESP projects, which have given me much useful experience and material. In particular, I am grateful for involvement in the Nigerian COMSKIP (Communication skills in English) Project (1988–91) and the Second Latin American Colloquium in ESP, held in Santiago de Chile, November 1990.

All the many errors and omissions which undoubtedly remain are entirely my own responsibility.

Abbreviations used in this book

EAP   English for academic purposes
EGP   English for general purposes
ELT   English language teaching
EOP   English for occupational purposes
EPP   English for professional purposes
ESL   English as a second language
ESP   English for specific purposes
EST   English for science and technology
EVP   English for vocational purposes
IL   Interlanguage
L1   First language
L2   Second language
LAC   Language across the curriculum
LGP   Language for general purposes
LSP   Language for specific purposes
TESOL   Teaching English to speakers of other languages
TESP   Teaching English for specific purposes
VESL   Vocational English as a second language

A note on the referencing system

The references in this book have been classified into ten sections. Section (A) consists of general books, which present an overview of ESP or which comprise collections of articles, and journals which are largely or entirely devoted to ESP. The other sections relate to the chapters of the book. Thus section (B) (Needs analysis) relates to Chapter Two and so on. In the text, the parenthetical reference numbers refer to the consecutive number assigned to each item in the bibliography.

Chapter One

Introduction

ESP today

The ESP enterprise

ESP is a major activity around the world today. It is an enterprise involving education, training and practice, and drawing upon three major realms of knowledge: language, pedagogy and the students'/participants' specialist areas of interest.

This book is addressed to teachers and would-be teachers of ESP. Because ESP teachers generally have a great variety of often simultaneous roles — as researchers, course designers, materials writers, testers, evaluators, as well as classroom teachers — the term ESP practitioner will generally be used.

ESP practitioners need training in ways of describing language, training in teaching language and training in designing language courses. In addition, and unlike those involved in EGP (English for general purposes), they need some knowledge of, or at least access to information on, whatever it is that students are professionally involved with, for example economics, physics, nursing, catering. Authentic materials (for example texts, recorded discussions, interviews, lectures) may be needed from these work or study situations to be developed as classroom materials. Thus ESP may be seen as dependent for its successful implementation on help and materials from specialists in many other areas of professional activity.

ESP may be seen as pluralistic, because many approaches to it are concurrently being followed around the world today. The full form of 'ESP' is generally given as 'English for specific purposes', and this would imply that what is specific and appropriate in one part of the globe may well not be elsewhere. Thus it is impossible to produce a universally applicable definition of ESP. Strevens (30, p. 109) suggests that 'a definition of ESP that is both simple and watertight is not easy to produce' and Hutchinson and Waters (15, pp. 18—19) prefer to say what ESP is *not*.

ESP is protean, as it is responsive to developments in all three realms of language, pedagogy and content studies. Changing interpretations of ESP over the years and in different parts of the world represent changing relationships between, and changing fashions in, these three realms of knowledge. Continental European studies in ESP, for example, have seemed relatively unconcerned with pedagogy but very active in aspects of language description. The pedagogy of ESP has always been important in Britain and North America, however, with Britain taking the lead in matters of syllabus and course design, practitioners in the USA and in Canada leading the way in matters of classroom-based practice and research (see the discussion in Swales (322, pp. 79–83)). Currently, I would suggest, there is a greater interest in the content with which ESP must be involved — the subject matter which ESP students have to study and work with through English. Content-based approaches to language teaching seem to be more discussed now, and not just in North America, where they have been most developed (see, for example, Tickoo (34)). If we consider the current focus in language description in Britain and the USA — genre analysis — then that too involves some engagement with content (and its institutional context) in a way that other approaches to language description have not.

Types of ESP

There are many types of ESP and many acronyms. Figures 1 and 2 show two versions of the 'ESP family tree'. A major distinction is often drawn between EOP (English for occupational purposes), involving work-related needs and training, and EAP (English for academic purposes), involving academic study needs. Cutting across these is EST (English for science and technology), mainly used for ESP work in the USA (especially the pioneering work of Selinker *et al.* (212)), which can refer to both work- and study-related needs.

A further important distinction must be made between those students who are newcomers to their field of work or study and those who are already expert (or on the way to becoming so), perhaps via the medium of their own language. This distinction, as Strevens (608, pp. 139–40) notes, 'is between English which is instructional and English which is operational'. Students who are newcomers to their field may need some instruction in the concepts and practices of that field. Experienced students 'require operational ESP materials, where the knowledge, the concepts, the instruction and the training are taken for granted, and where it is the ability to function in English which is being imparted'. Each situation has implications for the kind of content knowledge which the ESP teacher may need to deploy and for the degree of generality or specificity of the ESP course.

What is criterial to ESP?

A number of features are often thought of as criterial to ESP courses, but at the same time it is not uncommon to find courses which the organisers wish to think of as ESP courses but which do not appear to fit these criteria.

First, ESP is normally goal directed. That is, students study English not because they are interested in the English language (or English-language culture) as such but because they need English for study or work purposes. This has implications for the kind of activities and topics on the course. However, we should not assume that all students have chosen their work or study area. Students may wish to have practice

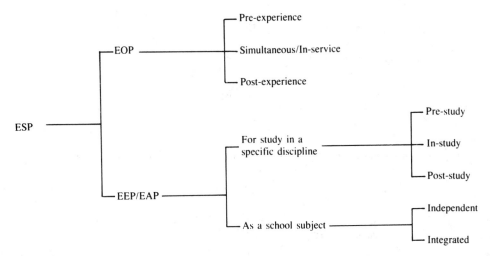

FIGURE 1   *The ESP 'family tree'.*

with general topics and activities, in addition to those shown to be relevant for their work or specialist study.

Second, an ESP course is based on a needs analysis, which aims to specify as closely as possible what exactly it is that students have to do through the medium of English. There are various approaches to needs analysis (see Chapter Two). Whereas needs analysis formerly focused rather exclusively on target or end-of-course requirements, now it is usual to take account of students' initial needs, including learning needs.

Other features of ESP courses may be seen as characteristics rather than criteria since they do not always apply, although they might be seen as corollaries of the two criteria described above. First, there is usually a very clearly specified time period for the course. This means that objectives should be closely specified and their realisation related to the time available. This implies collaboration and negotiation among all those involved with the course: organisers, teachers, sponsors and students.

Next, the students on an ESP course are likely to be adults rather than children. In some countries certainly, for example Egypt, there are vocational secondary schools where ESP rather than EGP is taught. In other countries there may be bilingual schools, for example in Germany, or English-medium secondary schools, for example in Turkey, where English and a content subject are taught together. More frequently, however, the students on ESP courses are in tertiary education or are experienced members of the workforce. A developing area, especially in the USA and Australia, is that of migrant education, involving language and work training for immigrants, who may already have many years of work experience behind them. In Europe, increasing activity is being devoted to equipping qualified workers to operate in more than one European Community language. It is often assumed that ESP students will not be beginners but will have already studied EGP for some years. However, ESP can certainly be taught to students who are beginning their study of the language (see the discussion on pages 22–3).

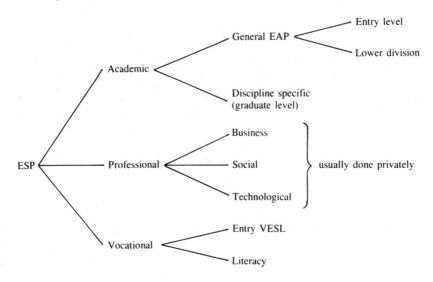

FIGURE 2   *ESP in the USA (Source: Johns (17)).*

Finally, ESP courses may be written about as though they consist of identical students, that is, that all the students in a class are involved in the same kind of work or specialist studies. This may certainly be the case in many parts of the world, but equally we can find many mixed ESP classes. For example, all the students may be engineers, but some may be electrical engineers and others mechanical engineers, and the two groups may not acknowledge that they have much in common. In some cases, an ESP class may comprise all the employees of a company: they will have shared knowledge of the company and shared overall objectives, but they will have very different job duties within the company. Even when students have identical job or study needs, however, they are still likely to be different in terms of the rate at which they learn English.

It may often be thought that a characteristic, or even a criterial feature, of ESP is that the course should involve specialist language (especially terminology) and content. I suggest, however, that an ESP course need not include specialist language and content. What is more important is the activities that students engage in. These may be specialist and appropriate even when non-specialist language and content are involved. We should be guided by what the needs analysis suggests and what we are institutionally capable of, and cases certainly exist where apparently general language and content are best.

In some cases, there is no absolute need for students to gain proficiency in English in order to cope with their work or study; they will manage well enough (or even very well) in their own language. However, there may be an institutional (or even national) requirement to study English, usually because of the known role of English as an international language of communication, trade and research. In such situations, teachers of English often select texts and activities from students' work or main subjects of study. As has just been suggested, the selection of specialist texts should not in itself make a course an ESP course. What is more important is a demonstrated need, which may be for specialist texts or for some other kind of material.

However, I do not wish to exclude people who would like to be members of the profession of ESP practitioner. What seems crucial, ultimately, is that courses are designed with particular students in mind, whatever their work or study needs and their personal preferences. As Richards (26, p. 215) notes: 'The concern of ESP with *delicacy of context* is something which distinguishes it from ELT in general.' Given the great variety of contexts and of ESP courses around the world today, perhaps what we are really involved in as ESP practitioners is not so much teaching English for specific purposes but teaching English to specified people.

What this book covers

In this book an attempt is made to review developments in ESP during the 1980s. Thus most references are to articles and books which have appeared in and after 1980, although some influential material from before 1980 is also mentioned. In 1980 the field of ESP still seemed relatively new and one bibliography of ESP which aimed to be fairly complete amounted to 500 references (Robinson (27)). Inevitably, some items were omitted, but since 1980 ESP activity around the world has expanded tremendously and the number of essential references is now at least 800 (this book) or, more realistically, many more. Again, many useful items have doubtless been omitted and, although an effort has been made to consider ESP activity worldwide, the main focus is on UK and UK-originated activity, with a lesser focus on work in North America and Australia.

Several excellent reflections on and accounts of ESP appeared during the 1980s (McDonough (22), Hutchinson and Waters (15), Widdowson (40)) and at least two invaluable collections of articles (Swales (32), Tickoo (35)). Reference is made to these, but on the whole the aim of this book is to consider the primary data: accounts of practical experience and reports of research. One essential source for these has been the journal *English for Specific Purposes* (44). Other excellent journals also exist but unfortunately not all of them always appear on a regular basis. One feature of ESP still is that much of the interesting activity that is carried on around the world is only reported in local publications (if it is reported at all), which may often reach people in other countries only by chance.

The approach adopted here is to work systematically through the process of ESP course design, reviewing the procedures which ESP practitioners employ at each stage. Thus needs analysis is considered first, and then approaches to the analysis of language in ESP. ESP syllabus design is considered, followed by approaches to methodology and to materials for ESP. Testing and evaluation are then dealt with. After this, the many and varied roles of the ESP teacher are discussed. The role of the ESP student would also merit a chapter but is considered alongside that of the ESP teacher. Finally, some of the many scores of current ESP textbooks are reviewed: those for the two largest areas of activity, business English and English for academic purposes.

From time to time the demise of ESP has been predicted. This has not yet taken place, however, and, as the following pages show, ESP is very much alive and well, albeit appearing in many different guises around the world. This book is an attempt to encapsulate the many forms of ESP as it is today.

Chapter Two

Needs Analysis

Needs analysis is generally regarded as criterial to ESP, although ESP is by no means the only educational enterprise which makes use of it. The best recent short accounts of needs analysis are by Berwick (55) and Brindley (57). The most thorough account is Brindley (56), and a useful resource book is Richterich and Chancerel (87).

Meanings of needs and needs analysis

Needs

The first, essential, point to make is that needs 'do not have of themselves an objective reality' (Brindley (57, p. 65)). 'What is finally established as a "need" is a matter for agreement and judgement not discovery' (Lawson (75, p. 37)); quoted in Brindley (57, p. 65)). The needs that are established for a particular group of students will be an outcome of a needs analysis project and will be influenced by the ideological preconceptions of the analysts. A different group of analysts working with the same group of students, but with different views on teaching and learning, would be highly likely to produce a different set of needs.

A number of people (for example Berwick (55), Brindley (57), Mountford (81), Widdowson (326)) have discussed the different meanings or types of *needs*. First, *needs* can refer to students' study or job requirements, that is, what they have to be able to do at the end of their language course. This is a goal-oriented definition of needs (Widdowson (326, p. 2)). Needs in this sense 'are perhaps more appropriately described as "objectives"' (Berwick (55, p. 57)). Second, *needs* can mean 'what the user-institution or society at large regards as necessary or desirable to be learnt from a programme of language instruction' (Mountford (81, p. 27)). Third, we can consider 'what the learner needs to do to actually acquire the language. This is a *process-oriented* definition of needs and relates to transitional behaviour, the means of learning' (Widdowson (326, p. 2)). Fourth, we can consider what the students themselves would like to gain from the language course. This view of needs implies that students may have personal aims in addition to (or even in opposition to) the requirements of their studies or jobs. Berwick (55, p. 55) notes that such personal needs 'may be (and often are) devalued' by being viewed as 'wants or desires'. Finally, we may interpret *needs* as *lacks*, that is, what the students do not know or cannot do in English.

Some of these views of needs have been paired, and the members of each pair seen as polar opposites, although the distinctions are not as clear cut as might be supposed. For example, we can contrast the views of *learners* and of *teachers*. Widening the scope of teachers to include *authorities*, we may note that, in some cases, there is a discrepancy between students' specialist course of study or job and the one which they would prefer. In such cases, we might expect students/learners and authorities/ teachers to have different views of the goals and content of the ESP course. 'Conflict' may also develop between learners and teachers in relation to 'a number of different facets of the learning process', including learning activities, strategies and materials, and language content (Brindley (56, pp. 103−12)). For example, the learners may want to employ rote-learning, a strategy which the teacher does not consider beneficial.

Another possible contrast is between *objective* and *subjective* needs:

> The first of these terms ... refers to needs which are derivable from different kinds of factual information about learners, their use of language in real-life communication situations as well as their current language proficiency and language difficulties. The second term refers to the cognitive and affective needs of the learner in the learning situation, derivable from information about affective and cognitive factors such as personality, confidence, attitudes, learners' wants and expectations with regard to the learning of English and their individual cognitive style and learning strategies (Brindley (57, p. 70)).

Very often, it is the teachers who will perceive the objective needs and the learners who will perceive their subjective needs. However, this is certainly not necessarily the case. Many ESP students have a clear view of some if not all of their objective needs. Conversely, 'many learners may not themselves perceive a particular subjective need (e.g. the need to develop confidence) which a teacher is capable of seeing' (Brindley (56, p. 138)).

Other pairings of contrasted views of needs include *perceived* versus *felt* needs (perhaps covering the same ground as *objective* and *subjective* needs) and *target* versus *learning* needs (covering the same ground as *goal-oriented* and *process-oriented*). The terms *product* and *process* have a range of uses here. As well as equating *product* with a target view of needs, and *process* with a learning view, we can try to identify the target-level products *and* processes which students will need to control at the end of an ESP course (see the discussion in Robinson (88)).

Target situation analysis

A needs analysis which focuses on students' needs at the end of a language course can be called a target situation analysis (TSA). This term is introduced and discussed in a useful article by Chambers (59). The best known framework for a TSA type of needs analysis is formulated by Munby (82), who presents a communication needs processor, comprising a set of parameters within which information on the students' target situation can be plotted. The Munby model has been widely studied and discussed. Among its useful features are comprehensive data banks, for example of micro-skills and attitudes, which can be used as checklists for the resultant syllabus. A helpful insight which Munby codifies relates to target-level performance: for certain jobs students may require only a low level of accuracy, of native-speaker-like ability etc. The TSA may thus pinpoint the stage at which 'good enough' competence for the job is reached.

The information sought for a TSA may relate to two different stages in the students' lives. Thus the English course may be preparing the students for a further training course, which will be conducted through the medium of English, after which the students will then take up jobs. The English language requirements of the training course and of the later job may well be different, but both need to be considered. For example, note-taking from books and answering examination questions may be needed for the training course, but the job may involve much discussion and negotiation in English and little reading and writing. Students will understandably want to practise examination-answering on the language course, but may also want to rehearse for their later jobs by doing a lot of oral work.

Present situation analysis

As a complement to TSA we may posit PSA (present situation analysis). A PSA seeks to establish what the students are like at the start of their language course, investigating their strengths and weaknesses. Richterich and Chancerel (87) give the most extensive range of devices for establishing the PSA. They suggest that there are three basic sources of information: the students themselves, the language-teaching establishment, and the 'user-institution', for example the students' place of work. For each of these we shall seek information regarding their respective levels of ability; their resources, for example financial and technical; and their views on language teaching and learning. We might also study the surrounding society and culture: the attitude held towards English and towards the learning and use of a foreign language.

An important issue is the relationship between the PSA and the TSA. For some people, including Munby (82), the PSA represents constraints on the TSA, which will have been conducted first. Munby (83) modifies this stand a little, allowing that political factors should be considered at the initial phase of needs analysis, but suggesting that factors relating to time, resources, and styles and traditions of learning should not be considered until the syllabus specification stage. For McDonough (22) the PSA involves 'fundamental variables', which must clearly be considered before the TSA. In practice, one is likely to seek and find information relating to both TSA and PSA simultaneously. Thus needs analysis may be seen as a combination of TSA and PSA.

The language audit

A combined TSA and PSA is provided by the language audit, used in language training for business and industry and described by Pilbeam (84). The language audit is used to plot the role played by a foreign language in a commercial or industrial enterprise. First, 'the precise language skills needed to carry out specific jobs' are determined, thereby establishing 'a *target profile of language skills* as part of a job description' and 'facilitating in selection of personnel for new positions' (Pilbeam (84)). In order to draw up this profile, the auditor/analyst must find out what tasks or activities people perform in their jobs (for example, chairing formal meetings, making presentations, writing telexes and memos) and must then decide what level of language performance is required for these tasks. Next, a *profile of present ability* needs to be established, showing the extent to which present personnel match up to their job requirements. This can be done by means of tests or, better, by means of an attainment scale and test battery (for example the ELTDU Stages of Attainment Scale and Test Battery; see Martin (80)) which will specify different levels of achievement of various tasks. Finally, the auditor must determine how much language training is needed (in terms of time and facilities required) to bridge any gap between the employees' present ability profile and the company's target profile. Such a language audit might be commissioned by a commercial company from a team of language consultants, as a preliminary to deciding whether to engage in language training or not.

Key methodological issues

Mountford (81, p. 28) suggests three sets of methodological problems related to needs analysis:

the problems of *perception*: whose analysis of needs?
the problems of *principle*: what should the analysis include and exclude as relevant content?
the problems of *practice*: how should the analysis be undertaken and applied?

Rather than seeing these as problems, let us simply treat them as factors to be taken into account, and consider them in turn.

Perception of needs

First of all we can ask: who carries out the needs analysis? This depends on the type of course or courses concerned. For a large institution or company an outside expert may well be called in — for example, from the British Council or from a language-teaching consultancy. Hawkey (67), (68) describes a five-week consultancy in Venezuela for the British Council. One advantage of having an outsider do the needs analysis is that he or she may be accorded special status and thus gain access to sources of information closed to the insiders. In addition, an outsider will bring a fresh pair of eyes to a situation and may be able to make an impartial assessment of what is required. However, an outsider may also bring alien cultural preconceptions and may hold rather different views on teaching and learning from the institution under analysis. An approach to needs analysis which, among other things, tries to guard against the ignorance and possible insensitivity of the outside expert is the 'ecological approach' to ESP of Holliday and Cooke (Holliday (69), Holliday and Cooke (70)). Rather than pursuing a Munbian type of exclusively target-oriented analysis, Holliday and Cooke suggest a 'means analysis' which researches into the local culture: its patterns of thinking and learning.

In many cases, however, the needs analysts are insiders, members of the institution which will run the ensuing course. As such, they should be familiar with much in the PSA, if not the TSA, and should thus be able to make relatively quick and informed decisions. However, as Ramani *et al.* (85) show, there are different degrees of 'inside-ness'. While lecturers in a university language centre, for example, may be familiar with the cultural norms and educational traditions of the country, they are still outsiders as regards the disciplinary cultures of the various university departments, being trained (most usually) in literature or applied linguistics, not in the natural sciences.

Who provides the information for the needs analysis? The sources of information are the potential students, the language-teaching institution (teachers and administrators) and those who are or will be concerned with the students' specific job or study situation. The students' sponsors might form a discrete fourth group. We might also want to consider past students. A basic problem can be that all these different sources of information have different views of what will be required on the ESP course. Further, these views may even be in conflict. Andrews (54) and Markee (79), both investigating the situation in Sudan, found a difference between the official view of the role of English and its actual role. They also found radically different perceptions of the role and target of the whole ESP project.

Principles of data selection

The type of information sought during a needs analysis is usually closely related to the approach to teaching and learning and to syllabus design followed by the analysts. (See the discussion of approaches to syllabus design in Chapter Four, pages 34–41.) For example, where the analysts favour a pedagogic approach which focuses on linguistic forms and their accurate reproduction by students, then needs analysis is likely to involve some study of the students' grasp of linguistic forms (probably through testing) and linguistic analysis of target-level texts. Students' needs will be expressed in terms of language items which must then be taught. In other cases, common for EAP, investigation will focus on the skills and sub-skills which are employed in certain study situations. For example, if reading is identified as an important skill, then investigators need to identify the types of text which must be read and the modes of reading employed for them: speed reading, reading for gist, scanning and so on. Any study of specific linguistic forms will be a secondary rather than a primary considera-tion. In recent years, also in EAP and more generally in ESP, we find an interest in the processes which students engage in and the strategies they employ, both when learning language and when engaged in their specialist areas of interest. A process-oriented needs analysis, then, would focus on information about these processes and strategies (see, for example, Jacobson (72)).

Ideally, of course, needs analysts should try to obtain information from a *range* of sources and viewpoints. Brindley (56, pp. 8−11) suggests a range of types of information to be sought from learners, teachers and others, adapted from Richterich and Chancerel (87). (See also Berwick (55, pp. 52−3.))

The practice of needs analysis

Schroder (91, p. 45) suggests that 'there are essentially four techniques for investigating needs': the questionnaire, the detailed interview, participating observation, and press ads. By press ads, he means that advertisements of job vacancies in the newspaper might indicate the language needs of the jobs. To Schroder's list we could add testing and the collection of authentic materials, such as audio and video recordings and documents from the students' workplace or specialist academic department.

Questionnaires

Examples of questionnaires are given in Richterich and Chancerel (87). If one has decided to use a questionnaire, then it is essential to try it out on a few respondents first to see whether the questions are comprehensible and whether the answers can be easily analysed and compared. A good account of preparing a questionnaire, which could be checked by computer, is given by Carrier (58). Lonnfors (76) describes the piloting of a questionnaire designed to be used as and when needed on future occasions to check on the continuing and developing needs of the different faculties of Helsinki University. One of her main concerns was that the questionnaire should be understood by laypeople, that is, non-linguists. The pilot questionnaire was administered to present and past students and to lecturers. There are obvious advantages in having some kind of ready-prepared questionnaire, which can be used at short notice for certain types of course and easily modified for others.

It is likely that the questionnaire will seek information for both the TSA and the PSA. For a new course or series of courses, one may seek information on a large number of points. For a repeated course, one may well focus on a particular aspect. For example, Horowitz (71), concerned with teaching academic writing, sought information on the range and nature of writing tasks assigned by lecturers, and the degree of control or instruction provided. He found that the written assignments fell into a small number of categories, several of which had not featured in previous studies of academic writing. He also found that a considerable degree of control or instruction was provided for the students, a factor not taken into sufficient account in contemporary approaches to the teaching of academic writing.

The advantage of a questionnaire is that it can be sent fairly easily to a large number of people; the disadvantage is that not many people will bother to fill it in and return it. The needs analyst has more control if the interview method is used.

Interviews

Mackay (77) advocates the 'structured interview' where, in effect, the interviewee is guided by the interviewer through a questionnaire. The advantage of this, suggests

Tarantino (95, pp. 35–6), is that the interviewer is able 'to help the respondents with linguistic clarification and to record their answers and explanations'. In addition, as Mackay points out, the interviewer can pursue any interesting new line of enquiry that develops, while at the same time having a planned agenda to refer to.

Observation

Questionnaires and interviews deal primarily with the respondents' opinions. The analyst needs to supplement these with direct observation: of successful target-level behaviour and of students' present, presumably defective, performance.

Svendsen and Krebs (94) describe the preparation of job-specific ESL classes which ran alongside vocational skills training at the actual worksite. They refer to Fanselow (66) on methods of data collection and on the importance of noting the role of non-linguistic communication. Svendsen and Krebs first conducted interviews with upper-level management, the department director, supervisors and the workers themselves in order to gain a thorough overall understanding of the nature of the job. They then made several visits to the workplace at different times of day, 'shadowing' the workers as they went about their work, noting the job duties, details of the environment and the nature of the spoken interactions that took place. Svendsen and Krebs continued their visits to the workplace, tape-recording the daily routines, even after the ESP course had begun. In addition to this, they collected samples of written documents used by the workers. Finally, they verified the accuracy of their data with experienced industry personnel.

Svendsen and Krebs stress the importance of establishing good relations with the industry staff: making only brief visits at convenient times; carefully explaining the purpose of the visits. Such good relations may take time to be established, of course. Industry personnel or (in the case of EAP) university or college departments may only start to co-operate *after* the first of a series of ESP courses has been successfully conducted.

Case studies

One particular type of observation is the case study, in which one individual is shadowed over a period of time. Schmidt (90) describes a case study from EAP in detail and suggests that 'the case study as a means of assessment not only identifies difficult linguistic features but provides information to support a process oriented definition of needs as well' (Schmidt (90, p. 201)). Schmidt selected an advanced ESL student of business administration (Yvonne) and attended classes with her for three weeks, taking notes, observing Yvonne and comparing lecture notes with her. Thus as well as gaining direct experience of the type of lectures being given, Schmidt could also study Yvonne's strategies for coping with lecture comprehension and note-taking. In addition, Schmidt interviewed the lecturer and made a study of Yvonne's examination-taking strategies. Schmidt suggests that the advantages of the case study method are that it gives 'the possibility of an in-depth study over a period of time, the opportunity to appeal to the student's intuitions about his or her difficulties and needs in more detail than in the oral interview or questionnaire, and the occasion for the curriculum developer to do direct observation of the student in the classroom and study situation to gain insight into the student's own methods of learning' (Schmidt (90, pp. 200–1)). The disadvantages are that this method of needs analysis is time consuming and that the results may not be generalisable.

Tests

Ideally, students should be tested before the start of the ESP course so that the course designers can have some idea of their present level of ability. The test may require students to perform target-level tasks, thus revealing which they are already capable of performing and where their deficiencies lie. (See the discussion of testing for ESP, pages 73–8.) The test should be reliable and validated, so that the scores can be easily interpreted. Vague assessments such as 'intermediate level' are of little help when course specifications are being drawn up. Failure to obtain an accurate idea of the students' initial level of ability can lead to serious problems and the hasty redesign of a course, as Saunders (320, p. 34) describes.

Authentic data collection

Authentic data collection refers to the making of audio or video recordings, for example of real-life business negotiations or of lectures in students' specialist departments, and to the collection of print material, for instance samples of commercial correspondence, samples of students' examination scripts, the books and journal articles that university students are required to read.

The analysis of the linguistic component of the material is discussed in detail in Chapter Three, pages 23–7. Here we might simply mention the importance of making an accurate record of the source of the data and noting such factors as how and for what it was being used and in what kind of situation. Thus if audio recordings of discussions or seminars are made, we need to know what actions and gestures accompanied the speech. If print material is collected, we need to know who used it and how, for example whether it was something read and closely studied or merely scanned, or whether it led to immediate action. A problem with the collection and analysis of authentic material is that it may be difficult to determine what is salient and useful and what is merely interesting.

Participatory needs analysis

A final type of needs analysis that may be identified is the participatory needs analysis, which involves the students more actively than in simply completing a questionnaire. Students might be invited to take part in a discussion on their needs (and wants), with the students able to make recommendations as to what should happen in the resultant course. Shaw (93) describes the use of a questionnaire on needs as a stimulus to a communicative class activity, during which students learnt to reconcile their individual needs with those of the class as a whole.

Students might also be asked to take part in further research, for example as to the nature of their subsequent work or study requirements. Where students have already started their specialist studies, they can report to the ESP teacher on the needs which emerge in the course of these studies. Johns (744) reports on the training of students in ethnographic techniques to enable them to study the academic community they are about to enter. Having identified the features of their target community, they may be more aware of what is needed to help them prepare for it. (See also Ramani (783).)

Conducting a needs analysis

Planning the needs analysis

Before embarking on a needs analysis we need to consider very carefully how much time there is available, both to do the actual collecting of the information and then to process and analyse it. We should also have some idea of *how* we are going to analyse and use the information. Mackay and Bosquet (78), in a very clear account of 'LSP curriculum development', warn that 'if the researcher assumes that the first step is to gather all possible information about the learner — his or her needs, the uses to which the language might be put, the expectations of the community — before deciding how the information will be analyzed and for what purposes it will be used, this phase is certain to end in frustration and is likely to end in the abandonment of the data' (Mackay and Bosquet (78, p. 11)).

It is also important to consider the likelihood of obtaining the type of data that we think we want. If the students have not yet arrived at the place where the ESP course will be taught, then can a questionnaire be sent to them? Can they be asked to take some sort of recognised test before leaving? What relevant material can they be asked to bring with them? Some of the problems of operating at a distance are discussed by Drobnic (64) and Hirayama-Grant and Sedgwick (288).

Another problem may be the difficulty of extracting usable information from sponsors or employers. This may be because the information is of a sensitive nature or because 'sponsors may be out of touch with the prospective students' actual needs. They may even insist upon imagined rather than established needs. Without special help, even the most enlightened of sponsors may be unable to offer more than a very crude analysis' (Allwright and Allwright (331, p. 58)).

Thus, when necessary, needs analysts must 'use their existing stock of knowledge' (Holliday and Cooke (70)) and make 'professional guesses' (Scharer (89)).

When should the needs analysis be carried out?

There is general agreement that as much as possible of the needs analysis should be completed before any course or series of courses starts. Richterich and Chancerel (87), and Holliday and Cooke (70) and others, however, also suggest that needs analysis needs to be repeated during the life of each course. This is most obviously because the PSA may change. As students become more involved with the course, their attitudes and approach may change. They — or their sponsors — may also become more ambitious and extend the targets towards which they are aiming. In the case of a large institution or company, we might imagine a repetition, on a smaller scale, of needs analysis at regular intervals, for example annually or every five years or so. Alternatively, this repeated needs analysis can be built into the formative evaluation (see the discussion on pages 65−6).

Accounts of practical experience

Richterich (86) presents a number of case studies in needs analysis, not all of them for ESP. Schutz and Derwing (92) give an account of a needs analysis project, as does Coleman (60), focusing on the complexities of needs analysis for a very large organisation. He suggests a two-stage needs analysis: 'The first stage would reveal the complexity and dynamism of the organization and then, at the second stage, attention would be paid to the specific needs of the organization's constituent units' (Coleman (60, p. 155)). Cumaranatunge (61) gives a good account of needs analysis for EOP (domestic aides in West Asia), using a wide range of methods.

An interesting account of an EAP needs analysis project is given by Hawkey. In Hawkey (67) he describes in detail the application of the Munby model (with appropriate practical modifications), which in Hawkey (68), referring to the same project, he sets in context. Hawkey had five weeks for his project, but on arrival (in Venezuela) found that the brief had been expanded to include materials production as well as needs analysis. Hawkey's approach combined informal interviews and observation and he notes that with both methods he was gaining information about both the TSA and the PSA. In addition, his classroom observation gave him ideas for the materials production. Hawkey stresses the importance to the project of the great amount of willing co-operation that he received from all concerned: students, English teachers, administrators.

On a very short course, or when a course has been arranged at short notice, a prior needs analysis may not be possible. In this situation, information on needs has to be obtained once the course has started. Knight (74) describes a one-off one-week course for German technical staff engaged in discussions on quality control with a firm of US consultants. The discussions had just broken down, which was the reason for the ESP course, and so the 'target' needs were actually very immediate. Knight did in fact obtain some information before the start of the course — from telephone calls, company literature and a textbook on quality control. However, he suggests that the identification of 'learner-related needs' is a product of the developing course and the developing rapport between teacher and students or clients. He stresses the importance of 'first-day analysis', which gives both overt information (through interviews, for example) and covert information (for example through simulations, which are a learning activity for the students but which give diagnostic information to the teacher). As the week progressed, it became clear that the reason for the breakdown was not what the clients had assumed and was perhaps attitudinal rather than linguistic, a conclusion which only emerged through simulation and discussion and which could probably not have been identified before the start of the course.

Specifying objectives; drawing up a contract

As a result of the needs analysis, we should be able to draw up our objectives for the ESP course. We might also wish to draw up a contract, to be signed by the course designers and the sponsors, which specifies what can (and cannot) be provided. The next stage is the design of the syllabus. It must be remembered, however, that the stages of needs analysis, specification of objectives and syllabus design are, in practice, often not discrete.

Chapter Three

The Analysis of Language for ESP

The relationship between ESP and linguistic analysis

Any ESP enterprise involves three realms of knowledge: language, pedagogy and content (the content of the students' specialist disciplines). The relationship between these is different for different ESP courses and depends on the views of the course designers concerning the description of language, syllabus design, and methods of learning and teaching language. At the needs analysis stage, ESP practitioners often take one of two paths: either texts (spoken or written) are identified, the language of which constitutes the language syllabus for the students, or some sort of language syllabus is identified and then texts are sought or created to embody that language. At the learning stage, some then advocate that students be exposed to the texts selected and, through appropriate activities or tasks, acquire the target linguistic features. Others adopt some form of explicit description and teaching of the linguistic features, perhaps not always embodied in texts.

Whether an ESP course contains a conscious focus on language or not, the course designers must be operating some sort of theory of language and of its relationship to ESP. Many theories of language and of its description are available and ESP has benefited greatly from work done in theoretical linguistics, applied linguistics and other disciplines such as psycholinguistics, sociolinguistics and sociology. (See Coleman (117) for a multidisciplinary survey of language and work, with contributions from a wide range of academic disciplines.) ESP practitioners can be seen as opportunistic in that they take whichever theories seem most appropriate to their purposes. Swales (225), (32) demonstrates how approaches to linguistic analysis for ESP have changed as fashions have changed in linguistics generally, but he also notes that 'older work does not automatically lose its value and relevance simply because it is old' (Swales (225, p. 17)). Thus, if we look at what is going on in ESP worldwide, we can find both older and newer approaches to language description in current operation.

For some ESP courses, students may be offered a fairly restricted set of linguistic options, and notions of 'register' and 'special language' (see below) may be invoked.

Such courses are likely to be short, closely focused on target-level needs and involving more of a training than a teaching approach (see the discussion in Widdowson (40)). On longer, more broadly based courses, where attention is paid to current learning needs as well as future work or study requirements, then the view of language and of which linguistic items need to be practised is a much wider one.

ESP has not been merely opportunistic by borrowing from elsewhere, for much linguistic work has been done under the auspices of ESP, often as part of needs analysis and the preparation of course materials. Too often such research is not offered for publication and so is not disseminated widely. Other research is only indirectly related to pedagogic needs. A considerable number of small and large ESP-related projects are carried out on master's level courses in applied linguistics, teaching English to speakers of other languages (TESOL) and teaching English for specific purposes (TESP), and for doctoral-level studies. Some of this work is published or otherwise accessible; much of it is not. What would be useful is a large-scale comparison of the findings and an indication of which areas have been sufficiently covered (if any) or neglected, of where fruitful comparisons and contrasts could be made, and of which approaches seem most productive. Van Naerssen and Kaplan (182) give a comprehensive account of linguistic research for EST, however, identifying the motivation for the research and the targets and posing a number of pertinent questions, some of which will be considered below.

Questions of theory and terminology

The central belief of anyone involved with a language for special purposes (LSP) is that no language is monolithic; that is, all languages comprise many varieties. The problem, however, is to determine the degree to which the varieties of any one language may differ from each other. A further problem for anyone wishing to investigate the matter is the great range of terms used. Some of the key terms are discussed below, with an indication of the theories they relate to and the significance they have for work in both ESP and LSP.

Variety

'Variety' is perhaps the most widely employed term and a well-established distinction is made between varieties according to user (for example, regional, temporal, social and sexual dialect) and varieties according to use (for example, in the workplace, in the home, at a social function) (see Halliday, McIntosh and Strevens (146), Gregory (142)). However, whereas varieties according to user were formerly thought to be fairly unchanging, it is now known that people can modify their original regional and other dialects. Conversely, workplace language, once thought to be confined to the work situation, can now be seen to affect a speaker's repertoire even in social situations. The distinction in linguistic usage between home and work is thus not always as clear cut as the analyst might wish it to be.

Register

The term most usually employed to cover varieties according to use is 'register'. Its constituent components are 'field' (topic), 'mode' (whether written or spoken) and 'tenor' (or 'style') (on a scale of formal to informal). The overall term, register, is sometimes also used for the component 'field'. Register has been a fruitful term, particularly in the field of stylistics, but also as the basis of research in ESP. The problem with register (and even variety) is that it can lead to reification; that is, a register of the language is identified and described, and then referred to as a discrete set of linguistic choices, seen as quite separate from the rest of the language. Thus we find, for example, 'the language of science', 'the language of medicine'.

Special language

The final development is the concept of 'special language'. Turner (242), in a very thorough and useful exploration of the terms 'special languages' and 'specific purposes', notes the 'rickety logical bridge from, for instance, "English for Bankers" (user) to "English in Banking" (domain), to arrive at "Banking English" (special language)' (Turner (242, p. 6)).

Special language or languages suggests the existence of general language or languages and LGP (language for general purposes). Illuminating discussions of what is involved here can be found in Varantola (244) and de Beaugrande (104). De Beaugrande (104, p. 6) writes:

> However, an LSP does not meet the requirements for a language in the usual sense … no LSP is composed exclusively of its own resources. Instead every LSP overlaps heavily with at least one LGP and is free to use any parts of the latter without express justification. One could not, for example, state the 'rules' which determine what parts of the grammar or lexicon of English may or may not appear in 'scientific English'; even such old stylistic restrictions as those forbidding 'sentence fragments' or 'slang' have been relaxed in recent years, especially within the discourse of computer technology. Hence we have more of a continuum than a division between LSP and LGP. (Varantola 1986)

A more useful term perhaps than 'special language', and surely a more accurate one, is 'technolect' (Lauren and Nordman (168), (20)), '-lect' suggesting, as in 'dialect', a form of a language, not an independent language. However, the term seems only to be used by Lauren and Nordman, who in fact entitle one of their 1989 volumes *Special language*.

Varantola (244, p. 10) suggests that 'special language' and 'general language' 'are good as working concepts but … resist clear-cut definition and delimitation'. One unequivocal definition is that of Sager, Dungworth and McDonald: 'Special Languages are semi-autonomous, complex semiotic systems based on and derived from general language; their use presupposes special education and is restricted to communication among specialists in the same or closely related fields' (Sager *et al.* (198, p. 69)). Lauren and Nordman (169, p. ix) write that 'the most advanced human thinking is expressed by special language'.

Specialist knowledge, not special language

Sager *et al.*'s work suggests that what is important first of all for the ESP researcher is the content of students' specialist disciplines: the knowledge and the conceptual networks that are involved. Hüllen (155, pp. 63−4) develops a concept of the 'stratification' of LSP 'according to the kinds of professional activities behind it', the strata being differentiated in terms of their relative abstractness or applicability (contact with material reality). This stratification model might usefully be applied to *all* users of a language, in fact. The broadest stratum would relate to the topics and concepts of daily life, understood and manipulated by all normal (native speaker) users of the language. These are the topics and concepts usually taught on language for general purposes (LGP) courses. Despite what Sager *et al.* suggest, these topics and concepts may also form an essential part of LSP courses, for example courses for medical personnel and hotel and catering staff who need to interact with the public. For all strata other than the broadest, we find that even native speakers have differential communicative ability, not because of their knowledge or lack of it of the linguistic system but because of their professional knowledge. (We should perhaps add leisure interest knowledge here. Is the discourse of the amateur photographer, actor, car mechanic and so on noticeably different from that of the professional?)

An important contribution to the study of the role of professional knowledge and conceptual networks was made by Selinker (205). Selinker describes a research project involving the study of an academic article in genetics by a group of ESL teachers and the discussion of their questions by a specialist informant (a lecturer in genetics). What emerged was that the teachers were not only ignorant of the meanings of technical terms, but that they could not identify when 'common language words' were being used technically, misunderstood the meaning — in context — of certain modal verbs, connectives and even punctuation and, because of their lack of specialist knowledge, did not in fact realise what the purpose of the entire article and its main content were. Zuck and Zuck (254) also show how English teachers and subject specialists can have a different view of the 'main idea' of a text. Other work which builds on Selinker (205) includes Huckin and Olsen (152) and Tarone *et al.* (235).

Common core

Having indicated that a concern with linguistic features should be secondary to a consideration of topics and concepts, let us return to the issue of language as such and to another variously interpreted term, that of 'common core'. This is penetratingly examined by Bloor and Bloor (107). They cite Quirk *et al.* (190), who write that 'we need to see a common core or nucleus that we call "English" being realized only in the different actual varieties of the language that we hear or read ... however esoteric or remote a variety may be, it has running through it a set of grammatical and other characteristics that are present in all others' (Quirk *et al.* (190, pp. 13−14)). Bloor and Bloor conclude that 'no speaker can have a command of the Common Core in a vacuum. Hence there is no reason whatever why the Common Core cannot be acquired from a so-called "special" variety just as well as from a more usual classroom variety' (Bloor and Bloor (107, p. 19)).

We might ask here what it is that the common core consists of. I suggest that it consists of the basic patterns of word, phrase and clause (or sentence) construction in English. Where one variety of English will differ from another is in the frequency of use of these different structural possibilities. A useful concept here is that of 'delicacy' (Halliday (144)). Thus, for example, while the noun phrase in English has the basic pattern of

m	h	q
(pre-modification)	head	(post-modification or qualification)

various combinational possibilities for items at m and q exist, and some of these possibilities may be more frequent in, say, certain types of engineering text than, for example, in certain texts on history. Similarly, while all clauses which one would accept as English fall into a small number of patterns, great variations are possible according to length, recursiveness and embedding, and on the basis of this it may be possible to distinguish a legal text from an elementary science one (see also the discussion in Robinson (28)).

ESP, LSP and language acquisition

In addition to elucidation of the term 'common core', Bloor and Bloor are concerned in their paper 'with the ways in which the LSP experience compels a new evaluation of certain theoretical positions in Applied Linguistics and Second Language Acquisition' (Bloor and Bloor (107, p. 1)). They argue that acquisition develops through exposure to language in context. 'A language learner is as likely to acquire "the language" from one variety as from another, but the use of language, being geared to situation and participants, is learned in appropriate contexts' (Bloor and Bloor (107, p. 28)). LSP, almost by definition, is language in context.

As well as invoking Krashen's distinction between acquisition and learning (Krashen (164)), Bloor and Bloor are here also utilising Widdowson's binary opposition of use and usage (Widdowson (251, pp. 1–21)). One important reason for the development of ESP was the realisation by those involved in teaching English as a foreign language that, while students might be acquiring some knowledge of English usage through EGP classes, they had not actually learned to use the language in the specialised contexts of work or study.

An interesting series of experiments which investigates students' acquisition and use of language in different contexts is reported in Selinker (206), (207) and Selinker and Douglas (208), (209). Selinker and Douglas suggest that learners' strategies vary according to 'discourse domain', that is, according to contexts which are important and/or necessary to the learners. 'The important SLA [second language acquisition] processes, such as language transfer, fossilization, and backsliding, as well as avoidance, and various communication and learning strategies, do not occur globally across ILs [interlanguages], but rather differentially within discourse domains' (Selinker and Douglas (208, p. 190)). Selinker and Douglas's method is to take comparable 'episodes' from the same learner's 'technical domain' and 'life story domain'. The research so far seems to show that some learners are more careful and more concerned to achieve effective communication in the technical domain compared with the life story domain (Selinker and Douglas (208, pp. 192−7)), while others are perhaps over-concerned in the technical domain and make errors which do not occur in the life story domain (Selinker and Douglas (209, p. 370)).

The nature of the relationship between context or domain and the learning and use of language is clearly vital to ESP and highly worth investigating. What can actually be done to help students both acquire and learn to use English appropriately in context is a matter of methodology (see Chapter Five).

Review of important approaches to the description of language

Changing approaches to linguistic analysis for ESP involve not only changes in method but also changing ideas of what is to be included in language and its description. Broadly, we might suggest that earlier studies focused on elements of the sentence and their construction; later, cohesion (particularly grammatical cohesion) was an important consideration. Attention then moved to the meanings of forms (notions and functions) rather than their structure and to the study of forms in context. Subsequently, approaches from discourse and conversation analysis and pragmatics were utilised. A good appraisal of approaches to the description of scientific language is given in Widdowson (252). Swales (32) gives not only an excellent presentation of the development of ESP but also a good guide to approaches to linguistic analysis for ESP. Here I shall deal with frequency studies, the rhetorical approach and genre analysis. These can be seen as occurring in historical sequence, but they may also occur concurrently, according to the needs of different course designers.

Frequency studies

Frequency studies have been important since the earliest days of ESP. The tradition seems to be particularly active in the former German Democratic Republic. Hoffman (148, pp. 114−15) writes: 'The peculiarities of LSP are first and foremost of a quantitative nature. It is the significantly frequent occurrence of certain speech elements, forms or structures that characterizes scientific writing and spoken discourse. As a consequence statistical methods play an important role in selecting an inventory for teaching purposes. . . . It is the word and the phrase levels that yield the best results, i.e. lists of typical lexical items which may serve as a highly effective teaching/learning minimum.' Further discussion of this is given in Hoffman (149).

Earlier and important frequency studies include Barber (101), which has stimulated a number of other studies, Ewer and Latorre (133), Huddleston *et al.* (153), Thakur

(236), Chiu (111), Porter (189) and Ewer (131), (132). Text selection is made on the basis of topic or domain — generally science, other domains being law (Gustaffson (143)) or government administration (Chiu (111)). The general conclusion from these studies is that 'science' is not a homogeneous linguistic entity, that writer's purpose and audience rather than topic are the determinants of linguistic form and that a variety of English 'may be characterized by a configuration of features all of which are found elsewhere, and none of which are themselves distinctive' (Porter(189)). Chiu (111) makes a similar point.

Frequency studies have been criticised for being only descriptive, not explanatory. Ideally, the two approaches should be combined, the description leading to an explanation, the explanation backed up by descriptive data. To some extent, Ewer combines the two in his 'The modals in formal scientific discourse: function, meaning and use' (Ewer (131)), in which he considers the meanings and roles of the modal auxiliaries in professional journals and academic literature. His work provides a more delicate explanation of modal meaning than that given in standard grammars of the language, whose corpora are normally derived from fiction, popular non-fiction and journalism. (For example, Quirk *et al.* (190). See also the discussion in Robinson (28, pp. 418−21) and the account of corpus selection for the development of the Cobuild dictionary in Renouf (191).)

Some more recent large-scale frequency studies attempt to relate the frequencies and clustering of grammatical forms to text type and rhetorical purpose (Grabe (140), Biber (106), Salager-Meyer *et al.* (202), (203)). Grabe also includes cohesion variables.

The rhetorical approach

A significant shift of approach in linguistic analysis for ESP was initiated by Selinker, Lackstrom and Trimble (212), suggesting that what was important was not so much the frequency of feature x or y but the reason for the choice of x rather than y in the developing text. The focus was thus on the text (specifically the conceptual paragraph) rather than on the sentence, and on writer's purpose rather than on form. This initiative was developed in a series of articles: Lackstrom, Selinker and Trimble (165), Selinker and Trimble (215), Selinker, Trimble and Vroman (216), Selinker, Todd Trimble and Trimble (213), (214), Todd Trimble and Trimble (240). A very practical and readable account of the approach is given in Trimble (241). Trimble in fact subtitles his work 'a discourse approach', but in it he is concerned with elucidating the rhetorical techniques and functions of written science and technology texts (or discourses), the aim being to identify the 'characteristics that make scientific and technical English writing different from other forms of written English discourse', noting that '"different" here means "different in degree" not "different in kind"' (Trimble (241)).

The rhetorical approach has been influential, especially in the USA. Pettinari (185) considers the alternation in a series of surgical reports of sentences with indefinite subjects and those with the dummy subject *there*, demonstrating how important it is to relate the grammatical description to the real-world role of the complete text. Several important studies have focused on the verb system, for example Tarone *et al.* (235). Tarone *et al.* consider the relative frequency of active and passive forms in two astrophysics journal articles, finding that (contrary to many assumptions about 'scientific English') *we* with an active verb occurs at least as frequently as the passive. What is important is that Tarone *et al.* try to identify the rhetorical reasons for the choice of active or passive, reasons that relate to the developing text and to authorial meaning and not to any prior stylistic decision. The approach is continued by Malcolm (176), who explores tense usage in scientific articles, finding that 'On the one hand, the same formula used for general English accounts for tense choices in EST . . . . On the other hand . . . tense formula is constrained by features unique to the genre of scientific articles.' These features in fact relate to the authors' necessity to refer both to the details of their experiments (past) and to their report (present or deictic function, as in 'We present the results . . . .'). However, one might conclude that the findings of both Tarone *et al.* and Malcolm pertain to academic journal articles in general, and not just to the domains of science and technology.

Genre analysis

A term used in Tarone *et al.* (235) but which up to that point was rare in ESP is 'genre'. Like all technical terms in ESP, it has various interpretations. For some writers, 'genre' seems to be the same as 'text type' and, as with the rhetorical approach, a genre analysis approach looks at the operation of language within a complete text, seeing the text as a system of features and choices. Selection is made according to the communicative purpose of the text producer. Salager-Meyer *et al.* (202), (203) did a 'principal component analysis' of medical English scholarly papers, divided into editorials, research papers and case reports, which are referred to as both 'sub-genres' and 'text types'. The results suggest a systematic difference between each text type or sub-genre according to the attitude of the writer to the reader: offering pure description in the case reports, advice and suggestion in the research papers, and judgement, value and instruction in the editorials. Salager-Meyer *et al.* appear to indicate that they see editorials etc. as sub-genres of the 'genre' of medical English, thus taking discipline or domain as the primary distinguishing factor between texts. For other researchers, 'text type' is superordinate to domain, so that the text type or genre of editorial might have the sub-genres of medical editorial, physics editorial, economics editorial and so on.

   Swales also used the term 'genre' for the first time in 1981 (Swales (222)), but for him it seems to imply much more than 'text type'. Like Salager-Meyer *et al.*, he considers author's purpose to be of central importance, but whereas they considered the effect of this on the selection of grammatical forms, Swales is concerned with rhetorical functions: 'Why is an author offering a classification at this point and what is its purpose?' (Swales (229, p. 12)). This authorial purpose is explained with reference to the wider professional culture to which the author belongs. Swales (222, pp. 10−11) has the following definition of 'genre': 'a more or less standardized communicative event with a goal or set of goals mutually understood by the participants in that event and occurring within a functional rather than a personal or social setting'. The standardisation of the event implies some regulation by the professional community, and the 'mutual understanding' suggests some induction into that community. The definition is further developed in Swales (229) and in Swales (230), where he introduces the concept of 'discourse community'. The members of a discourse community 'share common public goals', have 'mechanisms for intercommunication between members' and have 'discoursal expectations' leading to the development and use of distinctive text types involving specialised terminology, 'appropriacy of topics, the form, functioning and positioning of discoursal elements, and the roles texts play in the operation of the discourse community' (Swales (230, pp. 212–13)). Thus for Swales 'genre' involves not only text type but also the role of the text in the community which produces it, thus implying some study of institutional culture. The view of language which is presented here is, then, a social semiotic one (see Halliday (145)) and not a purely linguistic one. (See Swales (231) for a more extended discussion of discourse community and genre.)

A practical demonstration of what might be involved here is provided by Miller and Selzer (179). Their work suggests that in the analysis of any particular text we need to consider the 'generic' element, that is, whether it is broadly of the report, memo or letter etc. genre (or text type); the institutional element, that is, which company, department and so on it derives from; and the disciplinary element, that is, the topic, academic discipline etc. The study of institutional and academic culture is clearly of relevance here. A good introduction to the sociology of science is given in Bazerman (102), and a link between this and ESP is drawn by Myers (181). The approach is extended to economics and the writing of economics journal articles by Tinberg (238). Other work looks at the interrelationships between theories and researchers through analysis of the works cited in academic journal articles (citation analysis). This is considered from a discoursal point of view by Swales (227) and by Dubois (124).

A discourse analysis approach is also used in Swales (222), which is a pioneering study of the introduction section of forty-eight examples of the genre 'academic journal article', drawn from a wide range of academic disciplines. This has been an influential work, stimulating a number of further studies (Cooper (119), Crookes (120), Dudley-Evans (125), (127), (128) and Hopkins and Dudley-Evans (150)). Swales operates a 'top-down' approach; that is, he begins with a consideration of overall text organisation and any statements regarding choice of structure at the sentence level or below are related to that higher-level organisation.

Dudley-Evans (126) provides a good introduction to genre analysis, other systems of analysis and ESP, suggesting that ESP needs a system of linguistic analysis that demonstrates differences between texts and text types. 'Genre analysis may be used as a classificatory system, revealing the essential differences between both the genre studied and other genres and also between the various sub-genres' (Dudley-Evans (126, p. 2)). He further suggests that genre analysis within ESP is prescriptive (that is, able to make pedagogically useful recommendations), whereas register analysis, for example, is descriptive. The aim of discourse analysis, particularly the system of analysis of clause relations in written text developed by Winter and Hoey (Hoey (147)), is 'to describe relations that are found in all texts. It is concerned with similarities between texts' (Dudley-Evans (126, p. 5)). Nonetheless, Dudley-Evans and his students utilise the Winter and Hoey system, together with Swales's system of moves (Swales (222)), in order to examine the workings of individual texts. (Johns (744) also refers to the pedagogical usefulness of the Winter and Hoey system.)

Genre analysis is an exciting and fruitful development within ESP. It exemplifies the current importance of content, particularly the social and institutional aspects of that content. Even within a broadly genre analysis approach, however, other approaches may still be of use, for instance that of discourse analysis. Dudley-Evans and Henderson (129) combine insights from several approaches, including statistical (frequency) analysis for the study of vocabulary.

Vocabulary in ESP

For many people vocabulary, particularly specialist vocabulary (or terminology), is a key element of ESP. Despite this, vocabulary studies and, in particular, the teaching of vocabulary appear to have been somewhat neglected in ESP (see Laufer (167), Swales (224)). A number of aspects of the study of vocabulary in both ESP and LSP will be considered below, the central issue being to determine which aspect the ESP practitioner should most usefully be concerned with.

Specialist vocabulary and term formation

If we look at work in LSP, especially in Europe, we find that a large area of concern is that of specialist vocabulary or terminology. Sager (197, p. 98) writes: 'terminology is an applicable field of study concerned with the creation, collection and ordering of the vocabulary of special languages . . . this work is carried out by relatively few people for the benefit of all users of special languages'. Later he notes the 'assumption that specialized communication can be made more effective if terms are formed according to certain prevailing patterns which have a predictive value' (Sager (197, p. 99)). Alber-DeWolf (97, p. 167) suggests that 'a good knowledge of term-formation processes improves the reading skills necessary for reading foreign LSP' but most work in terminology is aimed not at teachers but at translators and, increasingly, at machine translation and the development of term banks (see Ross (193), Thomas (237)). Sager (197) makes the important observation that terminology is not so fixed as might be supposed. Several factors contribute to this: the speed of scientific development, its wider geographical and social spread, the duplication of research in different places so that there are 'group specific variations and synonyms'. Voracek (247) compares terminology across the natural sciences and the social sciences. He suggests that because political terminology 'can never be emotionally neutral, it can hardly be accurate and unambiguous and it will always cause problems to translators and interpreters'. Economics terms, while emotionally neutral, also cause problems of translation across economic systems (Voracek (247, pp. 15–16)). Thus while there may be value in compiling lists of terms for particular specialist areas, we must recognise the limitations of such lists.

Levels of vocabulary

Specialist vocabulary is identified as the first of three levels of vocabulary differentiated by researchers in ESP (specifically EAP) (see Martin (177), Swales (221), Inman (157), Loots (173), Baker (100) and King (163)). However, whereas Hoffman (149, p. 49) suggests that 'in the teaching of LSP attention is sharply focussed on the acquisition of special vocabularies', ESP/EAP practitioners generally agree that the specialist level is *not* the one to focus on.

The second level of vocabulary that has been identified is variously called semi-technical, sub-technical or general scientific/technical and comprises words which occur in a number of scientific or technical areas. Baker (100) gives six different interpretations of 'sub-technical', focusing on one of them, which consists of rhetorical/organisational items. 'These are items which signal the writer's intentions or his evaluation of the material presented' (Baker (100, p. 92)). What Baker is focusing on would seem to be similar to Martin's 'academic vocabulary' (Martin (177)), which consists of items necessary for discussing the research process and for analysing and evaluating data, whatever the academic discipline. King (163) also considers 'sub-technical' vocabulary, focusing on certain nouns which have a text-structuring and cohesive function. (See also Tadros (232), (233), (234) on cohesion.)

The third level of vocabulary is general and non-academic, such as would be central to an EGP course. Most ESP practitioners agree that it is the second level which should be taught on an ESP course — whatever interpretation of the second level is held. Phillips (187), (188), however, questions this (especially the concern with cohesion) and argues for consideration of the subject-specific vocabulary of a text, since this is what develops the unique 'aboutness' of the text, that is, its unique message.

Other views of vocabulary in ESP and of which levels should be taught come from work in listening comprehension (Johns and Dudley-Evans (582), Hutchinson and Waters (156), Farrington (134)). Here it is suggested that what can cause a problem for the non-native user of English is not specialist or even general academic vocabulary but the colloquial words, phrases and idioms made use of by certain lecturers. Some of this may be idiosyncratic, but some perhaps can be taught (Johns and Dudley-Evans (582)).

Personal idiosyncrasy is perhaps one of the concerns of Irgl, who looks at metaphor in commercial texts (Irgl (158)) and at synonymy in business and economics (Irgl (159)). He suggests that metaphor is particularly found in 'semiterminological collocations' (Irgl (158, p. 258)) and that we must be concerned not only with terminology but with 'the non-terminological parts of LSP texts, since there is interdependence between them' (Irgl (159, p. 276)). For business and economics, in particular, it would seem that understanding of the lexis (and style) of journalism might be important.

Semantic systems

A number of LSP practitioners have advocated the learning of lexical items according to semantic system. Hüllen (155) introduces the term *indexicality*, referring to the writer or speaker's presuppositions. In Hüllen (154) he examines a number of verbs, known to ordinary users of the language but which when used by international airline pilots have different indexical features and form a complete system. Gorm Hansen (138), working with student translators and interpreters on legal texts in Danish and English, suggests that the 'systems-oriented method' works better than the 'text-based method'. 'When applying the systems-oriented method the teacher would first give the students an outline of the systematics and the basic concepts of a given subject', thus setting the target terms in their 'functional reality' (Gorm Hansen (138, pp. 156−7)), each term deriving part of its meaning from its place in the system. As an example, Gorm Hansen compares the grounds for and the types of dissolution of marriage in England and Denmark. Because the systems are different, there is no exact translation for terms in either language. Each term must be considered not in isolation but in the context of the system to which it belongs.

Horey (289) refers to 'systemic language': 'the language that articulates the conceptual system of a subject' (Horey (289, p. 30)), consisting of sets of lexical items. Other semantic approaches are described by Rudzka-Ostyn — a 'cognitive approach' (Rudzka-Ostyn (196), Leow (171) and Wickrama (250)). Leow shows how important it is when reading law reports to be able to relate lexical items on a scale of more to less specific, and to be able to comprehend hyponymic relationships. She gives the example of a court case in which the appellant had discovered the remains of a snail in a partially consumed bottle of ginger beer. Comprehension of the report on the case would involve realising that 'decomposed remains of a snail', 'noxious element', 'defect' and 'act of omission' all referred to the same entity. Wickrama suggests utilising the techniques of componential analysis (also used by Hüllen (154)), which he suggests would be particularly appropriate for trainee lawyers as so much of the process of legal training involves the making of distinctions.

Vocabulary and structural patterns

As well as the semantic system to which a word belongs, we should also consider the structural patterns in which it occurs and the items with which it typically collocates. As Carter and McCarthy write, citing the work of Sinclair (218), 'collocations such as "vigorous depressions" and "dull highlights" may seem odd out of context; placed in their register-specific habitats of meteorology and photography, they are normal' (Carter and McCarthy (110, p. 36)). Roberts (192) refers to 'complex terminological syntagms', normally consisting of a key word (usually noun or verb) in collocation with an adjective, adverb, noun or verb, 'which together form a unit which not only is common in a given area of specialization but which often also serves to bring out the specialized sense of a given word. Thus, for example, the word *assets* has, in addition to its financial meaning, the general sense of qualities that serve as an advantage, support, resource, or source of strength; however, *assets* clearly takes on its financial meaning when it collocates with *liquidate* or *sell out* to form the syntagm *liquidate assets* or *sell out assets*' (Roberts (192, p. 155)). Roberts's work is aimed at the production of 'contextual dictionaries'. An earlier example of these is Spencer (219), (220), who looks at verb—object patterns in economics and law. For example, he takes the generic concept of 'make a law', showing that *make* itself is not in fact used, but listing which verbs are found and which nouns they take as objects, depending on the kind of 'making' involved.

One particular English structure which causes problems of identification and comprehension as a single lexical and conceptual unit is the nominal compound. Williams (253) reports on the higher incidence of nominal compounds in 'professional reading' compared with non-specialist texts and suggests ways to cope with the problem (Williams (253)). Others who have worked on nominal compounds include Olsen (183) and Salager (200).

Practical suggestions for the teaching of vocabulary in ESP

Swales (224) suggests that most studies of lexis and ESP have been 'language-centred', not pedagogically oriented. He reviews some ESP teaching materials and makes excellent practical suggestions. Other pedagogical approaches are presented by Fox (136), Bramki and Williams (108), Laufer (166), (167) and Ostyn *et al.* (184), all of whom urge the explicit teaching of vocabulary. The teaching of strategies for coping with new vocabulary items is suggested by Alderson and Alvarez (98). More work is obviously needed in this area, particularly workbooks for vocabulary activation and expansion.

Various resource books for students and translators exist, for example Spencer (220), mentioned above, Houghton and Wallace (151) and Godman and Payne (137).

How far can we use the research?

The above sections have offered a review of linguistic research which is available for the ESP practitioner to utilise. Many different approaches to the analysis of language are evident. It is for the ESP practitioner to decide which approach or approaches are most appropriate for the needs of the students and the design of the course. In some cases, direct information on language forms might be what is required. More often, probably, this information will serve as a resource for the development of the syllabus and the methodology.

How relevant is the research?

When one is preparing an ESP course, it is worthwhile finding out whether research already exists on the kind of language that the students might need. However, a number of cautionary points should be borne in mind.

First, the fact that research exists on the same topics or subject matter that the students are interested in is not sufficient to make that research useful. We need to know the source of the material that has been researched: its date and geographical origin. In addition, we need to know the level of the material: does it represent specialist to specialist communication, or specialist to non-specialist? What was the mode of the material? Was it originally spoken or written, prepared or unprepared? All these alternatives will have an effect on the language forms selected.

Second, we need to know the size of the corpus that has been researched. This can range from millions of running words of text (for example, Ewer and Latorre (133), Ewer (131), (132), Salager (199), Salager *et al.* (201)) to one text or journal article. Larger-scale studies may be able to arrive at reliable generalisations. Smaller-scale studies, however, may be able to go into more explanatory detail.

Third, we should note the range and domain of the corpus. Is the material from a broad domain, such as science or social science and, if so, how is it sub-divided? Or is a more limited domain being considered, for example journal articles in astrophysics (Tarone *et al.* (235))? In either case, we must consider the size of the claim being made: can or should we generalise on the basis of the results?

Finally, we should consider the nature of the items investigated and how they are determined. For example, statistical studies of sentence patterns can be difficult to compare because of differing interpretations of non-finite structures: these are variously interpreted as subordinate clauses and as phrases.

Good discussions on the collection and interpretation of data are given by Kennedy (162), who shows that there is a role both for informed intuition and for computer-based studies, and by Varantola (245), who compares the advantages and disadvantages of both large-scale and small-scale studies.

What is the coverage of the research?

Linguistic research in ESP has focused predominantly on formal written language, especially from academic sources. Studies of spoken language also often use academic material, looking at the features of lectures and seminars (see the section on EAP, pages 100–6). Other work has considered informal speech in lectures and laboratories (see page 28 above). Spoken interaction in business situations is considered by Lampi (650) and Williams (676), and in technical meetings by Lenz (170), all using the techniques of conversation analysis. Svendsen and Krebs (94) and Jupp and Hodlin (160) analyse the language of the workplace. On the whole, though, as Coleman (113, p. 7) notes, 'relatively little work is available which investigates language use in non-professional settings'.

Specialised text types which have been analysed include telexes, considered by Kitto (648), and by Zak and Dudley-Evans (679), who suggest that 'there is considerable evidence that the telex is replacing the letter as the main form of business correspondence' and that the common assumption that telexes have the same features as telegrams is not in fact correct. Recent evidence, however, indicates that the spread of the fax machine is causing a return to letter writing. Murray (180) looks at 'computer-mediated communication', suggesting that it shares characteristics with both speech and writing. Swales (228), (230) investigates the reprint request, in terms of both its form and its role in various academic discourse communities.

As far as one is able to tell, it seems that the data under investigation are in the majority of cases produced by native speakers. The rationale for this would be that what native speakers produce in the appropriate situations is truly authentic and thus suitable as a model and target. But a feature of ESP is that the language produced should be 'good enough for the job', not necessarily native-speaker-like. Additionally, many students of ESP require English for non-native-speaker to non-native-speaker communication. More knowledge is needed, following the lead of Selinker and Douglas (208), (209), of the communicative strategies and effectiveness of the non-native professional user of English. Some contributions have been made, for example by Zumrawi (255), who considered the presentation and simplification of the subject matter made by a non-native subject-specialist lecturer. Pettinari (186) compared surgical reports produced by native speaking and non-native speaking surgeons. Rounds (194), (195) investigated the linguistic usage of foreign teaching assistants in the USA. Salmi-Tolonen (204) compared European Community law in English with UK law documents, finding the former to be structurally simpler. Other related work is given in Selinker and Douglas (211). This is clearly an area for continued research, however. Since ESP is quintessentially language in use, linguistic research in ESP yields data that are of importance for the study and understanding of language and its function generally. Further, since English has become an international language because of its worldwide instrumental role (see Grabe (141); also Swales (226) on English as the international language of research), it is ESP situations and the functional communication of non-native to non-native that will illuminate the nature of international English.

Chapter Four

Syllabus and Course Design for ESP

Preliminary considerations

Definitions

This chapter focuses on what is involved in designing and setting up an ESP course or programme, the procedures that have been suggested and used and the types of syllabus. The term *syllabus* is used in the British sense, referring to a plan of work to be taught in a particular course. In many American publications we can find *curriculum* used with approximately the same meaning. (See the discussion on the use of the terms *syllabus* and *curriculum* in Brumfit (272, p. 9) and White (325, pp. 3−6).) Recent publications, however, contain work by North American writers using *curriculum* more in the British sense, involving issues of policy, planning and the complete educational environment, for example Johnson (297). Some of these aspects of curriculum planning are relevant for the discussion of course design (see below). Some of the references cited will be from general ELT curriculum planning and syllabus design, since ESP practitioners can learn from these, although recent examples, such as Johnson (297), show a mutual exchange of experience between ESP and general ELT.

Comparability of accounts

Numerous accounts of ESP courses exist, although many remain in unpublished form. Even those which are published reveal a great variety of approaches to course planning and design and the accounts themselves are written up in a variety of ways. It is therefore difficult to make comparisons. Bowers (268) complains of this and offers a matrix within which to locate different courses. The model essentially refers to classroom methodology, however. Swales (322) identifies a British−North American difference in accounts of course design, and urges attention to the decision-making processes. Thus writers should explain not just what they did, but why.

The input to course design: a dynamic interaction

ESP course design is the product of a dynamic interaction between a number of elements: the results of the needs analysis, the course designers' approach to syllabus and methodology, and existing materials (if any). All of these are mediated by the contextual constraints (see pages 41–2 below).

Any well-established ESP centre or other ELT institution has its own ideology relating to course design, to syllabus type, to the description of language and to the nature of language learning. In addition, the institution is likely to have a stock of its own materials, and knowledge and experience of commercially available materials. Even with an entirely new ESP project, the newly engaged staff members will have predetermined attitudes to course and syllabus design, and alongside the development of their first ESP course they will need to work on the development of a general institutional approach to course design, syllabus, methods and materials.

Thus the key question for any new ESP course is how far can and will the course designers modify their existing approaches. How far will the ESP course represent an innovation? This involves consideration of how far the existing approaches and materials match the results of the needs analysis. What modifications should be made? How far should and can the ESP course be revolutionary, requiring a radical rethink of approaches and the production of completely new materials?

Much of the excitement of ESP has come from just such radical rethinking and the resultant courses have advanced not only ESP but ELT as well. Clear examples, which led to the production of influential textbooks and articles, are the work of Ewer and Latorre in the 1960s (Ewer and Latorre (133), (281), Ewer and Hughes-Davies (280)); the courses in Tabriz, Iran, in the early 1970s, which led to the development of the *Nucleus* books (Bates and Dudley-Evans (263), Bates (262)); and courses in Lancaster leading to the development of *Interface* (Hutchinson (292), Hutchinson and Waters (156), (293), (294), (295), (296), Waters (378)).

Not every ESP course needs to be revolutionary, however. A common fear in the literature is that course designers are reinventing the wheel — through ignorance of ESP courses elsewhere in the world. We can also reinvent the wheel, though, by not using what we already have in our own institutions. What is needed is a judicious consideration of what can be recycled and a principled decision regarding the production of what is new.

The ESP syllabus

A syllabus, as suggested above, is a plan of work and is thus essentially for the teacher, as a guideline and context for class content. There may be value in showing the syllabus to students, so that they too can have a 'route map' of the course. The effect may be similar to that of using a published textbook for the course (rather than a series of handouts): the students can see that there is a plan and how the individual lessons fit together. Classroom research shows, however, that students frequently have a different personal plan for the lesson from the teacher, and at the end of a lesson

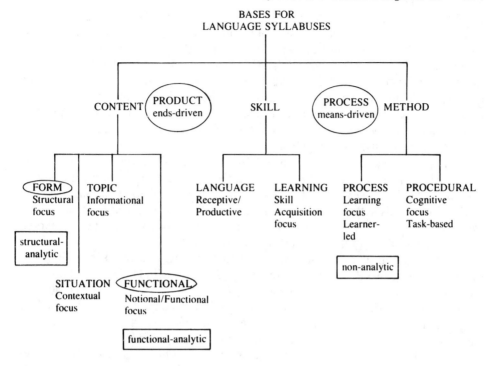

FIGURE 3 *Bases for language syllabus design (Sources: White (325); ovals, Breen (270); rectangles, Allen (256)).*

have a different notion about what has been taught (see the discussion in Nunan (312)). Process syllabuses (see below) try to overcome this discrepancy between student plan and teacher's plan, but for the other syllabus types the likelihood of such a discrepancy should be borne in mind.

Figure 3 combines three accounts of approaches to the ELT syllabus (Allen (256), Breen (270) and White (325)), which are useful as a starting point for discussion of the syllabus for ESP. Important questions are the following. How far are such syllabuses appropriate for ESP? How far do they offer a suitable conceptual structure within which to realise the objectives of the course? A key issue for ESP is the relationship in any syllabus of language, pedagogy and content (that is, the students' specialist subject area). Which of the three elements is paramount? How far do they combine? Let us explore these models in some detail and try to see how far they can be applied to ESP.

Content-based syllabuses: language form, language notion, language function

A basic distinction is between product syllabuses and process syllabuses. White uses the term *content* for *product* and suggests that there are several kinds of content syllabus.

The first is that of language form, consisting of an ordered set of language items, typically graded by supposed difficulty of learning. This syllabus has had the longest history in ELT and has also been very important in ESP. Important textbooks such as Herbert's (286) *The Structure of Technical English*, Ewer and Latorre's (281) *A Course in Basic Scientific English* and others are basically organised around such a language syllabus. For many ESP course designers, it is evident that this syllabus type is still a powerful if, to them, unacceptable model. Koh (301, p. 102), reacting against 'conventional ESP courses (which) do not meet the needs of . . . students', is referring to language-based syllabuses.

The major innovation in ELT in the 1970s was the development of the notional—functional syllabus (Wilkins (327)), in which the basic units are notions or concepts (for example, time, space) or functions (for example, greeting, asking, seeking clarification). This syllabus type was greatly developed within ESP, notably by the *Nucleus* series (Bates and Dudley-Evans (263)), based on concepts and, in EAP courses, for example Jordan (750), based on functions.

As with the language-form syllabus, the notional—functional syllabus can still appear to be a 'norm' for ESP. It continues to be found in EAP. Illuminating discussion of the syllabus and the methodology associated with it can be found in Allen (256). He identifies three basic syllabus types: A, B and C. A is structural-analytic, that is, language-form; B is functional-analytic, that is, notional—functional; and C is non-analytic, that is, process. Allen advocates focusing on type B and describes course and materials development based on this, and based on the *English in Focus* series (Allen and Widdowson (258)) but intended for ESL students in Canada. This demonstrates the general educational usefulness of an approach and materials developed within ESP, but also suggests fruitful borrowing in the other direction.

Content-based syllabuses: situation, topic

Situationally organised syllabuses can be found in English for business purposes, in some English for technology courses and in the 'English for social orientation' components of EAP courses. Bell (264) asks: 'Is there any possible way . . . of sequencing situations?' For some ESP situations, there may be an order. For example, in a business setting, the situations may be presented in the chronological order of a typical day's or week's work. In an EAP course, the situations may follow the sequence of a student's arrival in Britain or the USA: registering for a course, meeting other students, visiting the doctor, getting a flat etc., although it must be admitted that several sequences are possible here.

More important for ESP, however, is the topic-based syllabus, which deploys the content of the students' work or specialist study. One objective of the ESP course may in fact be to teach this specialist content. This is evident from some published ESP courses, for example Radice (667) and Mullen and Brown (310).

In the USA and Canada, combined language and specialist content teaching has been considerably developed under the umbrella title of 'Language Across the Curriculum' (LAC), and indeed many interesting developments which elsewhere would be termed ESP have occurred within LAC. A good discussion of this and useful references are given in Graham and Beardsley (284), as part of an account of a course in 'content, language and communication' for in-sessional pharmacy students. Other accounts are given by Allen (256), Mackay (307) and in Tickoo (34). Bhatia (265) discusses the issues involved. Comprehensive surveys are given in Brinton *et al.* (271) and in Mohan (309). (See also the discussion on pages 90−1.)

For many ESP courses, though, the specialist content is utilised as an organising device (or carrier-content — see Scott and Scott (321)) for the syllabus, in order to motivate the students and as a basis for the 'real syllabus' of language forms, functions or whatever the course designers wish to focus on.

Skill-based syllabuses

Figure 3 suggests that skill-based syllabuses are something of a half-way house between content or product syllabuses on the one side and method or process syllabuses on the other. By 'language skills', White (325, pp. 68−9) refers to the development, initially within ESP, of syllabuses focusing exclusively or principally on one of the four traditional language skills. Examples would be a course in writing business letters, or in oral skills for business people, or in academic reading. The actual content of the course, however, might be language forms or functions, as in content-based syllabuses.

More interesting developments have come not from considering just a four-way division of listening, reading, speaking and writing, but from looking at the constituents of these four skills. Various terms are used, such as sub-skills and micro-skills, not always in comparable ways by different writers (see the discussion in Fanning (282) and Bloor (266, pp. 18−19)). Some micro-skills, for example deducing gist, can belong to more than one language skill, in this case to both listening and reading, so that courses in 'learning skill' development may cover more than one of the language skills.

A useful framework for identifying micro-skills is Munby's taxonomy of language skills (Munby (82, pp. 123−31)). What is soon evident upon consideration of items in the taxonomy is that we are involved with more than language items. This point is illuminatingly developed by Bloor (266) in a comparison of ESP course design and courses in communication skills for native speakers of English. She tabulates the skills which are acquired naturally in a first language ('primary language skills') and those which are taught in the education system (Bloor (266, p. 21)). She suggests that 'much of the traditional language education of native speakers concerns the extension of such skills [primary language skills] to different fields and more mature contexts' (Bloor (266, p. 19)). Many of these skills which are taught to native speakers are included in Munby's taxonomy — hence Crombie's contention (279) that 'many EAP and higher-level GPE [General Purpose English] courses have a great deal in common with programmes which occupy the later stages of the English studies curriculum in secondary schools in the UK and USA'.

What seems to be involved is the development of cognitive as well as language skills. An important issue for ESP is the extent to which the development of cognitive skills should be an explicit part of the syllabus. Also important, and in need of further research, is the extent to which transfer of skill can be made from the first language to the second (see Green and Lapkin (285, pp. 136−9)).

Another set of skills which may form the focus for an ESP course are termed 'professional skills' or 'communication skills'. Linguistic accuracy is not ignored, but it is not the sole component. An example of a 'macro-skill' here might be 'making an oral presentation', the 'micro-skills' including control of gestures and body language, effective use of visual aids, as well as appropriate phraseology and terminology and clear pronunciation. Good accounts of professional communication skills courses are given by Huckin and Olsen (290) and Koh and Cheung (302). Both sets of writers react against a narrow focus on students' subject-specific concerns, opting instead for discipline or profession specificity. Huckin and Olsen, in fact, refer to 'generalised ESP'.

Method-based syllabuses: processes

Let us now consider method or process approaches to syllabus design, suggested by Breen as the major new paradigm. We can distinguish two sub-categories, one being variously referred to as method, process or learning process and the other as task or procedure. The first refers to the process or method of learning (in this case language learning) and is discussed in detail in Breen (269). The key feature of this approach is that what happens in the classroom is a matter for negotiation between the students and the teacher. There is thus a political aspect to the approach, namely a redefinition of the authority relations in the classroom. What students may opt to do might resemble any one (or a mixture) of the other syllabus types — for example, students may wish to follow a traditional language-form syllabus, the reason for its selection being that this is how students feel they would learn best. Parkinson and O'Sullivan (314) give an account of a negotiated syllabus in EPE (English for professional employment) for a course for immigrant professionals seeking employment in Australia. The focus of the programme was on sharing responsibility, problem-posing rather than problem-solving, and activating the work and life experience of the participants. (See also Auerbach and Burgess (260), Auerbach and Wallerstein (261), Clark and Silberstein (273), Tollefson (324) and Willing (328).)

The processes so far referred to are those for learning language. For ESP we can utilise a possibly different set of learning processes, namely those used in the students' specialist disciplines. Exploration of the methodologies of specialist disciplines is cogently argued for in Widdowson (326), (40, pp. 102−5). He examines the differing cognitive styles of the serialist and the holist, the convergent thinker and the divergent thinker, and considers the possibility that these styles match different subject specialisms.

Crocker (278, pp. 141−2) takes this a stage further and lists 'some of the major variables which seem to underlie the methodology of the disciplines in which I have had experience of running LSP programmes'. He contrasts the situation of 'technical students learning about safety procedures [who] cannot, in any real sense question the validity of information they are given concerning performance standards and safety regulations. Their task is to learn and apply. On the other hand, students learning seminar skills are required to adopt a critical stance towards the information provided. ... In the first instance, therefore, the relationship between information and user is non-negotiable, whilst in the second it is totally negotiable. This feature of negotiability can be treated independently of subject matter' (Crocker (278, p. 141)).

All this may seem to be a matter of methodology rather than syllabus. A key feature, in fact, of method-based syllabuses is that the distinction between syllabus and methodology to some extent disappears. None the less, the syllabus as such should suggest some sequencing of instances of methodological practice. The syllabus specification for the seminar skills course, for example, should have as one of the course objectives the development of a critical attitude, and should list a series of activities designed to promote such an attitude.

Other examples of discipline-specific methodologies are not common. Crocker (277) discusses a course in English for academic legal purposes, in which such legal processes as disambiguation and the application of abstract rules to specific examples of use were practised, utilising data from language, not from law. *Interface* by Hutchinson and Waters (295), (296) 'followed the methodology of the subject teaching' observed in local technical colleges, where 'a particular topic was presented, discussed and analysed; the knowledge thus built up was then used to solve a problem' (Hutchinson and Waters (296, p. 2)). McConnell (305) describes a course for technicians, utilising instructional principles derived from the technicians' work.

Flowerdew (283) examines Widdowson's suggestions (326), (40), in conjunction with considerations of cultural differences and studies of how good language learners operate. One problem which he identifies is that the dominant cognitive style for scientific disciplines may be in conflict with the style and strategies identified as belonging to good language learners. Flowerdew suggests that more research is needed and proposes that course designers conduct a 'task analysis of the intellectual abilities employed in the activities of the academic discipline for which the course is designed' (Flowerdew (283, p. 127)). The course designers would then 'relate this analysis to what is known about the intellectual abilities of the "good language learner" .... Once the two sets of intellectual abilities have been established and related one to the other, then they should be able to contribute to the design of courses which, it is to be hoped, will be more appropriate to the needs of our learners' (Flowerdew (283, p. 128)).

Flowerdew thus suggests an analysis of tasks as part of the input to a process syllabus. For other ESP practitioners, however, tasks can be directly utilised as the syllabus.

Method-based syllabuses: tasks

The procedural or task syllabus, consisting of a set of tasks or activities ordered according to cognitive difficulty, is associated in general ELT with Prabhu (318). Class time is devoted to performance of the tasks and attention is only consciously directed to language if this is necessary for completion of the task. A major concern throughout is that students understand the task and what they are doing, and do not act in a mechanical way.

Such an approach is clearly significant for ESP, since the basic need of ESP students is that, using the medium of English, they should successfully perform a work or study task. The most detailed development of a task-based approach for ESP took place within the King Abdulaziz University (KAU) project in Saudi Arabia. This is described in various articles by Horey (289), McAlpin and Wilson (304) and Harper (11). The theoretical underpinning is given in Phillips (315), (316).

The starting point for the syllabus, as described by Wilson (329, pp. 10−11), is a set of objectives which 'define the terminal behaviour required of the student'. A set of intermediate or enabling objectives is then set up to help the students attain the terminal behaviour. These enabling objectives are called tasks. The tasks reflect the structure of the terminal objectives, the difference between them being their level of complexity. Phillips (315, p. 98) gives an example of how teacher input and topic variables can be controlled in the preparation of a five-minute talk, used as an enabling objective to help students eventually to cope with a fifty-minute lecture.

An important feature of the approach is that 'each task has a conceptual, a linguistic and a physical aspect' (Wilson (329, p. 11)). This means that each task has an identified and relevant specific-subject content; is at an identified, appropriate and manageable linguistic level; and has an identified and appropriate performance requirement (for example, if students have to write in class, then this is because writing is required by the task and not just as a language practice activity).

Other accounts of task-based approaches are inevitably less detailed in their coverage than the KAU project. Xavier *et al.* (330), however, present an illuminating account of an innovation in ELT (EAP) in India, leading to the development of a task-based syllabus. Previously they had utilised a discrete skills approach (see the discussion on this above, pages 37−8), but found it unworkable. The innovation came about not through a study of theory but as a result of the teachers' experience in the classroom and with materials. Xavier *et al.* note that 'construction of . . . tasks has led to an alternative concept of materials. Materials are no longer viewed as merely texts to which students are exposed but as activities the learners must engage themselves in' (Xavier *et al.* (330, p. 18)). A good, short account of a task-based syllabus for EVP (commercial English) is given by Arnold (259). Further discussion of tasks is given in Chapter Five, pages 47−57. (See also Swales (231, pp. 73−82).)

Which syllabus to choose?

In the above account of syllabus types, I have discussed the main trends in ELT syllabus design and attempted to show how these relate to syllabus design in ESP. There are certainly other ways of encapsulating the features of ESP syllabuses. Indeed, in an earlier article (Robinson (28)), I interpreted skill- and process-based approaches in a slightly different way. Process approaches, in particular, are still under development and are the likely location for future research.

Figure 3 seems to represent a historical progression from left to right. This does not mean that we should jettison past approaches. Rather, we should treat all approaches as being simultaneously available and try to find what is most suitable for a particular situation. One reason for the continuing life of the language form and function syllabuses is that they are familiar to teachers. In a situation where teachers lack confidence and need a lot of support, such well-tried (although not necessarily evaluated — see page 65 below) approaches may be the best to adopt.

Swan (323) asserts: 'The real issue is not which syllabus to put first. It is how to integrate eight or so syllabuses (functional, notional, situational, topic, phonological, lexical, structural, skills) into a sensible teaching programme.' Swan is referring to general ELT, but as with much of this discussion of the syllabus his point is relevant for ESP. A glance at many published ESP courses (textbooks) will show that this is the case. Hutchinson and Waters (296), in their account of the development of *Interface*, are concerned to show that there is a language syllabus and that it matches that of other established courses.

However many parallel syllabuses there are for a course, one is likely to be primary, the organising principle for the course, with the other syllabuses subordinate to it. Allen (256), however, referring to both syllabus and methodology, advocates a variable focus within a course. Thus, for certain lessons the focus may be type A (structural-analytic), and at other times type B (functional-analytic) or type C (non-analytic). McDonough (765), in her discussion of the lack of a research base for EAP, considers syllabus implications, urging consideration of the process type, and argues in effect for a range of approaches within a course (McDonough (765, p. 22)).

As suggested above, the decision as to which syllabus type or types to employ will result from a judicious consideration of the students' needs and the objectives of the course, together with the institutional bias of the teaching institution. The latter forms part of the context of the ESP course and should be considered next.

Course design

Course design involves putting the theoretical decisions about objectives and syllabus into a context. There are various ways of viewing this context.

Constraints

In the epilogue of his *Communicative Syllabus Design*, Munby (82, pp. 217–18) writes that 'this book has not dealt with those variables which are concerned with that dimension of course design which is subsequent to syllabus specification'. These variables, which Munby describes as 'constraints upon the implementation of the syllabus specification', include such things as government attitude, the status of English, logistical and administrative matters, the students' motivation and expectations, and methodological issues. Munby's views on the relative timing of the needs analysis and the consideration of constraints was immediately and vigorously attacked, leading him to make some modification (Munby (83, p. 64)): 'Some constraints ... e.g. political factors affecting the target language and homogeneity of the learner group, should be applied at the needs analysis stage.' The other constraints are still considered to be subsequent to syllabus specification, though.

In practice, I would suggest, consideration of constraints occurs in conjunction with the needs analysis. Some of these constraints, notably those concerned with the students' attitudes and expectations, are an essential part of the needs analysis, especially one operating within a learner-centred framework. In such a case, rather than using the term *constraints*, it is probably more appropriate to use *fundamental variables* (McDonough (22, p. 15)).

ESP and language planning

An interesting recent development, but one which pertains to part of Munby's first category of constraints ('socio-political'), is both to apply the terminology and approaches of language planning (LP) to ESP and to treat ESP as an instance of LP (Kennedy (299), Markee (308)). Let us take the second point first. Kennedy (299, p. 73) suggests that the most frequent definition of LP is that 'it is the planning of deliberate changes in the form or the use of a language, typically at government level'. Clearly the development, by means of an ESP course, of a workforce with a command of a foreign language contributes to the national economy and such development needs to be part of government policy. As Kennedy notes, the implications of such policy may not always be fully worked out and the needs of those actually implementing the policy (course designers and teachers) may not be appreciated by the policy makers. This can in some cases explain the failure of otherwise well-designed language courses.

In other cases, as Markee (308, pp. 138−41) shows, ESP course designers may be able to make fundamental policy decisions, as for example of the choice of medium and form of language for instruction. He describes ESP work in Sudan, where the local language (Arabic) was given a role to play, despite its official proscription for class use. In other situations the issue may concern the dialect of English to use, the choice being not just between American or British English but involving other varieties such as Indian English, West African English etc. (see Kachru (298)). Such decisions as these, formerly seen as just some of the many to be taken by ESP course designers, can now be identified as important preliminary policy decisions, affecting both the wider community, of which the ESP course is a part, and all the subsequent practical decisions.

Management issues

Some of the features of the PSA (see page 9 above) are more appropriately considered here. These include the timing and location of the proposed course, the teachers and facilities available, and the time available for planning. The nature of these will affect course content. Discussion of the issues involved can be found in Robinson (319) and Swales (322, pp. 86−90).

A number of practitioners have written of problems related to the timing of courses (Johns (581), Skeldon and Swales (606)). In some cases, the course designers may have a choice in the matter and an early decision must be made as to whether the course should be full- or part-time, intensive or extensive. Pilbeam (317) weighs up the pros and cons of intensive and extensive courses in the business English context and discusses features of intensive courses.

In other cases, the timing and indeed the timetable of the course may not be negotiable. This may dictate the nature of some of the teaching activities; for example, if class sessions are infrequent (once a week), each session may need to be treated as self-contained, with no carry-over expected from one week to the next. Classes at awkward times, for example lunchtime, with some students arriving late, others leaving early, may need to be organised as group activities, with flexible starting times for each task.

An important consideration is the location of the course. Swales (322, p. 86) refers to 'uncertainties about the "home base" of Service English, its status and role and those of its staff'. Certainly where an ESP project is involved, which is likely to deal with large numbers of students over a number of years, it is important to decide as early as possible where the project should be located and with which other institutions (if any) it should be both physically and administratively associated. This decision will not be left just to the course designers, however.

On a more mundane level, the nature of the classrooms and their distance from the students' other places of work may influence decisions related to the syllabus and, even more, methodology. Interesting work is now being carried out around the world on coping with very large classes (which are frequently taught in lecture theatres with fixed seating) (see Coleman (275), Nolasco and Arthur (311)), but some of the more exciting and innovative communicative activities may be unusable because of the constraints of student numbers and location.

A vital consideration in course design is, of course, the number and capabilities of the teachers involved. The allocation of students to classes may depend first of all on the number of teachers available, and only secondly on the grouping of students by test scores or subject specialisms. The choice of methodology and materials is likely to be strongly influenced by what the teachers are able to do — or by how far the budget and timing allow for teacher training. If teacher time is limited, self-access work may need to be built into the course (although this then requires considerable designer/administrator input at the start of the course in order to set up self-access facilities). Wilson (329, p. 8) describes how the ideal syllabus approach (in effect, language across the curriculum) could not be implemented for what she terms administrative reasons: 'Few subject teachers at university level are trained to deal with the communication difficulties presented to students by English medium studies.' Hence 'a weaker statement of position' on the course approach had to be accepted and English courses offered as 'separate activities from the subject courses they are designed to make accessible to the students'.

A final specific issue is that of facilities, for example sufficient and good typists and functioning photocopying machines (and sufficient paper). Crocker (278, p. 136), noting that 'it is my experience that most attempts to improve the standard of language programmes require a mix of professional and administrative change' continues 'and to find out at an early stage that, for example, it is not possible to waive institutional regulations in order to offer a "market price" for a bilingual typist, can save much frustration and wasted staff time by avoiding a design which relies heavily upon locally produced materials'.

The overriding general managerial issue involves the amount of time that course designers have to do their planning (including their needs analysis). Too often, it seems, especially in the private sector, course designers have insufficient time. If there is plenty of time, then detailed course plans can be drawn up, with only minor modifications expected later. If there is very little time, then an *ad hoc* plan will be produced, to be worked through on a trial and error basis (see Crocker (278, pp. 147, 149–50)). Heyneman *et al.* (287) write that 'we now often begin classes with rather general objectives and then tailor our teaching to student needs as we become familiar with the students themselves'.

Even if there is time to make a detailed plan, however, contingency arrangements must be made, for the students may not turn out as expected. This is well described by Drobnic (64) and Saunders (320).

Procedures

Various procedural frameworks for course design exist. Litwack (303) gives a very structured account and calculates the amount of staff time needed to produce materials. Hawkey (67) specifies syllabus content following the Munby model. Mackay gives several accounts, in Mackay (306) focusing more narrowly on course content, and in Mackay and Bosquet (78) giving the administrative framework, as does Clyne (274). Crocker (278) gives the theory and rationale for decisions made in course design.

How far can we generalise from one course or situation to another? Board (267) describes an ESP project for the fisheries industry in Ecuador, one of the requirements of which was that the materials produced should be adaptable to other countries and other occupations. Baumgardner *et al.* (388) give the financial and managerial reasons for the different decisions regarding materials for two courses for engineers in Sri Lanka: for one course published materials were used; for the other in-house materials were specially written. However, O'Keeffe (313, p. 151) found that 'though different occupations need specific syllabuses, these syllabuses are rarely, if ever, unique. The technical words will differ from subject to subject but the language skills and functions, and the events and activities for which these language skills and functions are used, are usually common to a large group of occupations. Specificity does not necessitate uniqueness.'

Concluding remarks

There is a wide range of choices for course designers, although they may be constrained by past practices, institutional exigencies and personal predilections (see Courtney (276)). There is certainly no single model for an ESP course. An ESP course frequently requires a major input of time and resources — both financial and physical — on the parts of students, teaching staff and administrators. In addition, there may be an effect on the wider community. Thus the course needs to be recognised as an innovation, requiring appropriate managerial as well as pedagogical expertise.

The syllabus design stage is only part of the total process of course design. Too often around the world, excellent syllabuses have been devised and written up, but then have lain in offices and libraries gathering dust. Syllabus design must lead to (or, in some cases, be preceded by) developments in materials design and methodology.

Chapter Five

Methodology for ESP

Introduction

By *methodology* I refer to what goes on in the classroom, to what the students have to do. This has implications for what the teacher has to do, of course, which is discussed in Chapter Eight. The materials which are used (including visual and mechanical aids as well as books) are discussed in Chapter Six.

The key issues that we must consider in connection with methodology in ESP are the relationship between the methods and the students' specialism, and the place and nature of language practice. In addition, we might consider the relationship between acquisition and learning and between old and new knowledge and abilities. A further important issue, that of authenticity, is discussed in Chapter Six, pages 54–6.

Widdowson (40, p. 100) accuses ESP practitioners of leaving 'considerations of appropriate methodology entirely out of account'. The accusation is echoed by Markee (359, p. 9) and by Mountford (360). The reason for this may be the concern for rigorous TSA-type (target situation analysis type) needs analysis, popular in the late 1970s and early 1980s, attention being devoted to such needs analysis and to subsequent syllabus design rather than to methodological issues. Since then, however, there has been a developing awareness of the importance of a PSA (present situation analysis), a realisation that learners have personal and individual needs, and an acceptance that learning needs as well as target needs must be attended to (see Chapter Two, pages 7–9). Waters (378, p. 35) urges consideration of 'basic learning factors such as learner interest, enjoyment, creativity and involvement' in both methodology and materials. Hutchinson (353), acknowledging that 'we still know little about how people actually learn' sets out nine 'fundamental principles of learning' which he suggests 'can provide a reasoned basis for the interpretation of ESP language needs into an effective ESP methodology' (Hutchinson (353, p. 71)). These principles include 'Learning is a thinking process' and 'Learning a language is not just a matter of linguistic knowledge', both of which are relevant for the discussion below.

46

If we consider what methodological options are available in ESP, then an inevitable conclusion seems to be that there is very little difference from general ELT. Developments within the communicative approach, in particular, have been realised by both EGP and ESP and it is impossible to say who has borrowed from or influenced whom, or whether there have simply been separate but similar developments. A good review of 'Communicative language teaching in ESP contexts' is given by Swales (375). ESP practitioners can certainly learn a great deal from general ELT materials and methodological suggestions. The resultant difference might be that ESP can base activities on students' specialisms (but need not do so) and that activities can have a truly authentic purpose related to students' target needs. A recent highly critical account of 'Communicative theory and its influence on materials production' by Clarke (401) suggests that communicative theorists have failed to realise their claims. (Though Clarke's account is focused on materials, it is relevant to a discussion of methodology.) All the theories discussed by Clarke (for example, theories relating to the importance of reality and purposiveness) apply to ESP just as much to EGP and, as Clarke acknowledges, may in fact have been successfully realised in ESP.

In what follows, I shall discuss tasks, used here as an overall term and including role plays and simulations, case studies, projects and oral presentations. These can combine to form a task syllabus, but can also be found within a process syllabus, the focus during the task performance then being on the processes activated — whether general language learning processes or subject-specific processes.

Tasks

Overview: tasks in EGP

The best overview of tasks can be found in Candlin and Murphy (335). Candlin (334) offers the following 'working definition of language-learning task':

> One of a set of differentiated, sequencable, problem-posing activities involving learners and teachers in some joint selection from a range of varied cognitive and communicative procedures applied to existing and new knowledge in the collective exploration and pursuance of foreseen or emergent goals within a social milieu. (Candlin (334, p. 10))

Candlin acknowledges that elements in the above will be focused on to varying degrees in different situations. Later (334, pp. 14–16), he gives a typology of language-learning tasks. Coleman (339, p. 131) also gives a classification of tasks, depending on the source of the data used for the task, the mode of interaction and the degree of interaction predictability. Littlejohn and Hicks (356, pp. 70–2) list the following criteria for task design:

> extended discourse — learners should be involved in processing language beyond the sentence level;
> an information gap;
> uncertainty — learners should be able to choose what they want to say;

goal-orientation — there should be a purpose for communication;

real-time processing — the tasks should require learners to deal with language spontaneously.

In addition, Littlejohn and Hicks suggest that tasks 'should be motivating and absorbing and exploit the learners' prior experience' (Littlejohn and Hicks (356, p. 72)).

All of the above seems directly relevant to ESP.

Tasks in ESP

A detailed introduction to both theoretical and practical aspects of designing tasks is given in Nunan (364). Within ESP, the task-based approach was most developed in the King Abdulaziz University (KAU) project in Saudi Arabia (see the discussion on pages 39–40). A theoretical basis for the methodology is given in Phillips (315) (see also the earlier paper by Phillips and Shettlesworth (366) where they discuss the authenticity of classroom language). Phillips (315, p. 97) suggests that there are four key methodological principles:

reality control, which relates to 'the manner in which tasks are rendered accessible to the student';

non-triviality, that is, the tasks must be meaningfully generated by the students' special purpose;

authenticity, that is, the language must be naturally generated by the students' special purpose;

tolerance of error — errors which do not impede successful communication must be tolerated.

A good example of this task-based approach in action is found in accounts of the science activities course for first-year students in the Faculty of Medicine and Allied Sciences at KAU (Nolasco (362), Everett (346)). The behavioural objectives comprised linguistic and elementary science skills, for example 'to comprehend a set of instructions given orally or in writing', 'to carry out a series of operations working individually or in small groups, manipulating scientific equipment as required', 'to elicit information and seek clarification about instructions' and 'to write a report on the activity or experiment in the conventional form'. Further 'behavioural perspectives' emerged during the course, for example the appropriate way to handle scientific equipment, the need for scrupulous accuracy in recording results etc. (Everett (346, pp. 30–1)).

The activities included measuring heart beat rate, testing visual acuity and determining the constituents of some foods, and were sequenced according to degree of complexity. Although the target objective was the production of a written report, all the language skills were developed by the course, the students engaging in spontaneous, comprehensible (although not error-free) oral interaction during the experiments. All the tasks appeared to involve pair or group work, though individual work was possible.

Role play and simulations

Role play and simulations are often treated together and the terms have been 'interpreted in many different ways by teachers and textbook writers' (Sturtridge (374, p. 126)). Essentially, role play involves the learner taking on a different role and even identity from his or her usual one. A simulation is frequently longer than a role play and can allow the student to maintain his or her normal persona. Good accounts of simulations, from a mainly EGP perspective, are given in Sturtridge (374) and Jones (355). Sturtridge (373) deals with simulations in ESP. Sturtridge writes that 'in a simulation the learner is given a task to perform or a problem to solve; the background information and the environment of the problem is simulated. ... As a learning technique simulations were originally used in business and military training and the outcome of a simulation was of paramount importance' (Sturtridge (374, p. 128)). Sturtridge suggests that in language learning the outcome or end-product is less important than the language (the means) used to achieve it. I would suggest that in ESP the end is as important as the means, and may appear to be more so to the students.

A number of writers, both in EGP and ESP, suggest using non-ELT simulations. Jones discusses, among other simulations, *North Sea Challenge* (363), originally produced for native English-speaking sixth-form students, but taken up by EGP and later ESP students (Jones (355, pp. 28−9, 69−75)). Crookall (340) suggests that non-ELT simulations are more likely to be realistic and credible and to lead to more natural communication than ELT simulations, since the latter are too closely related to specific language points. He contends that 'when using simulations in ELT, we should not be concerned with language at all, but with the socially constructed situation and its meanings' (Crookall (340, p. 264)). He suggests that non-ELT simulations are particularly suitable for ESP and, further, may bring ESP and content-based language instruction (LAC, see pages 36−7) closer together. (See also Crookall (341) on the use of international relations simulations and on computers in simulations.) An example of an ESP simulation (for biochemists) which might seem too closely tied to specific language forms (namely those used in simple laboratory experiments) is described by Long (357, pp. 220−3), but Long shows how situational variation can be built into the simulation to help students develop communicative competence.

Other specially developed ESP simulations are described by McGinley (358) and Dubin (344). McGinley writes from the viewpoint of EAP, where, he suggests, simulations have not been common because of time constraints and because of excessively target-oriented needs analyses which disregarded students' personal need for speaking activities. Dubin describes how a simulation designed for a 'Business Argumentation' class was also used as a teacher-training device for the future teachers of that class. Hutchinson and Sawyer-Lauçanno (354) suggest reasons for the comparative lack of simulations in EST, providing two examples of EST simulations.

As McGinley's work implies, and as Hutchinson and Sawyer-Lauçanno suggest, simulations are generally thought of as involving primarily listening and speaking.

Littlejohn and Hicks (356), however, describe a writing simulation designed for lower-intermediate students of business English, involving the sending of various letters and telexes from and to a construction company by rival suppliers of equipment.

Case studies

The use of case studies is a well-established method for inducting future professionals into the job demands of business, medicine, the law and engineering. It would seem to be an ideal method for ESP. It involves studying the facts of a real-life case, discussing the issues involved and reaching some kind of decision and/or action plan. All the language skills are potentially involved: reading input documents, listening and speaking (discussing) and possibly writing some sort of summary or report. Importantly for ESP, especially where mature and professionally well-qualified students are concerned, case studies draw upon students' professional know-how, utilising the 'cognitive and behavioral styles' (Piotrowski (367, p. 229)) of their work rather than of the traditional language classroom. For students who are not yet fully qualified in their profession, the use of case studies helps to induct them into some aspects of the professional culture (see Charles (337, pp. 28–31)).

The case-conference, a recognised medical procedure, was used with qualified doctors by Allwright and Allwright (331). They discuss the selection of suitable cases to use and suggest that 'topic selection should be determined by a process of continuing negotiation between teacher and learners, as the course progresses' (Allwright and Allwright (331, p. 59)).

Piotrowski (367), Charles (337) and Sawyer (369) all describe work with business case studies, giving accounts of how such studies are normally used in the business world. Like Allwright and Allwright, they also discuss their own role as teachers in the case study situation (see below, page 81).

So far all the tasks or activity types have been of relatively short duration, typically one class period, albeit maybe a period of two hours (Piotrowski (367)) or ninety minutes (Allwright and Allwright (331)). A much more extended activity is that of the project.

Project work

A project typically lasts several days or even weeks and involves students in some out-of-class activities. It has a clear target or end-product, most often a written report. For Herbolich (351), however, the students not only had to write a technical manual but also had to construct a box kite! A good introduction to project work, with many examples, is provided by Fried-Booth (349). Although intended for the EGP class, the more advanced examples would be appropriate for ESP. (See also Fried-Booth (348).)

Project work is particularly appropriate to EAP, since 'doing a project' may well be a requirement for a university student, especially at the graduate level. Bloor and

St John (332) distinguish three types of project, depending on the students and their needs. The first is the Group Project, which involves the members of the group in real research. The example given is of a descriptive and evaluative survey of the university postal system. The second type is a Mini-research Project, for individual students, involving the use of questionnaires, surveys and interviews. The third and most common type is the Literature-based (or Library) Project, involving the individual student in extensive purposeful reading (Bloor and St John (332, p. 86)).

As well as rehearsing a target activity, project work may also involve activation of all the language skills and, importantly, at the discretion of the student. For example, the student may have to decide whether certain information is best obtained by interviewing someone or by reading about it (see the discussion in Robinson (368)). Bloor and St John argue that the processes engaged in during the project (both study processes and language activation processes) are as important as the product.

Oral presentations

A final task type which is common in ESP is the oral presentation. It may form part of one of the other types, for example one or more participants in a simulation may have to make a presentation. Students doing a project may have to make an oral presentation at the end, in addition to, or instead of, presenting a written report. While 'making a presentation' may seem to be a more limited activity than the other tasks discussed, it can in fact involve all the language skills, as Souillard and Kerr (372) show. Tudor (377), in an interesting article on using translation in ESP, shows how the student may need to use relevant L1 material as input to the presentation. Schofield (370) explains how the procedure for helping students prepare presentations, normally involving a lot of individual work, can be adapted to group work. Nesi and Skelton (361) give details of the oral presentation module of a one-year intensive EAP course for Algerian students in Britain. The students made several presentations during the year, even when at a very elementary level of English.

As with the other task types above, communication and professional skills are as important as language skills. Thus useful lessons may be learnt from what is done with native speakers (see Zawadzki and Saunders (380)). The professional skills focused on may relate to the business, technical or academic sphere. Dubois has extensively researched medical presentations (see the references in Dubois (345)). Thompson (376) looked at a range of academic disciplines. Chirnside (338) describes a whole course devoted to enabling students to give factual oral presentations, the topics being dictated by the students' concurrent studies in nursing. Peretz (365) describes an advanced reading course utilising students' content area knowledge and targeted towards a final oral report.

Task-based learning: concluding remarks

Clearly, there is a range of task types which can be utilised for ESP. All in some way mirror activities from the 'real world' outside the ESP classroom. However,

ESP practitioners disagree as to the desirability of closeness of fit between these activities and the students' specialist studies. Chamberlain and Baumgardner (336, p. 1) write of ESP teachers wanting 'materials to be more interesting and based on real life activities, and topics not necessarily to be too discipline-related'. Huckin (352, p. 64) refers to 'generalized ESP'. However, Bloor and St John (332, p. 85) write: 'We argue that project writing is an example of an activity which is directly relevant to target needs and yet provides the opportunity for process-oriented language learning. We also argue that there are advantages to the learner in using language which is subject specific rather than merely engaging in activities designed to develop general competence.'

General academic or scientific competence may have to be the target, though, when the students in a class represent a variety of specialisms. A solution here may be to use logical problems (Dorrity (343)). Flowerdew (347, p. 63) also refers to 'activating high-level problem-solving skills' through group discussions of such general topics as 'Pollution' or 'The development of alternative energy sources', although he acknowledges that, when groups are more homogeneous, more specific topics can be used. Souillard and Kerr (372) begin their course in oral presentations for science and technology students by getting the students to talk about 'funny gadgets', that is, humorous Heath Robinson-style (350) inventions.

At what stage is there explicit attention to language? Allwright and Allwright (331) refer to 'problems before solutions' and to a 'diagnostic approach', suggesting that linguistic problems should not be predicted before they are revealed in the course of real-life communication activities. Sturtridge (373, p. 34) suggests that the main linguistic input should come at the end of the simulation as 'in this way it can be more closely based on what the students themselves want to communicate'. Brammer and Sawyer-Lauçanno (333, pp. 146–7) write that 'the instructor has three ways of tackling the problem of language error correction: ongoing correction, note-taking and postactivity evaluation, and preactivity language exercises. All three should be used to obtain the most satisfactory results, although each has its drawbacks. Correction during the simulation can easily disrupt the activity. Postactivity evaluation sometimes gives the trainee the impression that we are more interested in the "look where you went wrong" aspects, unless it is counterbalanced by highlighting what the trainee did in fact manage to do correctly. Preventive language exercises are potentially unlimited . . . .' Littlejohn and Hicks (356, p. 83) suggest that 'the teacher's key role is in the debriefing after the simulation'. Wright (379, p. 108), however, notes both that 'our failing is perhaps that we do not do enough de-briefing work after role-plays' and that students 'easily tire of long post-mortems!'

Sturtridge (373, p. 34) argues that, as well as integrating all the language skills, simulations 'provide the learner with an opportunity to summon up and use all the language he has, which will extend far beyond what he has been "taught"'. Wright makes the same point, though not expressed so positively: 'Although the grammatical level of students may not be a deal higher than when we first taught them, . . . they learn to *use* their English' (Wright (379, p. 109)). Can the students do more than this through task-based work? Tudor (377), comparing students who used L1 material for their oral presentations with those who did not, suggests that those who did not use translation were working '*within* their existing L2 competence', whereas for those who used translation there was a '"perceived resource gap", i.e. the explicit recognition of the need for L2 input, and therefore a receptive attitude for the acquisition of new elements' (Tudor (377, p. 272)). Markee (359) suggests, somewhat speculatively, that the ESP classroom is particularly appropriate for study of the relationship between input and acquisition. His speculations have not been directly taken up, nor has there been any systematic evaluation of the results of task-based work. However, the general consensus is that task-based work is enjoyable and actively engages the students both as specialists and as human beings, all of which are pre-requisites for the acquisition of new language and the consolidation of old.

Chapter Six

Materials for ESP

In looking at the role of materials in ESP, I shall first discuss the important issue of authenticity, and then look at textbooks and in-house materials. After that I shall consider visual and mechanical aids, and such technical aids as video, word-processors and computers.

Authenticity

A key concept within the communicative approach, and one felt to be particularly relevant for ESP, is that of authenticity. It has aroused considerable discussion and a range of definitions of authenticity have been suggested (see Clarke (401)). Basically, when we refer to using 'authentic materials' in ELT, we refer to the use of print, audio, video and pictorial material originally produced for a purpose other than the teaching of language. At one extreme, this can be anything that is available to the language teacher but which was not produced for language-teaching purposes; at the other extreme, of particular relevance to ESP, it will be material normally used in the students' own specialist workplace or study situation. Additionally for ESP, we must consider whether the goals that we set are authentic with regard to students' real-world roles, and whether the tasks or activities that take place in the learning situation are authentic. The important questions to ask are how such authentic goals, tasks and materials should be selected and how they are realised within the language classroom.

A certain amount of authentic material may be collected as part of the needs analysis stage of course design. Alternatively, authentic text selection may follow the needs analysis stage. This is the procedure outlined by Mackay (306, p. 137). Scott (443, p. 24), having first made a selection of topic, refers to some of the problems that can occur in trying to obtain video recordings, attend classes and follow up references to print material normally used by the students in their specialist classes: 'In practice this is for the most part impossible owing to the usual constraints of time and the threat that recording and analysis of language might constitute to both native and non-native speakers of English.' As a compromise, Scott used lecture handouts and textbook references as guidelines for content and then sought 'relevant' material.

Morrow (432) urges that, in addition to topic, we consider function (or purpose), channel (whether spoken or written) and audience. The importance of audience is also noted by Greenhalgh (414), working with technical students in Egypt. Greenhalgh observed that a visiting British engineer consciously and consistently modified his language when lecturing to the students. Recordings of such modified speech would be more authentic for Greenhalgh's students than recordings of lectures given to native-speaker engineers.

Further development of the notions of audience and function is given by Widdowson (458). He suggests that with regard to scientific discourse, for example, there are three levels or types. Science 'as a discipline' is intended for 'scientist to scientist' and assumes a considerable amount of shared knowledge. 'Science as a subject' is 'science teacher to science student communication such as is found in textbooks'. Finally, 'science as a topic of interest' is 'journalist to general reader communication such as is found in newspapers and popular journals' (Widdowson (458, pp. 167–8)). Material from the last-mentioned category is frequently chosen for ESP courses; however, not because the students are 'general readers', but because such material is more accessible to the teachers and/or because the students do not share subject specialism.

For Widdowson, authenticity does not lie in the materials themselves but is created by the reader/hearer's response. He asks for 'a congruence between the language producer's intentions and the receiver's interpretation, this congruence being effected through a shared knowledge of conventions' (Widdowson (458, p. 166)). The language teacher's task, then, is to help the students develop an awareness of those conventions. The conclusion which Widdowson draws is that students should not be confronted with 'authentic materials' until they have sufficient awareness of the conventions to be able to react to them authentically. Thus such materials should not be used at the start of an ESP course. The question then is: what should be used, and what relationship does it have with the authentic materials?

Widdowson (459, p. 190) proposes a choice between simple and simplified accounts, the former being preferred. Simple accounts are specially written for students, bearing in mind the students' linguistic level, highlighting any rhetorical conventions that the students need to learn, and avoiding any idiosyncrasy of style. Simplified accounts, on the other hand, are 'doctored' versions of original texts. Simplification has been much attacked in the literature, but the objection would seem to be not that it is wrong in itself but that it has not been adequately done. This is because only vocabulary and syntax have been attended to, not the conceptual structure and the rhetorical patterning. Wood (464), looking at the rhetorical structuring of chemistry texts, shows how 'simplification, unless carefully carried out, may cause greater problems than it solves' (Wood (464, p. 126)).

However, Wood's analysis of certain types of chemistry texts leads him to suggest a new definition of authenticity, based on recurrent rhetorical patterns, some of which are realised by means of a limited set of linguistic forms. Authentic texts can actually be created by the ESP teacher or student, as long as they follow the regular rhetorical patterns. The level of difficulty can be controlled via control of the technical content or the linguistic realisation of the rhetorical patterns. Davies (405), by contrast, suggests that the information structure of a text is more significant than the rhetorical structure. She proposes a set of 'topic types' to which texts can be allocated. An authentic text for a student, then, could be one which belongs to the appropriate topic type for the student's specialism. Johns and Davies (747) suggest that students can be helped to identify the topic types with which they need to work and can move from shorter and easier examples of these types to longer more complex examples.

An alternative approach to those so far described is proposed by Bhatia (390), who advocates the use of 'easification devices' or 'access structures' which are presented alongside unsimplified original texts and help to guide the learner through them. Other suggestions regarding the selection and use of authentic materials (however defined) are given by Phillips and Shettlesworth (437) and Wilson (463). Phillips and Shettlesworth 'question the practicability of preparing specialised teaching material to a high standard when one is dealing with a diversified demand often on a "one-off" basis at very short notice'. They suggest using authentic materials and grading them according to 'accessibility' (for example, the density of new information in a text, the length of the text) and varying the complexity of the task demanded of the students (Phillips and Shettlesworth (437, pp. 24−5)). Wilson also suggests a set of criteria as a basis for text selection, including such aspects as the density of information, the cultural suitability of the material and the author's style (Wilson (463, pp. 48−9)).

Crocker and Swales (403, p. 265) write that 'we believe that one would want to ensure in an ESP course that the handling of the materials (i.e. the methodology) effects a compromise between techniques which are known to characterise "good language teaching", and procedures which derive from how the student operates in the domain of use'. Authentic materials, however selected, will not work well in the classroom unless the methodology is carefully considered. The danger exists that interesting-looking authentic materials are used in an uninteresting way because too much of the preparation time has been spent in looking for the materials and not enough in considering their exploitation.

Textbooks and in-house materials

Which to choose?

A common assumption in ESP is that the truly professional practitioner uses locally produced or in-house materials for teaching, not published textbooks. Swales identified this as a problem in 1980, and observed that 'this heavy commitment to materials writing has been intensified by the expectancies of the . . . institutions, which increasingly require their English departments to write all their own courses' (Swales (453, p. 15)). Materials writing thus contributes to the status both of the ESP practitioner and the institution, and the term ESP is seen to imply that every learning situation is unique. (But see O'Keeffe (313) on unique and recurrent elements in ESP. See also Jones (418) for a more recent discussion on the inherent contradiction offered by ESP textbooks: globally available materials for specific situations.)

I would argue that a real professional is able to make a principled choice between materials writing and the use of what is already available on the market. An example of such choice is given by Baumgardner *et al.* (388) in relation to two courses for engineers in Sri Lanka. For the degree course, published materials were used, the reasons being that there was only one adviser attached to the project who would be too busy to write materials, that there were funds to buy books, that suitable books were available on the market and that there would be a positive psychological benefit in the students having individual copies of the textbook. For the diploma course, by contrast, appropriate books and the funds to buy them were not available, whereas there was a team of people able to write materials. In addition, Baumgardner *et al.* believed that 'under favourable circumstances the writing of materials is an integral part of teacher training' and that 'locally produced materials incorporating local themes would be of more interest to Sri Lankan students' (Baumgardner *et al.* (388, pp. 97–9)).

Problems with textbooks

Allwright (384) asks 'What do we want teaching materials for?' and, arguing for greater appreciation of the role of the learner in the teaching/learning process, suggests that 'the role of teaching materials is necessarily limited' (Allwright (384, p. 8)). Other writers on the issue are in no doubt that teaching materials are essential. Nor are they opposed to the use of textbooks in principle. Rather, there is a fairly widespread feeling that the textbooks which are available are in various ways deficient.

Ewer and Boys (410) mount a strong attack on the EST textbooks then available, suggesting that 'the really fundamental factors of textbook design such as the validity of the linguistic contents, the accuracy of the explanations and examples given, and the number and coverage of the exercises provided' have been ignored in favour of considerations of approach and methodology (Ewer and Boys (410, pp. 87–8)). Taking the results of research by Ewer into the main communicative features of formal scientific and technological discourse (Ewer (132)), Ewer and Boys found a distressing lack of coverage of these features in the ten textbooks which they investigated (including one co-authored by Ewer himself — Ewer and Latorre (281)). They further found considerable inadequacies in the explanations and exercises.

Ewer and Boys ascribe some of these deficiencies to the fact that 'most EST textbooks are designed for, or are the outcome of, "remedial" or "supplementary" courses and assume that students already possess a knowledge of English .... . Unhappily, this is not at all understood by potential users, especially in developing countries abroad where the greatest demand for EST exists' (Ewer and Boys (410, p. 97)). Swales (453, p. 14) also notes that 'the textbooks are increasingly less self-sufficient in practice material and in coverage of skill areas', but ascribes this to constraints on publishers.

Another strongly worded attack on textbooks is given by Sheldon (446), (447) from a general ELT perspective. He writes of teachers' disappointment with textbooks, of 'a variety of common design flaws at one level, and a scepticism about the theoretical premises of many coursebooks on another' (Sheldon (447, p. 238)). Sheldon is primarily concerned, however, with helping teachers and course directors to be better informed about textbooks, so that they do not buy books which subsequently turn out to be unusable, a problem also addressed by Swales (453). Sheldon thus considers the usefulness or otherwise of reviews of textbooks and the criteria commonly used for textbook selection.

Advantages of textbooks over in-house materials

Pilbeam (438), posing the question 'Can published materials be widely used for ESP courses?', gives some criteria for evaluating ESP textbooks and, in effect, weighs up the arguments for and against both textbooks and in-house materials. In-house materials are likely to be more specific and appropriate than published materials and to have greater face validity in terms of the language dealt with and the contexts it is presented in. In addition, in-house materials may be more flexible than published textbooks (an advantage on a short course). Finally, the writers of in-house materials can make sure that the methodology is suitable for the intended learners.

It takes time, however, to write tailor-made materials. Pilbeam says that 'in the business world, where some companies commission writers to produce material specially for them, ratios of between 10:1 and 5:1 (writing hours : teaching hours) are not unusual'. Also not unusual, according to Pilbeam, is the result that the hastily written materials 'based on highly relevant spoken and written texts' have 'rather uninspired exploitation' (Pilbeam (438, p. 122)). One likelihood is that class activities are too tied to the texts and to their linguistic or factual content; not enough time has been expended on developing interesting and authentic tasks or on considering what learning processes are likely to be activated. Swales observes that 'the locally produced materials . . . show a striking resemblance to the published materials that have been rejected' (Swales (453, p. 11)). For example, the sequence and type of exercises found in the *English in Focus* (258) series has been widely imitated. Additionally, in-house materials may consist of much photocopied material from other textbooks.

As well as being time consuming, the production of in-house materials is relatively expensive, a point made by both Swales and Pilbeam and O'Neill (434). Pilbeam (438, p. 123) concludes that 'it is highly unlikely that one-off ESP courses justify the expense of producing tailor-made materials'.

O'Neill, responding to Allwright (384) and referring to experience with an ESP course, suggests that 'no other medium is as easy to use as a book' (O'Neill (434, p. 107)). The in-house materials are commonly in the form of 'showers of single-page handouts' (Swales (453, p. 18)), which can easily get out of order or lost. More importantly, a textbook is complete not just in the physical sense but in the sense that the whole term's or year's course is available to the students at once. Thus, if they wish, students can look ahead to see what is coming up, can refer back to what has gone before or to something that they might have missed, and can place a particular lesson in the context of the whole course. A textbook, especially a course book, provides a framework for a course, forming in essence a syllabus. This may appear to be unduly constraining in some situations, but for many students and for many teachers, especially less qualified or experienced ones, it is a positive advantage.

Despite what may have been implied so far, there is, of course, no polar division between in-house and published materials. The former can very often become the latter. Wright (379, p. 107) acknowledges that 'we write a lot of our own cases with the objective not only of finding new and lively things to do in class, but also of having the material published'. In other situations, what begins as supplementation to a published course develops to the extent that it is a course in its own right. Swales (453, pp. 20–1) offers a principled procedure for supplementation.

Materials evaluation

There are three types of materials evaluation: preliminary, summative and formative, the first two being more likely to focus on published or at least completed materials and the third to focus on in-house materials. Preliminary evaluation will normally take place before an ESP course begins and involves selecting the most appropriate from the publications that are available. It is obviously useful to have some sort of checklist of features which one wants the textbooks to have, and to rank these features in order of priority. No textbook is likely to be perfect, of course, and practical considerations, such as cost, may have to take precedence over pedagogic merit. Kitto (425) presents a course director's pragmatic approach to materials selection. Another case study, from the language training point of view, is given by Leckey (426). Sheldon (447) presents a general set of criteria which can be used for textbook selection, but notes: 'It is clear that coursebook assessment is fundamentally a subjective, rule-of-thumb activity, and that no neat formula, grid or system will ever provide a definite yardstick' (Sheldon (447, p. 245)). However, criteria such as those which Sheldon offers can help course designers to clarify some of their assumptions and preconceptions. Williams (460) and Breen and Candlin (393) give more interactive approaches to materials assessment, suitable for use on teacher training courses.

The other two types of materials evaluation are illuminatingly discussed by Alderson (381). Alderson first discusses performance (or summative) evaluation. This takes place at the end of a course and addresses the question of whether the materials have been effective. 'Typically, although not necessarily, performance evaluation makes use of tests administered before and after the programme' (Alderson (381, p. 147)). Other methods include use of a checklist, similar to that used for the preliminary evaluation, and use of questionnaires. Further discussion of summative evaluation is given on pages 65–73 below.

Alderson then discusses revision (or formative) evaluation, conducted while the course is ongoing, so that modifications can be made to the materials. He notes that 'revision evaluation of language teaching has received very little attention in the past, and relatively little is known about the usefulness of certain techniques' (Alderson (381, p. 151)). This still seems to be the case. The main techniques used, as with performance evaluation, are tests and questionnaires, plus interviews.

The function of a test in revision evaluation will be to examine the materials, not the students. Tests should be frequent, for example after each unit. Alderson suggests that 'errors on any item or group of items which have been made by sixty per cent or more of the students indicate that either the materials are too difficult, or the procedure or instructions for the exercises are causing problems' (Alderson (381, p. 151)). In addition to this, questionnaires may be given to both teachers and students, seeking information and impressions at the level of item, exercise and unit, rather than the course as a whole, though there may be problems in interpreting the students' responses. Teachers may be interviewed about their experiences with the materials and can be asked to annotate their copies of the materials as they use them, so that any problems or suggestions for improvement do not get forgotten. Alderson observes that 'the emphasis so far has been on paper and pencil type evaluation schemes', chiefly in the interests of standardisation, but suggests that more interactive methods of revision evaluation could be used, such as discussion and observation (Alderson (381, p. 154)).

Discussion and observation were among the methods used by Dudley-Evans and Bates (409) when evaluating the effectiveness of the *General Science* book of the *Nucleus* series (263) in Egypt (see also Dudley-Evans (408)). Face to face discussion with teachers had its drawbacks, however, since teachers were reluctant to voice criticisms and 'feedback tends to be rather disordered' (Dudley-Evans and Bates (409, p. 102)). The other methods used were questionnaires to teachers, visits by Egyptian senior inspectors to schools and discussions between inspectors and teachers, and seminars in which the authors discussed the book and the appropriate teaching methodology with the teachers and the inspectors. The materials under discussion were, of course, already published (and designed for a different part of the world). In response to the feedback obtained in Egypt, Dudley-Evans and Bates added reading passages to each unit and considerably enlarged the Teachers' Manual. Later, these revisions were made available worldwide. Thus Swales' complaint (Swales (453, p. 13)) that 'ESP textbooks never ... get revised' has in one case, at least, been listened to. (Another account of successful transfer of materials from one situation to another is given in Dudley-Evans (407).)

Producing materials for ESP

Several accounts exist of the genesis of ESP materials, often containing analyses of the exercise types involved. See, for example, Allen and Widdowson (257), Bates (262), Candlin *et al.* (394), (395), Jordan (419), McDonough (428), Morrison (431), Swales (452), (454) and Todd Trimble and Trimble (455). Too often, the underlying theory for the materials is based on speculation rather than detailed research, although Candlin *et al.*, Swales and Todd Trimble and Trimble are noteworthy for their careful analysis of linguistic and discoursal features. Accounts of large-scale projects, focused on or involving materials production, include Chitravelu (399), (400), describing the University of Malaya English for Special Purposes Project, Harper (11), describing the King Abdulaziz University project in Saudi Arabia, and Moore (430), referring to the project in Colombia which led to the production of the *Reading and Thinking in English* series (784).

Moore gives good practical advice, including a 'Procedural guide to producing a unit' (Moore (430, p. 45)), although he writes that his purpose 'is not to provide a recipe for materials production but to set out some of the procedures which team preparation helped to make explicit'. He suggests that 'a materials development project aims to eliminate some of the hit-and-miss procedures of materials production (e.g. by an individual teacher) by (1) using a coherent methodology (and) (2) being based on team planning and teacher evaluation' (Moore (430, p. 41)). Later, Moore offers six criteria to be applied to the activities created in the materials (Moore (430, p. 49)):

PURPOSE	Is the purpose clearly defined?
TYPE	Does the exercise type effectively and economically accomplish the purpose?
CONTENT	1. Is the ratio of language given/student task economic? 2. Are instructions to students clear?
INTEREST	Is it interesting?
AUTHENTICITY	Is it a meaningful task? Is it challenging?
DIFFICULTY	Does it contain distracting difficulties?

Gimenez (413) also gives a useful 'checklist for materials production in the context of ESP'.

Helpful collections of exercise types, especially for reading, are given in Scott and McAlpin (444) and Bates (387). Further useful practical advice is given by Chaplen (397), comparing the advantages and disadvantages of the team approach to developing materials for and teaching an ESP programme. He calculates that it takes at least ten hours to prepare an hour's worth of teaching material and that 'developing the first draft of a film-based unit generating 4−5 hours of integrated class activities can take a total of over 45 hours' (Chaplen (397, p. 3)). He suggests that the advantages of a team approach to materials production are quality, since materials can be scrutinised and checked by people other than the writer, and continuity, because a team approach requires clear guidelines for everyone to follow. The disadvantages are that individuals do not always perceive the relationship of their materials to the whole course, that far too much material gets produced and yet people underestimate the amount of time needed to produce and to revise it, and that, because all the classes must keep in step, teachers may have to concentrate on getting through the materials rather than ensuring that the students are making good progress. Chaplen concludes that strict control is needed to prevent materials developers attempting overly ambitious revisions, to ensure that there is sufficient time for adequate consultation between developers and colleagues, to ensure quality, and to ensure that materials are geared to the average, not just the brightest, students.

Technical aids

Visual and mechanical aids

As well as print material, focused on above, one would expect that for teaching ESP there would be a rich supply of authentic visual and mechanical material. There is not a great deal of discussion of this in the literature, however. Kalinyazgan (421) and Souillard (450) describe the use of pictures and diagrams to practise oral and aural skills with technical students. B. Robinson (439) discusses the use of a piece of hardware with engineering students (in this case a bicycle pump), in order to give the students, who were beginners in engineering, some understanding of engineering concepts and thus provide them with genuine meanings to convey in their language practice. Diagrams of the hardware were also available, to give the students practice in diagram interpretation. Other accounts of working with equipment are given by Nolasco (362) and Everett (346) in connection with the KAU Science Activities Course.

Video in ESP

Video is probably still not as much or as inventively used in ELT, let alone ESP, as it might be. Important questions to ask are (1) is video being used to replicate what could be done with other media or is it making a unique contribution, and (2) how exactly does video contribute to students' learning. A useful set of 'frameworks for the exploitation of video in the language classroom' is given by Tudor (457); Tomalin and Stempleski (456) is a reference and resource book for using video in the classroom; MacWilliam (429) discusses the relationship between video and comprehension; and Kennedy (423) gives an overview of ESP and video.

Perhaps the commonest use of video for ESP is in EAP. Recordings can be made of regular lectures and seminars or, if this is not feasible, lecturers can be invited to give lecturettes (very short lectures) in the recording studio. Simulated seminars can be video recorded as can role plays of tutor−student interactions. Obvious exploitation is to have students make notes while watching the recorded lectures and discuss selected features of both the lectures and the seminars. The advantages over audio recordings are that attention can be paid to gestures and body language and that information given on the blackboard, overhead projector and on slides can be captured on the recording. Accounts of material of this type are given in Sturtridge *et al.* (451) and Geddes (411). Williams (461) describes a course in listening comprehension and exam answer writing, using ready-made video recordings.

Other practical suggestions for work with ready-made recordings originally intended for use with native speakers is given by Kerridge (424), Lynch (427), Sheerin (445) and Willis (462). Willis notes how short a segment of video (four and a half minutes) is sufficient for a session. Lynch explores the opportunities afforded for follow-up 'by the medium and technology of video', for example having students produce their own alternative soundtrack for the video (Lynch (427, p. 6)). In both these cases we assume that the topic of the video material is relevant to the students' studies; in fact, Lynch refers to 'content familiarity', which enables students 'to discuss a given process *before* they watch the tape' (Lynch (427, p. 6)), a technique also used by Williams (461). Charles (398) and Crocker and Swales (403), however, address the situation where there may not be a recording which has topic relevance for the students. As an alternative, and distinguishing carrier content from real content (see Scott (443)), they consider process and system relevance, in both cases extracting generalisable material about procedures from sports recordings (football and cricket respectively). Crocker and Swales (403, p. 262) suggest that 'the key feature for materials is appropriacy to a learning or teaching need, but appropriacy can be constructed between what is available and what is required'.

In all the above cases, reference is made to group work. Bevan (389), however, describes self-instruction with video. The practical experience of creating a video is recounted by Bonamy (391). It was realised that the original recording, of a UNESCO adviser giving a demonstration, was too difficult to use with students at the beginning of their course. An audio tape was made from the soundtrack and used to help prepare short simple accounts of some of the content of the video, these simple accounts then being video recorded. The final materials consisted of two or more of these simple accounts, followed by the corresponding extract from the original video recording, together with back-up worksheets and visual aids. Candlin *et al.* (396) describe the making of a videotape of a business case study session with two purposes in mind: to have an example of a case study to show future students, and to have material for visual and linguistic analysis. A less formal use of video recording is for the purpose of feedback. For example, after a simulation students may watch a teacher-made recording of the simulation, focusing variously on linguistic features, on indicators of successful or unsuccessful communication, on appropriate body language etc.

Word-processors and computers in ESP

A brief review of the use of word-processors and computers in LSP is given by Hahn (415). St John (440) discusses the practical applications of word-processors in helping students with writing problems. In general, it seems that the greatest use of computers is in LSP research into the formation of term banks and machine translation (see various articles in Lauren and Nordman (20), (21)). Pedagogical use of computers for vocabulary work is described by Baten *et al.* (386) and Fox (136). Nyns (433) describes the teaching of reading for professional purposes, using semi-structured self-access work with computers as a complement to class activities. An interesting component is the 'dynamic dictionary', tailor-made for the specific students and texts. Other practical accounts of working with computers and preparing materials are given by Atlan (385), Botha (392), Danchik (404), Johns (417), Phillips (435), (436) and Skehan (449). Phillips reminds us that the computer should be the servant, not the master: 'Current work in CALL gives the overwhelming impression that the program designers are responding more to the challenge of the chip than to the purposes of the pupil.' He urges that software should not be written 'in isolation from considerations of how the activities thereby created relate to actual learning contexts' (Phillips (435, p. 31)). Kay (422) distinguishes between 'learner tools' and 'trainer tools' and urges more trainer training both in the pedagogical use of computers and in information technology skills. An obvious use of computers is for self-study, as described by Sampson (441), but Davies (406) shows how they can also be used for group interaction. Another obvious use is in testing, referred to by Alderson (381, p. 151) and Cousin (402).

Scarbrough (442), reviewing software for ELT, comments on 'the relatively narrow range of language-practice techniques available' in the programs he viewed. 'Essentially there are just four types of program: gap-filling, text manipulation, text reconstruction, and simulation' (Scarbrough (442, p. 301)). Scarbrough concludes his review with the suggestion that 'the most interesting next stage of CALL development may well lie in the elaboration of techniques for the incorporation of . . . real-world information-handling uses of computers into the language learning process' (Scarbrough (442, p. 310)). An interesting example of this suggestion is provided by Hollis (416), describing work with airline reservations agents in Saudi Arabia. He writes of 'blurring the distinction between the classroom and the work situation in the interests of authenticity', and is enabled to do this by means of video and, even more, through the flexibility of the computer system.

Chapter Seven

Evaluation and Testing in ESP

Evaluation

Introduction and definitions

'Evaluation can be defined as "the discovery of the value of something for some purpose". This is necessarily vague, since the specification of "something" and "value" depends on the specification of the "purpose".' Thus wrote Alderson (381, p. 146). Murphy (518, p. 15) writes that 'evaluation is concerned with describing what is there, and placing some value judgement on what is found'. With regard to ESP, we are seeking to establish the effectiveness and efficiency of teaching programmes. Testing, often equated with evaluation, is only a part of it. We shall here concentrate on the evaluation of courses and programmes as a whole. Textbook and materials evaluation is discussed in Chapter Six.

According to Alderson (381), McGinley (513), (514), Mackay (515), Murphy (518) and Swan (530), evaluation has been neglected in ESP. McGinley notes how often ESP materials and programmes are written of as successful despite there being no account of any objective measurements of this success. Swan (530) suggests eight possible reasons for the underdevelopment of evaluation in ESP, including the shortness or even one-off nature of ESP courses, the time-consuming nature of evaluation and the lack of any felt need for evaluation. In the 1990s, however, there is a greater concern for the cost-effectiveness of courses and, even more, of large-scale projects, and so a need for evaluation is now being felt.

Useful articles which give an overview of evaluation in ESP are those by Bachman (476), Brown (484), Mackay (515), Murphy (518) and Rea (523). Also useful are Elley (493) and Moody (516). The most detailed account of an evaluation project in ESP is Celani *et al.* (486), which describes the evaluation of the Brazilian ESP project for the period 1980−6 (see also Celani (485)). Other references, such as Long (507) and McCormick *et al.* (512), derive from general education or general ELT, not ESP.

A basic distinction is made between *formative* and *summative* evaluation. Formative evaluation is carried out during the life of a course or project and the results obtained can be used to modify what is being done. Summative evaluation, on the other hand, is carried out when the course or project is finished and when it is clearly too late to do any 'fine tuning'. Rather, a decision will be taken as to whether to repeat the course or not, or, in the case of a 'one-off' course, whether money has been well spent or not. Obviously, for any particular course or project, both types of evaluation can be undertaken, as was the case with the Brazilian ESP project evaluation (Celani *et al.* (486)). A type of summative evaluation not often feasible, and therefore not often carried out, would occur some time after the end of the course, for example six months or a year or more after. This would attempt to ascertain the effectiveness of an ESP course in preparing students for their subsequent work or study experience. Such evaluation is referred to as 'ultimate evaluation' by Swan (530) and is also discussed by Alderson (465).

A further distinction can be made between *process* and *product* evaluation. A process evaluation may be concerned with teaching and learning strategies or processes, and administrative and decision-making processes. A product evaluation will look, in particular, at student product such as examination results, essays etc. Rea (523) suggests a link between formative and process evaluation on the one hand and summative and product evaluation on the other. Long (507), however, in a useful discussion of the terminology, suggests important differences between these four approaches. Brown (484) suggests that the three 'dimensions' of evaluation, namely formative versus summative, process versus product, and qualitative versus quantitative, are 'complementary rather than mutually exclusive' and that 'all available perspectives may prove valuable for the evaluation of a given program' (Brown (484, p. 229)). Lynch (511, p. 39) writes that 'the strongest approach to evaluation is one that combines as many methods, qualitative and quantitative, as are appropriate to the particular evaluation context'. Lynch presents a 'context-adaptive model' for evaluation that can be utilised in a variety of language-teaching contexts.

As with needs analysis, it is useful to pose a series of 'wh-' questions to guide one through the essential points related to evaluation. Thus:

WHY carry out an evaluation?
WHAT is the subject of the evaluation?
WHO carries out the evaluation?
HOW is the evaluation carried out?
WHAT NEXT: what will happen to the results?

Why carry out an evaluation?

Considering the list of 'wh-' questions above, it might seem that there is some overlap between evaluation and needs analysis. Brown (484) notes that 'it is worth considering the possibility that the difference between needs analysis and program evaluation may be more one of focus than of the actual activities involved' (Brown (484, pp. 222–3)). Information on needs is certainly needed for the evaluation. Richterich and Chancerel (87) see needs analysis as an ongoing process, acknowledging that students' needs may change as a course progresses. An evaluator would wish to know of changed needs and whether these changes had been responded to or not. Knight (74), discussing one-off short courses, refers to monitoring, meaning in this case on-the-spot needs analysis. The term 'monitoring' could equally well refer to formative evaluation and perhaps in the case of such very short courses the distinction between identification of needs and formative evaluation becomes blurred. Kennedy (499), however, gives a useful comparison and contrast between needs analysis and formative evaluation.

Both formative and summative evaluation can be undertaken to provide data as input to possible change. Thus evaluation is being used as part of quality control. Any or all aspects of a programme may be changed, hopefully for the better, as a result of information obtained from the evaluation. In other cases an evaluation may function as a source of information and experience, but not necessarily lead to change. Summative evaluation of a one-off course will not lead to an improved version of that same course, but can serve as a resource for others thinking of running similar courses. A further reason for carrying out an evaluation may be to ensure that money is being or has been well spent.

Bell (479) suggests twenty-four possible purposes for an evaluation project, including 'to guide any curriculum changes', 'to document events', 'to measure cost-effectiveness', 'to determine curriculum-related in-service needs of staff', 'to identify any unintended outcomes of the program' and 'to clarify objectives'. Murphy (518, p. 13) suggests that the purpose of evaluation is threefold: 'assessment, accountability, awareness'.

Beauchamp (478) aimed in her study to assess the effectiveness of different models for ESP course design for immigrant workers (overseas-qualified engineers and overseas-trained hairdressers and electricians). It was hoped that such an assessment would 'assist in the refinement of national policy' regarding matters such as 'recognition of overseas qualifications', 'overall funding of educational programs for overseas qualified persons', 'targeting of client groups' and 'modes of delivery' (Beauchamp (478, p. 3)).

For any particular evaluation project, it is important that the evaluator manages to establish the purposes of the instigator of the project. One reason may be to justify a decision that has already been taken. Thus a prestigious outsider may be called in to evaluate an ongoing or even completed project, but what is required is the expert's approval. For political reasons, any negative comments or suggestions for change would be unwelcome. Alternatively, support may be required for a decision that has already been made to cancel or change a programme. Bell (479) refers to 'hidden agendas' for evaluation exercises, including providing 'ammunition for pre-determined decisions' and being 'seen to be evaluating'.

What is the subject of the evaluation exercise?

An evaluation exercise can be very wide-ranging or very limited in scale. The subject (or object or target, various terms being used) may be a whole ESP project or course, or just one or some aspects. Long (507, p. 417) suggests that formative evaluations 'typically look at such factors as teachers' and students' attitudes toward a curricular innovation, or at the usability of new instructional materials as they are tried out in the classroom for the first time'. Kennedy (499), for example, describes the formative evaluation of a set of new ESP reading materials in Tunisia. An ordinary classroom teacher could well carry out a short-term evaluation of a particular exercise type or of a method of classroom organisation, aiming only at the improvement of his or her own teaching rather than at any widespread dissemination of results.

A summative evaluation may look at virtually all aspects of a programme, possibly with a particular interest in cost-effectiveness. Mackay (515) suggests thirteen areas of investigation in the analysis of the LOOT project (an imaginary case based on a real project), including the administrative procedures, the students' attitudes and behaviour, and the physical conditions and equipment, and ten sources of information. Mackay writes: 'We felt that such a framework avoided the pitfall into which evaluation studies frequently fall, namely to focus exclusively on student product' (Mackay (515, p. 113)). The 'suggested evaluation package' in McGinley (513) is shorter, but combines formative and summative evaluation and focuses on the methods, including individual lesson evaluation, tests and attitude questionnaires.

Rea (523, p. 90) emphasises that 'different areas of evaluation are important to different people, at different times, and for different reasons'. For example, teachers and materials writers will want to know about the effectiveness of the materials and methods, 'host institutions, on the other hand, will be more interested in the overall impact of the project . . . and in the evaluation of student achievement. Where there are heavy expatriate involvements, they will wish to monitor the progress of the localization process.' There may thus be several different targets for the evaluation to suit the different interested parties.

Who carries out the evaluation?

As with needs analysis, a basic choice must be made between the outsider and the insider. For large aid-funded projects an outsider is typically brought in. One assumed advantage of an outsider is that such a person has hitherto not been involved in the programme and hence brings an objective approach to it. While an outsider may be free of local politics and prejudices, no observer is truly objective. The evaluator will have his or her own views on language teaching methods, administrative procedures etc. and could well be unsympathetic to local practices. Further, he or she may need more time than is given to become aware of local needs and constraints.

In the introduction to one of the accounts of the King Abdulaziz University (KAU) project (1975–84) in Saudi Arabia, Horey (289) refers to several different stages of evaluation and different types of evaluator. During the establishment phase (1975–7) outside experts were called in for brief 'appraisal' visits. Later, in the evaluation phase (1982–4), 'a three faceted approach emerged. The ELC [English Language Centre] would conduct an internal evaluation, the Supervisor General [the Saudi head of the ELC] would commission an independent university evaluation and the British Council would also produce an independent evaluation based on the observations of its English Language Officer in Saudi Arabia and those of a visiting team . . . . Within the ELC an Evaluation Officer was designated' (Horey (289, p. 25)).

Who are the insiders, if they are used? They are most likely to be the course designers and the teachers, but students also may be involved and, in the case of in-company language training, a representative from the management. Bachman (476, pp. 115–16) concludes that formative evaluation, especially, is most appropriately carried out by the 'program development staff'. The Brazilian ESP project, which was designed from the start to be participatory in nature, involved a significant number of teachers and students in the evaluation process. Celani (485) gives details of how this worked and considers the validity of 'an internally organised evaluation'. As a compromise, however, an outside consultant was also involved. Waters (531) describes an attempt to involve students in evaluation, his purpose being both to obtain information about the course from them and to provide them with a learning experience. Potts (522) and, in particular, Lewkowicz and Moon (504) considerably develop the role of the student in the evaluation process.

An important point to bear in mind throughout is that evaluation can be seen as threatening. Teachers, in particular, are likely to feel that the objective of the evaluation is to 'check up on them' and too often it is assumed that any resultant evaluation document will be negatively critical. Thus it is very important that the evaluators win the confidence of those from whom they seek information. Thus, Bell builds a communication stage into the principles of procedure for conducting an evaluation and suggests: 'inform audiences and any others (particularly those potentially threatened by your evaluation) of the purposes and methodology plans' (Bell (479, p. 29)).

Confidence will increase if the evaluation is seen to have beneficial results, for example an improvement in teaching conditions, reward for endeavours etc. The evaluation project is even more likely to be successful if those whose efforts are being evaluated are also involved in the evaluating, which then becomes a team effort, not just the task of one individual. Kennedy (499), and others, refer to 'ownership'. Thus if participants in an ESP project in general and in an evaluation project in particular are given a share in the responsibility for its success, that success is a little more assured. Waters (531) acknowledges the hazards that students may face in taking on such a responsibility but concludes that the gains are worthwhile. An important factor in all this is the appropriate choice of technique for obtaining information.

How is the evaluation carried out?

Many of the basic procedures for data collection are the same as those that can be used for needs analysis. Thus, some or all of the following may be utilised:

    questionnaires
    checklists
    rating scales
    interviews
    observation
    discussion
    records
    assessment

A useful table of procedures is given in Brown (484, p. 233). Nunan (520) gives details of methods for collecting data for the analysis of what goes on in the language classroom, all of which are invaluable for evaluation. A very important consideration is that the procedures employed should be manageable, cost effective in terms of time and money, and appropriate for the situation. Bell urges: 'know how the data will be analysed when you construct the instrument' (Bell (479, p. 31)). The Brazilian team record that 'data analysis took much longer than we (rather naively) imagined at first, and data collection took time' (Celani *et al.* (486, p. 17)). Elley (493), in a practical approach, explores the need to 'tailor the evaluation to fit the context', and to accept the constraints of the real world. Bachman writes that 'data collection procedures, particularly testing and scaling, are often surrounded with an aura of complexity . . . but . . . this need not be the case . . . the amount and type of information gathered should be determined by the kinds of decisions to be made. In the majority of programs perhaps the most useful information is of an informal and subjective nature. That is not to say, however, that it cannot be systematic' (Bachman (476, pp. 114–15)). Brown, too, stresses the value of qualitative data, but urges that it be used 'in a principled and systematic manner' (Brown (484, p. 232)).

Questionnaires

Various people have written about the construction and design of questionnaires and some of the problems involved, for example Mackay (77) and Richterich and Chancerel (87), both in relation to needs analysis. Smith (529) discusses the use of questionnaires for in-company course evaluation, and urges a closer match between the questionnaire and the course it relates to. He also notes the training function of questionnaires. The Brazilian evaluation report gives examples of the questionnaires drawn up for students, ex-students, ESP teachers and subject specialists, and discusses their design and piloting. Mackay (515) describes the development of 'a pool of approximately 150 questions' which was 'selectively drawn upon' to produce a number of questionnaires, the responses to which could subsequently be compared and contrasted. Obvious problems with questionnaires are their length, possible misinterpretation of questions by respondents and failure of respondents to return them.

Checklists

A checklist is much shorter than a questionnaire and can be used when the evaluation is focused on small-scale aspects of a programme, for example one component, such as speaking skills, of a syllabus. As with a questionnaire the questions may be closed (Yes/No/Don't know), which are easiest for computer checking, or open ended. Additionally or alternatively, rating scales may be used which, suggests Bachman (476, p. 114), are particularly effective.

Interviews

Face-to-face interviews are time consuming but provide the opportunity for more extended exploration of the points than do questionnaires or checklists. Ideally the interviews are planned and systematised; that is, the same or related questions are asked of each interviewee. (See Nunan (520, pp. 60−2) for transcribed examples of interviews.)

Observation

Mackay (515, p. 115) writes that 'classroom observation is essential to furnish the evaluator with assumed important process variables that characterize the work in the classroom'. He discusses the preparation of appropriate observation sheets, suggesting seven headings under which to collect data. Mackay's LOOT project evaluation seems impossibly ambitious, however. Long (507) also discusses classroom observation and suggests a much reduced and more manageable set of classroom behaviours to observe.

As well as the classroom processes, it may be possible to observe past students in operation at work, to see whether their ESP course has prepared them effectively or not.

Discussion

One method used by the Brazilian team was class discussions on aspects of the ESP project, followed by a report from each class summarising what had been said. As well as being a once-and-for-all session reviewing all aspects of an ESP project, class discussion can form a regular part of the programme, the topic being, for example, a review of all the activities of the past week, the content of one particular part of the programme, for example speaking activities, or the general approach to methodology etc.

Records

Records form an essential part of the data for an evaluation exercise. Ideally, records of the project or programme will have been kept from the beginning. These include the original planning documents, statements of needs, aims and objectives etc. They can later be matched against subsequent developments. Other types of record, introduced specifically for evaluation purposes, include teachers' lesson records, for example in the form of a checklist which can quickly be filled in after each lesson or each type of lesson being evaluated. Teachers and students may also be asked to keep diaries of their experiences on a course — to be presented, perhaps in edited form, to the class or just to the evaluator. Murphy-O'Dwyer (519) describes the use of diary keeping as a method for evaluating a teacher training course. Another type of record-making, more of a one-off class activity, is the writing of letters or postcards to real or imaginary friends describing aspects of the ESP course.

Assessment

Assessment traditionally includes tests and examinations, the evaluation of students' projects, written work etc., the evaluation or assessment being carried out by teachers or evaluators. Brindley (482) investigates a wide range of procedures for assessing students' 'language gains over a course of instruction' (Brindley (482, p. 1)) and suggests the involvement of the learners themselves in the process. Other ideas on student self- and peer-assessment are summarised in Lewcowicz and Moon (504, p. 47).

The above techniques may be employed by teachers, students or evaluators, that is, people who are temporarily or permanently outside the regular teaching and learning programme. Some techniques, for example discussion and some types of record-keeping, are clearly participatory and can form part or all of a regular class activity. Some types of observation, too, may be carried out by class members. Further, while all the techniques discussed may form part of a planned evaluation project, there is no reason for them not to be used in a more *ad hoc* way by individual teachers and classes. Murphy (518, p. 10) refers to the 'growing acceptance of the ordinary teacher's capacity for *action research* — evaluation by another name' so that the teacher may be more or less permanently conducting evaluation — into his or her own methods and into elements of the prescribed programme. As Alderson notes: 'Evaluation is a crucial and integral part of the instructional process . . . . As materials developers, ESP teachers or researchers we should be concerned continually with asking ourselves whether our courses are producing the effects we intend and if not, how we can improve or replace them for better effect' (Alderson (381, p. 154)).

An important consideration is the reliability of the evaluation instruments or techniques being used and the validity of the results. Celani *et al.*, in their very careful account of the Brazilian evaluation project, admit to some problems and small doubts, but they had deliberately chosen a qualitative rather than a quantitative approach and noted in the beginning (Celani *et al.* (486, p. 9)) that 'objectivity is impossible'. Long (507) acknowledges that we have to accept some crudity.

One way of building in some cross-checking of results is by *triangulation*, that is, by targeting the same point by means of two or more techniques of evaluation, for example seeking information on an aspect of classroom methodology by means of observation, class discussion and a rating scale. Alternatively, information on the same point can be obtained from different sources, for example by administering the same questionnaire or interview to different types of respondent. This again suggests that the evaluation project must be manageable in size, without too many aspects being investigated at the same time.

What happens next?

What happens to the data collected during an evaluation exercise? How is it reported? Is it written up and, if so, who receives copies? What action is taken? It is important to have some answers to these questions *before* the evaluation is carried out. At the same time, however, it is essential to be prepared for unexpected outcomes to the evaluation.

With formative evaluation, we might expect some modifications to be made to the course, the materials etc. Kennedy (499) describes some of the action taken with reference to the reading course in Tunisia: in response to students' comments, more oral work was provided, and summary writing and some work on vocabulary was introduced. Some aspects of the methodology which students were not happy with were not altered, however, as it was felt that in time the students would become accustomed to them. Kennedy notes that the most illuminating feedback came from students' comments on the success and failure of each unit. These comments 'often revealed genuine problems which, if not resolved, could have caused the failure of the course'.

A summative evaluation will have a less obvious follow-up as the programme being evaluated will have already been completed. The design of future programmes, however, will hopefully be influenced by the results of the evaluation. In some cases new initiatives may be suggested. For example, the evaluation of an EST textbook in use in West Bengal, India, suggested that what was needed was not modifications to the textbook (as had first been assumed) but a systematic programme of in-service teacher training (Robinson (525)).

Testing

ESP testing is a relatively neglected area. In 1983, Alderson and Waters wrote that 'only a limited number of articles have been published in the area of ESP testing . . . . No substantial body of experience, expertise or instrumentation appears to exist in the area of specific purpose testing and evaluation' (Alderson and Waters (474, p. 41)). Six years later, Alderson writes: 'It is rather sobering and perhaps depressing to note the minimal attention paid to testing within ESP . . . . Language testers, with very few exceptions, have ignored the ESP challenge, and there are very few papers, articles or books discussing testing in ESP' (Alderson (467, pp. 87−8)). The ESP challenge derives from the fact that the ESP student has a definite target, namely adequate performance in a study or work situation. Both at the start and at the end of an ESP course we need to know how near a student is to achieving adequate performance. What type of test can measure this?

Performance-based testing

Language (and other) tests can be either norm-referenced or criterion-referenced. 'A norm-referenced test score provides information about an individual's relative rank with reference to other individuals who have taken the test' (Bachman (477, p. 248)). For criterion-referenced tests, on the other hand, 'test scores are reported and interpreted with reference to specific context domain or criterion of performance. They thus provide information about an individual's mastery of a given content domain, or level of performance' (Bachman (477, p. 248)). (See also Brindley (482, pp. 47−56)). Tests for general purpose English are typically norm-referenced, whereas those for ESP are typically criterion-referenced, although Skehan (527) suggests that criterion referencing is really only feasible when very narrowly defined job specifications are involved. One of the tasks of the ESP test designer is to determine the exact nature of the criterion, or, more probably, criteria, for judging adequate performance. This will require the assistance of experts in the specific work or study area that students are or will be involved in.

Theoretically, an ESP test would consist of performance in a real-life situation.

This is normally not practicable, so what is more common is simulated real-life peformance. 'In this case the entire testing situation is contrived, although in such a way as to represent what are deemed to be the pertinent aspects of the real-life use context' (Wesche (534, p. 29)). A good example of this is given by Morrison and Lee (517), describing the use of a simulated academic tutorial as a testing device to identify first-year Cantonese speaking students at the University of Hong Kong who might need extra help with English. 'To simulate the atmosphere of teacher-led group interaction, it was decided to test students in groups of four or five, with one . . . staff member playing the role of "tutor", and two others serving as non-participant evaluators' (Morrison and Lee (517, p. 85)). The students were given material on general interest topics to read beforehand and then discuss in the 'tutorial', which was videotaped. Sample videotapes were evaluated by both language-teaching and subject-teaching staff, according to the students' demonstrated proficiency in English, ability to communicate and academic potential. There was a high degree of agreement between the language-teaching and subject-teaching staff.

Allison and Webber (475) give a good review of performance-based (or performative, as they term it) tests for communication skills courses for EAP. They support the use of performative tests 'where the primary aim of the activity is to reinforce teaching and learning', but are 'less convinced of the advantages of performative testing for selection purposes, and specifically when recommending students for future courses of study' (Allison and Webber (475, p. 199)).

More complete, publicly available, examples of performance-based EAP tests are the British Council's IELTS (International English Language Testing System, formerly English Language Testing Service (ELTS)) test and the Associated Examining Board's TEEP (Test in English for Educational Purposes) test, both designed to assess the amount of preliminary English language tuition needed by students planning to pursue tertiary-level or further education courses in Britain. Each test consists of sub-tests or tasks which replicate what students might be expected to have to do on their subsequent courses of study. All four language skills are potentially tested. (There is some choice as to how many sub-tests candidates may take.) Details of both tests and sample papers are given in Weir (533). (See also British Council (483) and Westaway (535) for details of the test, and Coleman (489) for research on one component of the test.) Skehan's review of the state of the art of testing (Skehan (528)) summarises reaction to the ELTS test.

The TEEP test was based on extensive research into the needs of overseas students attending courses in the UK (see Weir (532)). The ELTS test, by contrast, is based not on empirical research but on the assumed needs of hypothetical typical students, following the model of needs identification given in Munby (82). Accounts of more recent experiences in the development of performance-based academic tests are given in Wesche (534), in relation to the Ontario Test of English as a Second Language, and Williams (536). See also St John (526) on the Joint Matriculation Board EAP test.

Although the components of the tests referred to above may simulate academic tasks (for example, writing an essay using material from several authentic texts in a source booklet), the test designer may want to go further and try to isolate the constituent sub-skills for such tasks. This is suggested by Low (508), describing the construction of a test which modelled the writing of a tutorial paper. Sub-tests, which modelled the sub-skills involved, included proof-reading, writing text from a pictorial input and writing text from note-cards (Low (508, p. 252)).

How specific should the content be?

The tests already referred to can be said to have valid content in terms of the tasks that the test candidates are required to perform. Another aspect of content is that of subject matter or topic. A key question in relation to ESP tests is how close the subject matter of a test should be to the students' specialist discipline. Students are likely to demand that it be very close, in which case the test designer may wonder whether content knowledge may then compensate for linguistic deficiency. This issue was addressed by Alderson and Urquhart (472), (473). Summarising the results of the third and largest of their studies, Alderson (466, p. 28) writes that 'what this study appears to have shown is that background knowledge does have an effect on text comprehension and test performance. The relevance to ESP testing is the apparent disadvantage some students suffer when taking supposedly neutral tests.' A problem with 'parallel' tests with different subject matter, however, is that true parallelism is difficult to achieve and to demonstrate. 'There is no doubt that ESP test construction presents a host of problems which are avoided by the "one test" solution. This does not make the latter the best solution, merely the more convenient' (Alderson (466, p. 28)). A move towards greater convenience has been made for the IELTS test, which now has three parallel forms (life sciences, physical sciences and arts), whereas previously there were six (general academic, life sciences, medicine, physical sciences, social studies, technology).

Clapham (487), reviewing research such as that of Alderson and Urquhart (472), (473), suggests that 'language proficiency levels seem to play at least as important a role as background knowledge in the comprehension of reading texts', but 'background knowledge is not easily assessed' (Clapham (487, p. 4)). Clapham's own research did not consider background knowledge as such, but asked whether choice of subject area had an effect on students' reading success. Clapham interprets the results cautiously, but suggests that they indicate that just one academic module would be sufficient for IELTS from an empirical point of view. However, more should be retained, in order to preserve face validity.

The above investigations have all focused on reading. Douglas and Selinker (492) and Douglas (491) report on research into field- and domain-specific testing of oral abilities. (See also Selinker and Douglas (208), (209)).

Predictive validity

The use of tests such as the ELTS test and the TEEP presupposes that some sort of correlation exists between linguistic proficiency and academic success, that a test of present linguistic performance can be the basis for a prediction about future academic performance. There are two issues to investigate here: the relationship between linguistic proficiency and academic success, and the selection of criteria for judging academic success.

Rea (524), reviewing the literature, finds 'varying degrees of association between language proficiency and academic performance' (Rea (524, p. 145)). There are, of course, many factors which might contribute to academic success or failure, including general intellectual ability, financial stability, health and so on. As a result of her study of the University Screening Test (UST) at the University of Dar es Salaam, Rea concluded that the UST did have predictive power in that 'students who score below a certain level on the UST stand a greater chance of failing in their academic subjects than those who score above this level' (Rea (524, p. 152)). The issue is also examined by Graham (494), who argues that 'while the research clearly shows that many factors other than English proficiency are important to academic success, there may be for each institution, or even for each program, a minimum level below which lack of sufficient proficiency in English contributes significantly to lack of academic success' (Graham (494, p. 505)).

Light *et al.* (505) and Low and Lee (510) address the issue of the criteria for judging academic success. A common criterion, against which language screening tests are referenced, is that of students' grade point average (GPA). However, in the study by Light *et al.* there was a low correlation between results on the language test (the Test of English as a Foreign Language (TOEFL) test) and students' subsequent GPA. A greater correlation was found between TOEFL scores and the number of graduate credits earned. Light *et al.* suggest that 'criteria for academic success other than GPA and credit hours earned should be examined; such criteria might include professors' evaluation and students' perceptions of their own success' (Light *et al.* (505, p. 259)). Investigation along such lines had already been carried out by Low and Lee (510), reported by Low (509), who makes the important point that 'academic grades are standardly given for the academic content of a piece of work and in many cases the marker tries consciously to ignore problems deriving from the language in which that content is couched' (Low (509, p. 164)). In Low and Lee's study, content area lecturers used a questionnaire (which they themselves had helped construct) to record their reactions to the linguistic content of students' assignments. These reactions were then matched with the students' initial language test results. Some significant correlation was found, but Low and Lee are extremely cautious about building upon this.

Non-EAP tests

The discussion so far has focused on tests for EAP. Clearly there are tests for other areas of ESP, notably for English for business, such as the Business English Test (502) and the London Chamber of Commerce and Industry's English for Business tests (506). Both offer a mixture of realistic tasks, and hence a measure of performance testing, and language-oriented activities, for example gap filling and answering short comprehension questions.

The London Chamber of Commerce and Industry's tests are proficiency tests, which may be taken by individuals in order to gain a qualification. The Business English Test was prepared for training institutions to use as a placement test, for companies to use as an assessment test and for both to use as an achievement test at the end of a course of instruction. It is banded or scaled (as are the ELTS and TEEP tests), with results being allocated to bands or scales which relate to job performance requirements. A description of the design of a placement test for banking staff, related to a performance scale, is given by Land (501).

Candlin *et al.* (395) describe the extensive research which led to the development of materials for teaching communication skills to overseas doctors working in Britain. Another product of the research was the TRAB (Temporary Registration Assessment Board, later PLAB — Professional and Linguistic Assessment Board of the UK General Medical Council) test, used as a screening measure for such doctors. It consists of a number of sub-tests, some of which measure linguistic proficiency, some medical knowledge and one, in the form of an interview, which involves an element of simulated doctor–patient interaction, which tests both linguistic and medical competence. Coleman (488) describes the design of tests for dentists.

Alderson *et al.* (470) is a report on proficiency testing for migrant professionals in Australia, giving extensive exemplification of different test types for the four language skills.

The link between testing and teaching

In their analysis of the reasons for the neglect of testing in ESP, Alderson and Waters (474, p. 43) discuss the influence of tests on teaching:

> This 'washback' effect of tests on teaching is a well-known and frequently deplored fact — teachers all too often teach to the test instead of doing what they feel to be best for their learners, regardless of the test. The negative aspect of washback has long been recognised. What has remained less noted is the fact that the washback effect is actually neutral as to good or bad — the test will exert an influence on the teaching regardless of whether it is a good or bad test. So if a bad test can have a bad effect on the teaching, a good test can have a good influence on the teaching. And since the test will always in our experience have some effect on the teaching, the simplest way to innovate in language teaching is to improve the test.

The experience of Hughes (497), introducing a new test in English for academic purposes at an English-medium Turkish university, bears out what Alderson and Waters suggest. 'The test had a considerable impact on teaching and learning in the Foreign Languages School. It is my belief that this was due almost entirely to the fact that the test was criterion referenced and based directly on the English language needs of undergraduate students. In these circumstances, teaching for the test (which may be regarded as inevitable) became teaching towards the proper objectives of the course' (Hughes (497, p. 145)).

Further discussion of the washback effect is given in Pearson (521), in a useful review of the relationship between teaching and testing. He suggests that one of the uses of a test is to give evaluation or feedback. 'Here the washback effect is engineered, so that test results can help teachers, syllabus constructors, and the writers of course materials to change and develop both themselves and their materials' (Pearson (521, p. 102)). Tests are thus part of the broader process of evaluation, which in itself contributes to the teaching and learning process. Corbett (490) mentions that one of the aims of a short oral interaction test used in the KAU project was to 'encourage the students to think about their purpose in learning English, and their attitudes towards their English studies' (Corbett (490, p. 171)). The test took place in class time and was to be seen as a routine part of the course. Finally, Holliday (495), in a discussion of 'project work as an evaluation device', shows how observation of a key classroom activity can be used to assess both students and teachers, and also the role and effectiveness of materials.

Chapter Eight

The Role of the ESP Teacher

The role of the ESP teacher is a controversial issue. A variety of interpretations will be presented here. An important point to consider, from the start, is that there is no single, ideal role description. ESP courses, and the institutions around the world which offer them, are so varied that there can be no single model for the ESP teacher. We can certainly find conflicting viewpoints about the qualifications and capabilities needed by the ESP teacher and of the tasks which the teacher is expected to perform. Good collections of viewpoints can be found in a special issue of the *ESP Journal* (vol. 2, no. 1, 1983), devoted to teacher training and ESP, and in British Council (550).

After reviewing the different jobs that the ESP teacher may be expected to perform, I shall consider the degree to which the teacher should be knowledgeable about the students' specialism. After that, I shall look at different kinds of team teaching and, finally, at teacher training for ESP.

A job description for the ESP teacher

What kind of person?

Strevens (608, p. 41) writes: 'Who is the ESP teacher? Almost always he or she is a teacher of General English who has unexpectedly found him/herself required to teach students with special needs. The experience is often a shock!' Strevens goes on to suggest that the shock may be a mixture of the welcome and the unwelcome (Strevens (608, p. 42)). The shock may be unwelcome because the teacher's training in English is more likely to be in literature than in language. For non-native speaking teachers of English, then, added to any doubts that they may have about their competence in the language, there is likely to be fear that they may not cope with their students' areas of specialism. Many native speakers may share the fear; others, however, may welcome ESP because they have qualifications, or at least a strong interest, in another discipline. In the KAU project in Saudi Arabia, qualified science teachers as well as ELT trained teachers were employed.

Williams (614, p. 91) emphasises the personal qualities needed by the ESP teacher:

'At the chalkface, such personal attributes as enthusiasm, the ability to develop and administer a course, work-rate, rapport, and a knowledge of the students' world are equally as important as the ability to write teaching materials or perform a Munbyian needs analysis.'

'Knowledge of the students' world' is ambiguous, as it could cover both the students' culture and personal concerns as well as their specialism. A good teacher should surely be interested in all of these, as Adams Smith (539) seems to suggest. She identifies three qualities as being important for the ESP teacher, namely an interest in the students' specialist area (or at least an open mind about it), an interest in the learners' language and 'a readiness to respect students, whether adults or near-adults, who have chosen a demanding profession about which they may already know a great deal more than their English teachers' (Adams Smith (539, p. 38)).

A good account of the knowledge and skills needed by the industrial language trainer is given by Lavery (588). Noting that 'Industrial Language *Trainer*' is the 'fashionable' term for 'language teachers in industry', he acknowledges that 'it is difficult to draw up a profile of the "typical" language trainer'. However, 'fluency in a foreign language is a prerequisite', in order to be able to sympathise with the difficulties of the students, to achieve credibility as a professional instructor and to conduct business in the students' country. Further, Lavery asserts that 'knowledge of behaviour sciences, analysis of training needs, counselling, feedback skills and cost effective training planning are all vital in the transformation process from language teacher to industrial language trainer' (Lavery (588)).

Perhaps the key quality needed by the ESP teacher is flexibility: the flexibility to change from being a general language teacher to being a specific purpose teacher, and the flexibility to cope with different groups of students, often at very short notice (see Heyneman *et al.* (287)).

The teacher's roles

First and foremost, of course, the ESP teacher is a *teacher* and many writers agree that the qualities of good teaching generally, and of language teaching specifically, are also required for ESP. Kennedy (586), referring to ESP teacher training, suggests that the principles 'may be derived from educational, language teaching and ELT domains', with only the exemplification of these principles being specific (Kennedy (586, p. 52)). Strevens (608, p. 44) writes:

> The methodologies of ESP conform to the same model of the language learning/teaching process as does any other form of language teaching. That is to say, the basic teaching activities are these:
> — Shaping the input
> — Encouraging the learner's intention to learn
> — Managing the learning strategies
> — Promoting practice and use.

However, while in some situations the ESP teacher may be viewed as a 'purveyor of information about the language and as [an] orchestrator of its acquisition' (Swales

(609, p. 9)), in other situations 'our task is very often not so much a language-teaching one — many of the courses we are involved in are too short to enable a great deal of progress to be made in this direction — as teaching techniques or strategies' (Deyes (558, p. 58)). Deyes is referring here to training students in reading strategies, which, he suggests, involves getting students to perform a familiar task (reading) in a new way and for a variety of purposes. In order to do this, Deyes suggests that the ESP teacher must assume the role of 'empathiser', first seeing things from the students' perspective before leading them towards an ESP approach (Deyes (558, pp. 58–9)).

As well as being a regular class teacher of language or strategies (or both), the ESP teacher may well teach individual students, especially when these are adults. Piotrowski (367), describing the use of the case method with business people, states that in addition to leading class discussions on the cases (which he or she will have previously selected and prepared), the teacher will also act as a consultant. This involves diagnosing each student's language and communication needs, discussing these with each student and planning individual programmes for improvement. The area of EAP, in particular, may involve a considerable amount of individual consultation work, for example helping students, and also academics, with the writing of theses and research articles.

The ESP teacher does not only teach, however. Very often, he or she is involved in designing, setting up and administering the ESP course. Mackay (594, p. 58) notes the 'integrated nature of the ESP activity. Virtually all the tasks involved in planning, mounting, teaching, coordinating and administering may be required to be performed by one person or by a small number of people operating as a well-knit team.'

Some of these tasks will call upon very particular capabilities. Conducting the initial needs analysis, for example, may require considerable diplomacy in order to gain the information one needs, to gain access to the students' work environment, to obtain authentic documents. Negotiating skills may be required when dealing with the students' employers or sponsors, in order to gain acceptance for the kind of ESP course which one thinks the students need. Campany (553) suggests that 'from the side of the language trainers, it is necessary to develop effective methods of communicating the nature and purpose of the programme to non-specialists'.

In order to design the ESP course, the teacher needs to employ analytic techniques: whether linguistic, discoursal or ethnographic. In other words, the teacher/course designer should be able to select, in a principled way, the language items, or discourse features, or elements of the disciplinary culture which need to be taught. (See Chapter Three for a discussion of language analysis for ESP. See Swales (229) (230) and A.M. Johns (744) for discussion of disciplinary culture and the contribution of ethnography to ESP.) Having designed the course, the ESP teacher is then likely to be involved in materials preparation — frequently under time pressure. Angela Lilley (591), describing a short course for bankers, refers to the 'considerable organisation' that was required to 'prepare in advance a wide variety of materials . . . packaged according to level' to enable tutors to 'tailor the course to the students' needs'.

During the course, and certainly at the end, the ESP teacher is likely to be involved in evaluating and testing, quite often devising the tests as well as administering them.

Finally, the teacher may well have to write reports on the students and on the course as a whole. In some cases, there will also be later follow-up consultations with some or all of the students, perhaps even a short refresher course.

Problems

A number of aspects of ESP teaching are seen as problematic. Some of these are problems within language teaching generally. Large classes, for example, common in many parts of the world, can be the norm both for pupils beginning the study of EGP and for university students following EAP courses. In addition, the classes may be of mixed ability. A particular problem for ESP course organisers may be deciding whether to group students by specialism, in which case classes may be exceedingly mixed in terms of linguistic level, or whether, at least at first, to group by language level. Even grouping by specialism, however, may not always be easy: different types of engineer, for example, may not always acknowledge that they have much in common. Classes held for the employees of a company may be exceedingly mixed in terms of both job specification and ability in and attitude towards language (see B.J. Robinson (601)).

A third problem, generally considered to be more common in EGP but also found in ESP, is that of motivation. In many parts of the world, university students, for example, may not see the value of their ESP course, perhaps because they did not choose to study their specialism or because they know that they can in fact pass their subject examinations without a knowledge of English. Very often, university EAP courses are at the start of a student's university career, and the student may not appreciate the value of the course until much later.

A fourth problem, voiced by all types of teachers everywhere, relates to status, pay and conditions. What is an appropriate teaching load? How much preparation time is realistic? Lack of sufficient preparation time is a commonly mentioned problem among ESP teachers. The issues of status and conditions generally have been much discussed, particularly in relation to EAP and the provision of 'service English' in universities around the world. T. Johns (581) lists five problems, ranked in order of importance: low priority in timetabling (so that classes are at awkward times of the day or week), lack of personal and professional contact with subject teachers, lower status than subject teachers, isolation from other teachers doing similar work, and lack of respect from students. Johns concludes that the fundamental issue is that of professionalism: how far is the service English teacher viewed by others as a professional; how far do EAP/ESP teachers regard themselves as professionals? (T. Johns (581, p. 22)). See also Skeldon and Swales (606) and Swales (609). As Early (563, p. 44) notes: 'The ESP teacher typically leads an uneasy existence housed in a curriculum unit which exists on the margin of the academic world. It is not a situation which is conducive to a strong sense of professional identity.' Rivers (599, p. 66), urging that ESP/EST be 'approached systematically by well-trained, or self-trained, specialized teachers', suggests that, otherwise, 'it will not gain the respect of specialists in other areas of foreign-language departments. It will then continue to be fobbed off on junior faculty, or senior faculty with low registrations in courses in their own faculty, on the assumption that teaching language is teaching language and anyone can do it.'

A fifth and final problem area is found particularly in language training for business and industry. Here, short intensive courses are increasingly the norm, being seen as cost effective for the company and more manageable for the busy employees than longer extensive courses (see Pilbeam (597), Johnson (583)). The content may be very specific indeed, requiring a high degree of knowledge and skill from the teachers. The intensity of the course, possibly a sense of pressure and a desire to cram in as much as possible, may affect the teachers as well as the students. In addition, 'the learner may already be exhausted before beginning the course because of pressure of work or too much travelling. If the course is held on-site in the company, the learner is often distracted by his own work problems which may seem more important to him than the course' (Johnson (583)).

Possible solutions

There is no easy panacea for any of the problems described above. A real solution to the problem of large classes requires both political and economic change at government level. The problems of impossibly mixed classes and very short preparation time also derive from economic, and perhaps also political, causes relating to the situation of the institution offering the courses. ESP teachers need to take a tougher attitude towards their conditions of employment, but the realities of the job market can make this a risky step to take.

One thing that ESP teachers can do is to try to develop their professional competence. This may involve specialising in a particular discipline or profession, or undergoing further training, or carrying out research alongside one's teaching. Kennedy (587), addressing 'some recurrent problems in ELT and ESP', argues for teachers to carry out 'action research': 'I want to suggest that we should create conditions whereby the teacher himself undertakes research in his classroom which can feed back into his own teaching and so create the possibility for self-renewal so important for teaching' (Kennedy (587, pp. 10−11)). As Kennedy notes, the teacher is normally 'at the bottom of the decision-making hierarchy', so that such action research (albeit small scale) helps to give the teacher some degree of control over his or her own professional life. Research leading to publications is urged by Swales (609, p. 12) and by A.D. Lilley (592, p. 192).

Where an ESP operation is being set up for the first time, then appropriate structures and conditions need to be established from the outset. Adams Smith (540) and A.D. Lilley (592) both describe the setting-up of ESP/EAP units and their attempts to ensure their status and independence.

Practical suggestions about dealing with some of the ESP teachers' problems are given by Nolasco and Arthur (311) and Coleman (275) on the topic of large classes, and by Johnson (583) on the topic of intensive courses. Strevens (608), referring to 'the gap between the *learner's knowledge* of the special subject and the *teacher's ignorance* of it', recommends three techniques: 'Become familiar with the ESP course materials', 'Become familiar with the language of the subject', and 'Allow students to put you right!' (Strevens (608, pp. 42−3). These are not as easy as they sound, however. The first point is addressed in Chapter Six. The second and third recommendations are considered below.

How much should the ESP teacher know of the students' specialism?

Conflicting views

'I believe that ESP situations are infinitely varied and that no principle or practice of any significance can be valid for all of them' (Crofts (557, p. 147)). This perception certainly applies to the issue of how far the ESP teacher should be expert in the students' specialism. There are conflicting views on the issue, and although various courses of action are suggested, none will apply to all situations.

Several key variables should be borne in mind. First, a great deal depends on whether the students are experienced in their specialism or not. Are the students pre-experience, post-experience, or are they studying their specialism concurrently with English? In each of these three situations we might expect the students to have different views regarding the teacher's engagement with their specialism. Second, we must consider the sponsor's requirements: in some cases these may include specific teaching of (aspects of) the specialism. Third, we should consider the students' views regarding the role of the teacher and the nature of English language teaching. If the students expect that the teacher should be an authority, they may find it hard to accept a teacher who is forced to admit ignorance of their specialism. If the students believe that English language teaching should consist of practice in grammar and general vocabulary, they may well be, at the very least, disconcerted when the English teacher appears to be teaching their specialism. Finally, we must consider what help is available to the ESP teacher. Is an appropriate ESP textbook available? Is the teacher working alone or is there an ESP team, able to share in the needs analysis, the syllabus design and the materials preparation? Are there helpful specialist informants around for the ESP teacher to consult? Has the teacher enough time to learn something of the students' specialism?

Strevens (608, p. 42) recommends: 'Become familiar with the language of the subject', and refers to the 'educated layman'. Is this possible, is it appropriate? Adams Smith (539, p. 38) writes that 'some of the finest ESP teachers I have met could probably pass their students' subject area examinations very creditably'. However, Abbott (537, p. 35) asks: 'How many disciplines can the EST teacher be expected to acquire a "layman's outline knowledge" of? To what level should the teacher strive in each of these? Would such a level of knowledge be achievable? Yet mightn't a little knowledge be a dangerous thing?' B. Robinson (600, p. 32) suggests that 'for the pre-university ST student and the student technician, the EST teacher will need a grasp of sub-O level concepts (surely no great imposition for a postgraduate teacher): the modes of thought of science he has to some extent already, as they only differ in degree, not quality, from those of other Western academic disciplines of which applied linguistics is one.' Greenall (569, p. 24), however, asks: 'Can the EST teacher be expected to absorb the values and symbols of science without the thoroughgoing training which scientists have?' He attacks the 'bicycle pump syndrome' and the temptation for the EST teacher and course designer 'to choose what he himself understands' (Greenall (569, p. 25)).

What the research shows

A pioneering piece of research which addresses the issue of the ESP/EST teacher's knowledge of the students' specialism is Selinker (205). He observes that 'teachers seem to be put into one teaching situation after another which is clearly untenable, such as having to teach students to read subject-matter material which we ourselves have trouble in understanding' (Selinker (205, p. 190)). Selinker demonstrates that for ESP teachers to understand a scientific text properly, they would need to know the concepts and presuppositions involved. Ignorance of these means that the text as a whole is not understood. Attention is then likely to be devoted to lower level features of grammar and vocabulary. However, these may not be properly understood either, as their role in the overall discourse (and in the scientific area generally) is not understood. Selinker comments that in some cases 'reliance on conventional linguistic wisdom proved misleading, if not inaccurate' (Selinker (205, p. 205)).

Smaller scale research by White (613) and Zuck and Zuck (254) has similar findings to Selinker. White and Zuck and Zuck found that language teachers and subject specialists interpreted specialist texts differently and set different comprehension questions on them. The language teachers tended to focus on low-level issues and to be concerned with the identification and reproduction of facts. The specialists, however, were more concerned with interpretation. White's informant commented that the text under consideration (a legal text) should not be 'viewed in isolation', each text being 'part of a large body of related information' (White (613, p. 12)). Whereas White (the language teacher) had set several comprehension questions on the text, the specialist had set only one and in fact was more likely to test students' understanding by giving them a problem to solve.

Classroom-based research is reported on by Arnold (542), describing an attempt to relate the science content of ESP to scientists' judgements of the validity of the content as science. Tape recordings of ESP classes were played to subject specialists and a textbook was evaluated. It was found that 'some of the examples introduced into the lessons were scientifically-speaking imprecise (or just plain wrong!) and usually relying upon layman's notions of terms, or half-remembered secondary school teaching' (Arnold (542, p. 2)). The textbook, too, was thought to present an imprecise, layman's view of science. Some of the errors which occurred were due to the textbook; others occurred when the students asked questions about content which the teacher was unable to cope with. Arnold further notes that 'it is extremely difficult for a non-specialist to know which level to pitch his explanation at' (Arnold (542, p. 4)).

Accounts of experience

Despite awareness of the problems discussed above, a number of ESP practitioners would seem to share the views of Scott-Barrett (602), who writes that: 'Undoubtedly, a knowledge of the technical area will be of great help to the language trainer. However, it is not a pre-requisite for successful technical training.' Scott-Barrett suggests that a needs analysis for technical students reveals 'that in terms of skills and micro-skills, there are many overlaps with other, non-technical, areas of language training for industry. Therefore an experienced trainer will be able to transfer the ideas and strategies s/he has used with other learners in other fields to the teaching of technical English' (Scott-Barrett (602)). The chief value of experience and of knowledge of the students' specialism is to give the teacher confidence.

Lack of confidence is one of the 'real difficulties' addressed by Sheerin (603), referring to classes with experienced doctors. She shows that with careful preparation, and access to relevant reference material, it is possible to cope. She acknowledges, though, that 'it is useful to have a final line of defence in the shape of an English doctor whom the teacher can consult towards the end of the course on any problems that have arisen and that the teacher and the doctors together could not solve' (Sheerin (603, p. 40)). Sheerin notes that many of her imagined difficulties did not arise. She was able to understand the technical material sufficiently and found that the majority of errors made by the doctors were of general English. The 'specialist errors' were usually recognisable to the teacher and could in most cases be resolved using reference materials (for example specialist dictionaries). Sheerin cautions that 'in attempting to improve one's specialist knowledge in one small area, it is very important not to lose sight of or underestimate the importance of one's role, which is that of language teacher and *not* medical specialist' (Sheerin (603, p. 41)).

In some situations, however, for example that of Chirnside (338), 'a sizeable amount of subject information has to be provided . . . students' motivation is powerfully and exclusively instrumental, resulting in resistance to and sabotage of overtly linguistic activities' (Chirnside (338, p. 141)). The students referred to were second-year university students, following the English course concurrently with their specialist studies (nursing). Chirnside does not discuss what difficulties, if any, she had with the content of the ESP materials. The units of the materials consisted of the following stages: input, feedback, reproduction and expansion. In the input stage, the focus was on content. 'The students believe that they are seeking information, as indeed they are. This use of text as an information source makes the input stage highly communicative . . . linguistic models are not presented by the teacher, nor indeed will a rigid selection of models have been made for the students' (Chirnside (338, p. 143)). Language work comes in the feedback stage, but this stage also involves 'recap of the salient features' of the content. The teacher must then be 'in command of the information content' in order to 'possess the flexibility which is essential to assess the content correctness of student utterances' (Chirnside (338, p. 144)). A time lapse was needed between the feedback and the reproduction stages in order to avoid student boredom, because both stages dealt with the same information content.

Student boredom with familiar content is one of the problems mentioned by Crofts (557) in an excellent discussion of his experience in a variety of ESP teaching situations. 'When students are very familiar with a topic, they will be bored with any treatment of it as not familiar, and they will tend to draw on their existing knowledge rather than on the information or point of view presented in the ESP materials' (Crofts (557, p. 147)). In these cases, the students may well know more about their specialism than the ESP teacher and it may be possible to observe Strevens' injunction: 'Allow students to put you right! Do not be above letting the students correct your solecisms in the subject' (Strevens (608, p. 43)). However, Crofts' 'sad experience', when asking students to explain points, was 'that usually either none of them can, or they disagree with each other, or they give an explanation that seems wrong and later is found to be wrong' (Crofts (557, p. 148)).

Practical suggestions

Crofts suggests that 'the ESP teacher's most acceptable and effective role, in addition to that of pure language teacher, is not as a pseudoteacher of subject matter students have previously learned or expect to learn in their specialist studies or occupations, but as a teacher of things *not* learned as part of courses in these specialisms' (Crofts (557, p. 149)).

One approach is to teach some of the background to the students' specialism, material that the specialist lectures assume, often wrongly, to be already known to the students. A similar suggestion is made by Hutchinson and Waters (156). They suggest that foreign students entering British tertiary-level colleges need to be taught the layman's science that the college lecturers will build upon in their classes. A second approach is to get the students to try to apply the theories which they have studied to practical situations and problems. Third, the ESP teacher may take material which is known to the students but present it from a different viewpoint. Finally Crofts suggests focusing on the metalanguage of ELT (the teacher's or the textbook's explanations and instructions) as an instance of language use, but using the methodology of the students' specialism. This suggestion is similar to that advocated by Widdowson (326).

Webb (612), referring to the ESP teacher 'coming under fire in turn from subject matter teachers, specialists, and at times his own students', writes of 'a "no-man's-land", claimed by neither linguists nor subject specialists, across which we must lead our students'. Some ESP teachers realise that certain essential knowledge is not taught by the specialists, for example awareness of the importance of safety procedures in the laboratory or workshop (see Burkart (551)), or the need for appropriate dress (see Crocker and Swales (403)).

All the above suggestions clearly require some preparation and knowledge on the part of the ESP teacher, even if they do not require the teacher to be an expert in the students' specialism. As Scott-Barrett (602) notes: 'The greatest contribution which the client can make to the development of a successful training programme is time.' In addition, the client (or sponsor) should provide the ESP teacher with 'as much relevant documentation as possible in advance — e.g. product brochures, technical specifications, instruction manuals, etc.' (Scott-Barrett (602)). This documentation is essential both for the development of teaching material and as a source of knowledge for the teacher. Reed (598), referring to a course to enable French technical instructors to be able to explain the workings of agricultural equipment in English, writes that 'two English teachers would receive a week's general training, in French . . . on the technology and operation of tractors and agricultural equipment . . . . One teacher would make a visit to the company's agricultural branch in England, to learn about its operations and to collect documentation' (Reed (598)).

Above all, however, it seems that what the ESP teacher must do is collaborate in some way with content specialists. There are various kinds of collaboration. These are discussed next, under the general heading of team teaching.

Team teaching

An overseas student's failure to keep pace with his course or with his research is rarely attributable to 'knowledge of the subject' or 'knowledge of the language' alone: most often these factors are inextricably intertwined. If their work is separate, it is difficult for the subject teacher, and even more so for the language teacher, to take account of that intertwining. In the triangle of which the three angles are the student, the subject teacher, and the language teacher, each needs a certain type of assistance and feedback from the other two (Johns and Dudley-Evans (582, pp. 7—8)).

The solution proposed by Johns and Dudley-Evans, and others, for the kind of situation referred to above is *team teaching*. This is generally discussed in the context of university level ESP/EAP, but some instances of it in other contexts, for example banking (Angela Lilley (591)), can be found. There are several different types of team teaching, although each type shares some features with the others. I shall first consider the type which involves two teachers (the ESP teacher and the specialist lecturer) being present in the classroom together. Then I shall consider subject—language integration, which may involve only one teacher teaching at a time. Next, after a brief consideration of North American types of team teaching, I shall look at a variety of more limited examples of collaboration and co-operation.

Two teachers together

A pioneering and much discussed case study of team teaching with both the language and the subject teacher present in the classroom together is that of Johns and Dudley-Evans (582). They describe a pattern which they devised at the University of Birmingham whereby over two terms each year, in several departments, a weekly class was taught jointly by either Johns or Dudley-Evans (as language teachers) and a subject specialist. In the first term, the focus was on lecture comprehension; in the second, on writing examination answers. For a number of the lecture comprehension sessions, the language teacher arranged for a specialist lecture to be recorded. He was not present during the recording, but listened to the tape afterwards and prepared a worksheet on it. The team-taught session focused on the students' answers to the worksheet questions, with the lecturer who had actually given the lecture being present to cope with issues of content, and the language teacher to help with language points. In the second term, the specialist lecturer involved selected examination questions. He could then discuss his expectations in terms of the content of the answers, while the language teacher could help with linguistic and thematic structuring. These team-taught classes were an addition to the normal timetable and were restricted to ten to twelve of the linguistically weakest students in each department. Johns and Dudley-Evans give extensive examples of their materials, which contain useful ideas even for sessions taught by the language teacher alone.

Other examples of such team teaching are described by Guezguez (570), referring to a course on computing and English; Jackson and Price (578), referring to a course in communication skills for engineers; and Chamberlain (554), referring to a basic course in the language of mathematics. However, in these three cases the courses were self-contained, whereas those described by Johns and Dudley-Evans were adjuncts or back-up to other classes. For the course taught by Jackson and Price, both the engineer and the language teacher were present in the twenty sessions taught over two terms, either of the teachers initiating a topic and developing it. In Chamberlain's case, the maths/engineering specialist (who had ESP experience) wrote the course and took on the task of 'initial presentation and organising activities . . . he was really to be in charge . . . . The task of the language teacher was . . . to act as a constant check to see that any questions or problems of structure, vocabulary, or pronunciation were given immediate attention' (Chamberlain (554, p. 107)).

Subject–language integration

Subject–language integration refers to a situation where there is normally only one teacher present in the classroom, who is then involved with both language and content. The material being taught, however, has derived from some earlier collaboration between language teacher and subject teacher. The term is used by Dudley-Evans (559), relating his attempts to replicate the team teaching situation of Johns and Dudley-Evans (582) in Singapore. It was not possible to have language and subject teachers together in the same classroom because of the teachers' heavy teaching load and some subject teachers' fear of being observed by a language specialist. As in Birmingham, Dudley-Evans worked on listening and writing. He recorded some live lectures in the subject departments and then prepared worksheets on these, which were checked by the subject lecturers. The students worked on the lectures in the language laboratory. For the writing, Dudley-Evans and the subject lecturers jointly planned assignments, which Dudley-Evans then worked on with the students. The finished assignments were marked by both the language teacher and the subject teacher.

Earlier examples of subject–language integration, cited by Dudley-Evans (559), are by Ivanic (577) and Henderson and Skehan (573). Ivanic and her colleagues were fortunate in that collaboration between subject teachers and language teachers was formally supported by the institution (a UK college of further education) and language teachers were members of content course development teams. However, Ivanic comments that the principle of subject—language integration 'is very untidy in practice . . . . Pay schedules do not allow for two teachers in one classroom' (Ivanic (577, p. 49)). Ivanic describes various modes of integration, which could involve the language teacher taking some responsibility for teaching content or the subject teacher becoming involved with language work. After the 'intensive collaboration' over materials preparation for one course, English for Dressmaking, the two teachers involved 'now feel that either of them could teach the course independently' (Ivanic (577, p. 63)).

The course described by Henderson and Skehan (573), and also Skehan (605), involved the teaching of both English and introductory economics to groups of students from Iran. The two teachers involved planned the course together and met frequently to review progress. 'A common body of materials was covered by the two teachers working in the fixed order of (1) self study to (2) English class to (3) economics class' (Henderson and Skehan (573, p. 44)). On some occasions new economics content was first presented in the language class and Skehan (605, p. 23) observes that 'the traditional distinction between specialist (economics) teaching and language (English) teaching was blurred'.

North American approaches

Most of the work so far discussed has emanated from Britain. Other related and very interesting work has developed in Canada and the USA. Some of the approaches are part of the Language across the Curriculum movement (LAC), where content classes, mainly for native speakers of English, contain some language work. LAC methods and materials can also be used for non-native speakers, both in EGP and in ESP classes.

Shih (604) gives a very useful review of content-based approaches to academic writing in an ESL situation in the USA. Some of these approaches involve the language teacher in the teaching of content; others involve back-up work in support of separate content classes. Shih outlines five different approaches (Shih (604, pp. 632−3)).

The first approach is 'topic-centered modules or minicourses', involving all the language skills, and with the focus on comprehending new content. This presupposes some content knowledge on the part of the language teacher, or at least a willingness to acquire some. 'Topics with the greatest potential to hold student interest may not also be areas in which ESL instructors are knowledgeable' (Shih (604, p. 635)).

The second approach is 'content-based academic writing courses', that is, 'composition courses organized around sets of readings on selected topics'. Specialist lecturers can help here by providing topics for students' written assignments, and by commenting on the content of the finished assignments.

The third approach involves 'content-centered ESP' courses, another term for which is 'sheltered' courses, in which specialist material is taught to classes consisting exclusively of 'at risk' non-native speaking students who have been taken out of the full specialist class. Shih reports that any of the following may apply: subject-area instructors teach the course, language teachers who happen to have the necessary content knowledge are employed, team teaching is used, materials aimed at a general or lay audience are used (Shih (604, pp. 638–9)).

The final two approaches involve back-up or adjunct language work, linked to selected specialist courses. This may take the form of classes which run parallel to the specialist subject class. Alternatively, individual consultations between language teacher and student may be arranged. Shih writes that for the adjunct classes 'what is needed, minimally, is cooperation from subject-area instructors and ESL faculty willingness to step into subject-area classrooms and keep up with class events' (Shih (604, p. 640)).

A detailed account of an adjunct programme is given in Snow and Brinton (607). In addition they provide formal evaluation of their programme, something lacking in all the other cases I have discussed. Snow and Brinton emphasise that much consultation and discussion is needed between language and content teachers. 'Throughout the instructional period, weekly meetings are scheduled to ensure continued cooperation between the two teams of instructors' (Snow and Brinton (607, p. 559)). Also vital to the success of the programme is adequate financial and administrative support.

Co-operative teaching

Co-operative teaching (Adams Smith (538)) is a useful term for smaller-scale collaboration between language and subject teachers than that of some of the cases described above. Adams Smith suggests that 'there are massive difficulties in the way of establishing real team teaching between disciplines as dissimilar as English and biochemistry or mechanical engineering, among them being near-total mutual incomprehension of purpose, subject matter and pedagogical approach, together with conflicting schedules, different commitments to research, and problems of basic attitude' (Adams Smith (538, p. 76)).

Adams Smith describes a very interesting series of 'limited teaching situations' which as well as motivating students seems to have motivated the specialist lecturers to welcome more contact with the language unit. One pattern was for the language teachers to show specialist content films, backed up with worksheets. At the first showing, the focus was on comprehension and language work. At the second showing, a specialist lecturer was present, to answer questions of content and to relate the content to current research. Subsequently, the specialists took the students on visits to their departments and laboratories. Other limited teaching situations involved the study of reading materials suggested (or requested) by the specialists, guest lectures, note-taking on regular lectures and joint oral examining of students by specialist and language teachers.

Further examples of co-operative teaching are provided by Morray (595), Hansen and van Hammen (571), Gee *et al.* (568) and de Escorcia (564). In the South American situation (that of de Escorcia), 'full team teaching' (in the sense of two teachers being simultaneously present) may be inappropriate because the specialist lecturer's English is not good enough. In this situation, the pre-class co-operation will be conducted in the local language.

A very good set of practical suggestions for contacting and co-operating with content lecturers is given by Brennan and van Naerssen (548). They focus on informal rather than formal means of contact. Among other things, they videotaped a content lecture and then, with the students, compared the language teacher's notes on the lecture with the lecturer's notes, taken when he viewed his own performance on video. The students made two sets of notes: during the live performance of the lecture, and when watching the video. In other cases, the language teachers were able to obtain model answers for student assignments from the subject lecturers. Whereas in many cases it was the language teachers who made the first move, in others the subject lecturers approached the language teachers, who then sometimes had to 'press the content lecturer for more background . . . in order to pinpoint more precisely the problems' (Brennan and van Naerssen (548, p. 203)).

Benefits of the approaches described and conditions for their success

The above discussion of team teaching may imply that it is the ESP teacher who has most to gain. However, there are many ways in which the subject specialist may benefit and, as a result, the student too. Dudley-Evans (561, p. 25) summarises the benefits of team teaching as follows:

1. *The student* is given the opportunity to see how well he is measuring up to the requirements of his department, and to catch up on work not fully understood.
2. *The language teacher* is able to see at first hand what difficulties the students are having with their subject course, and to learn a little of the way communication takes place in a given subject.
3. *The subject lecturer* receives feedback on how well he has been communicating with his students.

Johns and Dudley-Evans (582) observed that some, although not all, of the subject lecturers involved began to make improvements in their lecturing style. Skehan (605, p. 27) suggests that 'subject specialist teachers may be partially trained in sensitivity to language use (in terms of form, function and lexis)'. More specifically, Ivanic (577, p. 53) writes that the language teacher can 'advise the subject teachers on the wording of their examination questions and handouts. This has led not only to more realistic reading demands for the students but also to a greater understanding on the part of the teachers of the difficulties caused by the language of the subject.'

A further benefit of team teaching, noted by Jackson and Price (578, pp. 40–1) and Chamberlain (554, p. 107), was that the interaction between the two lecturers created a higher level of involvement among the students, helping to overcome their fear of asking questions and of engaging in discussion.

The key requirement throughout is communication: communication between and among all members of the triangle formed by students, ESP teachers and subject specialists. However, as Chamberlain (554, p. 101) points out, when considering the ESP teacher's institutional isolation (see the discussion on page 82), too often language teachers do not communicate enough among themselves.

In some cases, it might seem that what has been found out through team teaching, especially co-operative teaching, should have been found out at the needs analysis stage. However, there is not always enough time to carry out a sufficiently detailed needs analysis before the start of a course, and it is often difficult to obtain the information desired. Once a course has started and the students are around, perhaps even coming into contact with the subject specialists, problems can become apparent — but then so too can a desire to do something about them. The ESP teacher often has to be patient, to work at a gradual building up of contacts and human resources.

An important first condition for successful team teaching of any type is that both specialist department and language department (or individuals in each) recognise that there is a problem and that some form of collaboration is needed to help solve it. Johns and Dudley-Evans (582, pp. 21−2) suggest that a 'clear framework' must be 'agreed in advance for the pattern of activities, and the responsibilities of each side . . . defined'. In addition, they 'attempted to reduce intrusion on the subject-teachers to a minimum, while exploiting the help they could give us to the maximum'. Finally, they suggest that it is important that the group of students is homogeneous — in terms of language level as well as specialism.

Henderson and Skehan's case (573) is probably rather unusual in that their course 'was the central concern of all the teachers involved: indeed in terms of organisation they were as accountable to the Course itself as to their own university department'. In addition, both lecturers involved 'could claim some expertise in the speciality of the other' (Henderson and Skehan (573, p. 41)). Skehan in fact suggests that 'we may reach a stage where ESP teachers are generally expected to have introductory knowledge of two or three subject areas' (Skehan (605, p. 26)). Other writers, however, suggest that subject−language integration is most appropriate when the students are at a low level in the specialism, so that the language teacher can soon cope with the content. Examples are some of the cases described by Ivanic (577), and the course described by Houghton (576), which was the same programme as the course described by Henderson and Skehan (573) and Skehan (605).

Ultimately, the issue we are involved with here would seem to be that of autonomy, as Arnold (543) suggests. He argues that, to achieve effective teaching in the ESP situation, 'it is absolutely crucial that both the subject specialist and the English teacher should be prepared to give up some of that autonomy which has traditionally been held to be theirs' (Arnold (543, p. 7)). Each needs the advice and guidance of the other and will never be truly effective without it.

Teacher training

Just as ESP situations and institutions vary widely, so too do types and methods of teacher training for ESP. Around the world we can find pre-service and in-service courses, courses for new graduates and refresher courses for experienced teachers. Some courses will retrain teachers of EGP, or even teachers who have taught subjects other than English. Some courses will be in-house at a language school or ESP centre; others will be conducted in a university or college teacher training department.

The first issue to consider is whether the course should be general or specific. McDonough (593), reviewing the options, refers to 'narrow-angle' and 'wide-angle' courses, and goes on to describe a wide-angle course. This would seem to be appropriate when the trainees are from a variety of backgrounds and teaching situations, or, as in the case of many pre-service trainees, do not yet know where they are going to teach (see Harmer (572)). Some courses, however, particularly in-house courses and some refresher and retraining courses, may be tied to particular types of students and particular specialisms, and so can be narrow angle. The short refresher courses described by Dudley-Evans (408), for example, were very specific, being designed to help Egyptian teachers work with a particular ESP textbook.

The second issue to consider is whether a wide-angle course is in fact any different from a general EFL/ESL teacher training course (see Kennedy (586)). There seems to be a widespread opinion that, if possible, the ESP teacher should at least have the same training input as any teacher of EGP, the question then being whether the ESP teacher needs something additional. Certainly the ESP teacher needs to develop the same knowledge and awareness of educational and pedagogical issues as any other teacher. Houghton, referring to the role of the language teacher in team teaching situations, suggests that 'the language adviser will need to make use of learning and pedagogic theories in his contribution to the solution to problems. Thus he must be a competent teacher with an interest in education and learning theory as well as ESP' (Houghton (576, p. 32)). Several of the ESP teacher training courses described or suggested in the literature seem to be extremely well designed courses, applicable not just to ESP but to language teaching generally (see, for example, Harmer (572), Kennedy (584), de Escorcia (565) and, above all, Ewer (566)).

Some ESP teacher trainers advocate an ESP approach to designing the training course; that is, the use of needs analysis and a precise specification of objectives (for example, Kennedy (585), Calderbank and Holliday (552)). This ESP approach is particularly apparent in the attention to the study skills and language needs of non-native speaking trainees.

If the ESP teacher training course contains more than the EGP teacher training course, however, what will the extra components consist of? A good set of headings under which to consider this issue is provided by Ewer (566, p. 10) when he lists the difficulties which a teacher of EGP may face when transferring to ESP. Ewer suggests that the difficulties are the following: attitudinal, conceptual, linguistic, methodological and organisational. Let us consider each of these in turn.

By *attitudinal difficulties*, Ewer refers to the fact that the traditionally arts or humanities trained teacher of English (who may also have studied English literature rather than English language) may have a very negative attitude to science. (We might extend the meaning of 'science' to include anything outside the humanities.) An important function of the teacher trainer, then, will be to try to overcome the trainees' dislike (or even fear) of science. A good way to do this is to involve the trainees in scientific activity in a small way, for example by having them observe and meet practising scientists, by putting them in the role of students and teaching them some scientific material, or by getting them to conduct a small-scale experiment or other practical activity. A by-product of this practical work may be new insights for the trainees about ESP methodology. Holmes (574), describing a short course for Egyptian teachers, the main aim of which was to build up their confidence when dealing with scientific material, gives a good example of such a practical approach. The course helped the teachers overcome not only their attitudinal difficulties but also their *conceptual difficulties*, by giving them 'an appreciation of what science is about and how scientists work' (Ewer (566, p. 10)).

Several ESP teacher trainers refer to the necessity to help trainees with *linguistic difficulties*. This is discussed in a general way by Kennedy (584, pp. 44−5). Others address the situation whereby ESP students and teachers often have to cope with longer texts than are found in EGP classrooms. For example, Akermark (541), while cautioning against creating 'a mystic aura around the teaching of ESP/EST', suggests that trainees might need 'extensive practice in adapting "heavy" chunks of . . . technical descriptions in service manuals to effective teaching points' (Akermark (541, pp. 40, 41)). Good practical training in linguistic analysis for ESP teacher trainees is described by A.M. Johns (579) and Tarone (611). Johns trained the Chinese ESP teachers with whom she was working to do textual and discourse analysis of their own ESP textbooks. In this way, they were able to generate data for practical classroom work and, at the same time, to produce research papers on their analyses. Tarone, working with native speaker trainees, suggests that they need training as field linguists on registers of English. 'Our trainees tend to rely on their own intuitions as native speakers too much, and at first fail to realize that their intuitions may not be accurate for STE [scientific and technical English] . . . . What this means is that even greater emphasis needs to be placed in our program on background information relating to language variation, and the way in which structures and items may be used differently within different fields or vocations' (Tarone (611, p. 69)).

Under *methodological difficulties*, Ewer includes problems arising from the age of the students (older than many EGP pupils), new classroom methods (perhaps related to students' disciplines) and new attitudes to error (more tolerance being shown than in the past) and to evaluation (employed more frequently than in the past). Abbott (537), however, cautions against following new 'orthodoxies' too enthusiastically and suggests that teacher training programmes for ESP must vary from country to country and situation to situation. Thus methodological training will vary from situation to situation and in some places 'older' approaches will be more appropriate.

A good way of providing training in methodology for ESP teachers is to involve them in materials production. This is advocated by Baumgardner *et al.* (545), who suggest that 'the writing of materials is a very important aspect of teacher training. It ensures that teachers will become more involved in the work of the course and will as a result teach the course materials with more understanding and confidence' (Baumgardner *et al.* (545, p. 147)).

Finally, Ewer refers to *administrative difficulties*: 'a substantial proportion of EST teachers will, as supervisors, have to cope with administrative problems for which their conventional training has entirely failed to prepare them' (Ewer (566, p. 10)). This important issue is addressed by Swales and L'Estrange (610), who describe a short course in ESP administration, using a case study approach. At the time of their article (1983), attention to administrative training for students on graduate courses in TESOL of any type was rare. Now (1990), it is a little more common. Given the many roles of the ESP teacher which have been referred to in this chapter, training in management and administration would seem to be a valuable part of an ESP teacher training course.

Conclusion

Being an ESP teacher is not easy. One of the prime requisites would seem to be flexibility — and a willingness to try new approaches and methods. Whatever the training that is given to an ESP teacher and whatever the situation, it is probably the case, as Strevens suggests, that 'becoming an effective teacher of ESP requires *more* experience, *additional* training, *extra* effort, a *fresh* commitment, compared with being a teacher of General English' (Strevens (608, p. 43)).

Chapter Nine

Issues and Approaches in Business English and in English for Academic Purposes

Business English

Introduction: what is business English and who needs it?

Business English, a term used in many publishers' catalogues for a subset of ESP books, caters for a multitude of users and activities, among whom there can often be very little similarity. Business English courses and materials can serve both the occupational user of English (for example the manager of a company, an accountant, a secretary) and the student (for example the student of business, banking, economics or management). (See the discussion of 'business language' in Johns (645, p. 4)).

The term business English implies the existence of a discrete form of the language. Pickett (664) calls business English an *ergolect* (or *work language*), suggesting that 'an ergolect operates at the level of *lexis* and at the level of *transaction*, hardly at all at the level of grammar' (Pickett (664, p. 11)). What is distinctive about business English, compared with other ergolects, is that

> it is a *mediating language* between the technicalities of particular businesses ... and the language of the general public. It is not purely for intra-group communication. This is not surprising since business and commerce are by definition an interface between the general public and the specialist producer ... (Pickett (664, p. 6)).

Business transactions are likely to be similar whatever the nature of the particular business; the particular business, however, will affect content and lexis.

Business language has been insufficiently studied, compared for example with the language of EST, a point noted by Johns (645). Johns (645) and Pickett (664) both give overviews. Other studies look at particular text types or aspects, for example telexes (Zak and Dudley-Evans (679)), and oral interaction (Lampi (650), Neu (660), Williams (676)). An important finding, made by Williams in particular, is that the language taught in textbooks is different from that used in real life. Williams concludes that 'more real data is needed about what language is used in different situations before we as teachers and coursebook writers can begin to select what to teach for different situations' (Williams (676, p. 53)).

However, as well as attempting to discover the authentic linguistic realisation of discourse functions (which are often at the level of the sentence or below), we also need to know what strategies speakers use when conducting complete transactions. Micheau and Billmyer (658) make a start on this, concluding that 'where language content was once the focus of our curriculum, interactional skills have now become a topic of discussion in their own right' (Micheau and Billmyer (658, p. 95)).

Three points must be made here. First, native speakers of English who are new to the work of business may have just as much need of lessons in discourse skills and strategies as non-native users of the language. Hence we might expect, and indeed can find, business English textbooks which aim to cater for both native and non-native English speakers. Second, as an international language, English is used as the means of communication in business transactions between people none of whom is a native user of the language. Thus, any study of authentic business English language must include data on the forms and strategies employed by practising business people who are non-native speakers of English. Third, more consideration needs to be given than at present to cultural aspects of business communication (see Cowcher (631)). Currently, too much attention is focused on the business practices of western Europe and the USA, any cross-cultural adjustment being made in the direction of the West.

Business English textbooks: why are so many so general?

There are a very large number of business English textbooks available on the market; only a few can be considered here. A striking feature is the large number of general books, which seem to differ very little from coursebooks for EGP — working through a standard set of structures, teaching much common core as well as some work-related vocabulary, and dealing equally with all the skills. There are several reasons for this. First, the role of business English as a 'mediating language' (see the discussion above) implies that it must bear much similarity with everyday language. Second, the wide range of people who might identify themselves as students of business English may suggest a market for general coursebooks (and also for some more specialised books; see below). Third, we may note that in the private sector, particularly, language schools offer 'open door' business English courses. As the students are not likely to be homogeneous in terms of work experience, a general textbook applicable to a range of business situations may be the most appropriate one to use (see the discussion in Gowdridge (638)).

These general business English coursebooks thus often have very general aims. Jones and Alexander (646) is 'a flexible learner-centred course in communication skills for people who need English in their day-to-day work'. White and Khidhayir (675) aims 'to provide students with the practical language skills needed to communicate effectively in a wide range of business situations'. The target audience, too, is very broadly defined, often with both practising business people and students of business (or commerce or management) being catered for by the same materials. Brieger *et al.* (620) is aimed at 'the specialist or non-specialist student of business English'. White and Khidhayir (675) is designed 'for adults who need English for professional as well as social purposes' and 'for adult students of business English'.

These books clearly meet a need. They appear to fulfil what are surely common expectations of a language textbook/coursebook: namely, that it should be reasonably complete in its coverage of language forms and functions, usable as a reference source, and fairly lively and interesting.

Business English textbooks: what types of specificity are there?

More narrowly targeted business English textbooks may be designed for a specific type of student. Knowles and Bailey (649), for example, is a carefully designed low-level course in listening comprehension and conversation skills for Japanese business people.

Many books are skill specific. Hanks and Corbett (639), while aimed at a wide audience, is specific in its focus on listening. Hughes *et al.* (642) also focuses on listening, utilising recordings of unscripted authentic conversations between business people.

Listening and speaking combine in a business situation which requires everyday language and topics: socialising with clients. Ellis and O'Driscoll (634) focus on this, as do Coulton and Rossiter (630) and Hollett *et al.* (640). Listening and speaking also combine for telephone skills, dealt with by Bruce (622), Naterop and Revell (659) and Palstra (662).

We might expect something different from general English for reading and writing, since many of the written text types in business English are specific to the business world, for example invoices, quotations, company reports, memos. Carrier (623) and Spiro (673) aim to develop reading skills using a variety of business text types. Cotton (626) and Land (651), however, both use texts from business journalism and seem to activate language knowledge more than reading strategies.

A number of textbooks focus on business letters, for example Beresford (618), Littlejohn (654), who has a more genuinely communicative methodology than most, Methold and Tadman (657) and Wilson (678). Comfort *et al.* (625) deal with business report writing, although the tasks suggested in the book do not seem to produce very much extensive writing. Doherty *et al.* (633) work through a range of written text types, building up to a long report. The topics are drawn from factory life, but the approach to writing seems similar to other good, recent work in writing, for example in EAP.

Other specific types of business English textbooks include Palstra (663) on telexes and Kerridge (647) on presenting facts and figures. Cotton and McGrath (628) is a language laboratory course, focusing primarily on vocabulary acquisition in the area of international trade.

For books which are specific as to work area, we can note that there may be some teaching of content as well as language, for example Radice (667), (668). Books on management and managerial strategies seem to be a growth area and, as Trickey observes, 'in the last few years, language training and management/communication skills training have begun to overlap significantly' (Trickey (674)). Scullion (672), indeed, aims his book at native users of English as well as non-native. In fact, one might have thought that, for some of the situations that Scullion includes, managers would be unlikely to use a language other than their native one — be it English or something else. Ardo (615), a very lively and unorthodox book, seems to be only minimally a language practice book and much more a workbook of management strategies and attitudes.

Within the management field, in particular, an approach which can lead to a good variety of meaningful language practice is that of the case study (see the discussion in Chapter Five). A recent attractive and very authentic-seeming example is by Casler and Palmer (624). Trickey, however, suggests that 'the more authentic and sophisticated published materials are, the more inflexible and "user unfriendly" they become for the trainer; this is because *another* person's or company's world has been so effectively recreated that it is difficult to provide transfer to the learner's own highly specific world of work' (Trickey (674)). Thus, rather less authentic and more easily generalisable sets of case studies can be of value, for example Pote *et al.* (666) and Sawyer-Lauçanno (670).

Nearly all the books so far referred to seem basically designed for classroom and interactive use, although there is a tendency for publishers to claim that they can also be used for self-study. As Badger (617) shows, this aim is frequently not realisable. More investigation is needed into the design of effective self-study material. Useful self-access and reference material, however, is provided by the *Bilingual Handbooks for Business Correspondence and Communication* (Davies *et al.* (632)). In general it can be said that there are too few reviews of business English textbooks. Users' reports based on extensive classroom use of the materials would be particularly useful. In addition, more research is needed along the line suggested by Williams (676).

EAP (English for academic purposes)

Is EAP part of ESP, or ESP part of EAP?

EAP (English for academic purposes) accounts for a large amount of ESP activity. A recent review of EAP is presented by Jordan (751), and he begins by discussing the relationship between EAP and ESP. (See also Blue (688, p. 96).) For some practitioners, EAP is a branch of ESP, the other major branch being EOP. EAP is thus specific purpose language teaching, differentiated from EOP by the type of learner: future or practising student as opposed to employee or worker. EAP can appear to be very general in scope, however, as the same courses and materials can be aimed at students from a wide variety of academic disciplines. Within such general courses, we might find components aimed at students from specific disciplines. In these cases, we might wish to view EAP as the more inclusive term, with ESP work a subordinate part of EAP.

A further term to consider is *study skills*. This can be seen as identical in coverage to EAP, or as a part of EAP. Here it will be viewed as a part of EAP (see below).

The type of student typically catered for on EAP courses is either already on or about to enter a college or university course, either at graduate or undergraduate level. A few courses cater for school-age pupils, and some work has been done for university teachers and researchers (see Ramani (783), Swales (800)). Collections of articles which deal largely or entirely with EAP include British Council (690), (691), (550), Cowie and Heaton (700), Harper (11), Mackay and Mountford (23) and Robinson (787).

Are the concerns of EAP specific to English?

An important issue in EAP is whether what is taught is specific to the English language or in fact universal. Are EAP students being taught things (strategies, processes, concepts) which do not pertain to their own language communities, or is it the case that academic activity is the same, or at least broadly similar, around the world, whatever the language? The general consensus is that the concerns of EAP are not specific to English, but that many students are aiming at a higher level of academic achievement through English than in their first language. Thus they are learning academic strategies for the first time through English — and they may subsequently try to apply what they have learnt to operations in their first language. A good example here would be of reading in an academic context. Amongst other things, an EAP course might help students with speed reading, reading for gist, distinguishing main points from subordinate ones or supporting detail. Student difficulties here could derive not so much from lack of knowledge of the English language but from poor or undeveloped reading ability in their first language.

An important related issue is that of learning and teaching styles: first, are these universal or are they culture specific; second, are they discipline specific? The evidence suggests that culture is a significant factor in students' academic success. This is discussed in British Council (691), Mead (769), Mohan and Lo (772), Smithies (796), (797), Weckert (807) and Willes (809). See also Reid (785) on students' preferred learning styles. The question of 'the cognitive style of the specific purpose' is challengingly raised by Widdowson (326), and discussed by Flowerdew (283). As Flowerdew suggests, more research is needed. At the moment there is insufficient hard data available on which to base a discipline-specific EAP course which takes properly into account the learning and teaching style of that discipline. (But see Hall *et al.* (719) and the discussion on pages 38—9.)

EAP course design: common core or specific?

Even if we cannot base an EAP course on the learning-style of a particular academic discipline, we may be able to focus on discipline-specific topics and texts. This is done in some EAP textbooks, for example Jordan and Nixson (753) and Mead (770), focusing on economics. The books in the Cassell EAP series focus on medicine (D.V. James (737)), general engineering (Johnson and Johnson (748)), agriculture (Yates (813)), and earth sciences (Yates (812)). The format and exploitation is similar in each, suggesting that the authors believe that students require practice in the same strategies and tasks, whatever the discipline.

However, it is often difficult to ensure that all the students in a class are following the same academic discipline. Also, undergraduate and pre-undergraduate students may not, in many cases, have chosen their major specialisation yet. Thus a popular basis for the design of EAP courses is a range of topics and texts from several disciplines or of general current concern (for example, ecological issues).

The 'several disciplines in one course' approach seems to be favoured by American textbook writers, particularly for reading and/or writing courses. Examples are Bachman (685), Currie and Cray (701), E.S. Lynch (760) and Rornstedt and McGory (788), all using extracts from a variety of undergraduate textbooks. Some reading courses take texts from several related disciplines, for example the social sciences (Haarman, Leech and Murray (718), Stevenson and Sprachman (799)) or science (Long *et al.* (759)). Some British EAP textbook writers and editors favour adapted or specially written texts on topics of general interest, for example Adkins and McKean (681), Johnson (749) and the *Reading and Thinking in English* series (784).

The assumption underlying these 'common core' textbooks would seem to be that the strategies focused on are common to all disciplines and to all types of student. A further development of this assumption, perhaps, is the idea of taking the business of studying itself as the topic of a course, with sub-topics such as 'how to use the library', 'attitudes to the learning of vocabulary', 'types of academic writing'. This approach is adopted in K. James *et al.* (739) and in K. James (738).

Obviously, before an EAP course is set up or a textbook or coursebook written, some sort of needs analysis should be carried out. Academic needs analyses are reported on by Johns (73) and by Weir (96). Christison and Krahnke (697) and Horowitz (71), however, show that much more precise detail is required than had been obtained in previous surveys. Horowitz's work suggests that close attention must be paid to the academic requirements not just of particular disciplines but of actual specialist lecturers. Thus a truly specific EAP course would be specific to a department or even a lecturer of a particular faculty in a particular university. This is the situation for adjunct classes in North American universities (see pages 90–1).

Reading in EAP: what are the issues?

Reading is probably the most generally needed skill in EAP worldwide. An important question is how far success in reading is helped by practice in the other language skills. Activation of knowledge of the language through writing and speaking can feed back into reading. However, very often there is too little time on a course to do more than focus on (silent) reading and little motivation to do so. In Latin America, for example, for many disciplines, much if not all of the basic material is available in the students' first language (Spanish or Portuguese), which is also the medium of instruction. The need for English is limited to the skill of reading and the content of the texts is likely to be discussed in the first language (see Sinderman and Horsella (794)).

A second issue in EAP reading is how far knowledge of the topic can compensate for linguistic difficulties in reading a text. This has been researched, in relation to LSP, not just ESP, by Ulijn in particular (see Ulijn (803); also Alderson and Urquhart (472), (473), Koh (756), Mohammed and Swales (771)). The evidence appears to be that, as might be expected, subject knowledge does have a role to play. However, work on language as such is still clearly important (see Evans (711)) and thus a key target for research is the identification of the particular structures and types of vocabulary which cause most difficulty in reading (see, for example, Bramki and Williams (108), Williams (811)). A good approach to the issue of what grammar (and vocabulary) teaching is necessary to aid reading is provided by the 'minimum discourse grammar' of Deyes (704).

In order for teachers and students not to spend too much of a reading class in studying grammar, it is important to identify the purpose for which a text needs to be read. In an influential article, Johns and Davies (747) suggest that in EAP (and in ESP generally), texts are 'vehicles for information', not 'linguistic objects'. They suggest a methodology for studying written texts, such that the focus is on the information in them and not primarily on the linguistic forms used to realise that information. Attention to the use of the information in a text is also emphasised by Adams Smith (680), who argues for a greater degree of intellectual involvement in the reading class than may always apply. Intelligent and challenging comprehension questions may help students to think, not just to manipulate language. A necessary development of what she suggests would be to try to match the intellectual tasks to what is required in the students' specialist class. Adams Smith's ideas are built on in accounts of reading courses by Frydenberg (714) and Alderson and Lukmani (682).

Important current concerns in reading in EAP are classroom management and the nature of the reading process itself. How should the classroom be organised, especially when it contains students with very different levels of competence in English? One solution is to have tasks of different degrees of complexity, to be applied to the same texts (see Nunes (776)). Another idea, appropriate to large classes, is to have a set of 'standard reading exercises' which can be applied to a range of texts (see Scott *et al.* (792), Holliday and Zikri (731), Holliday *et al.* (730)). In these situations, it would seem that what is most appropriate for the students to read is not ready-prepared textbooks but extracts from textbooks and articles supplied by their specialist departments or faculties. Some of the activities suggested are also suitable for self-study, perhaps an obvious approach to the development of reading ability (see Armanet and Obese-jecty (684), and Kharma (755)).

Writing in EAP: process or product?

The current debate on the merits of a process or a product approach to learning is clearly apparent in the area of teaching writing. Here the features of the product method can be clearly shown:

Model text → comprehension/analysis/manipulation → new input → parallel text and compared with the features of the process method:

> Writing task → draft 1 → feedback → revision → input → draft 2 → feedback → revision → draft 3

Like many 'innovations' the process approach was not so new, having been employed for many years in the teaching of English as a first language. Within ELT, its methods seemed to bring a way of getting students to write more and to write more fluently. Such results are clearly of value to EAP, and certainly process ideas have had an effect on EAP materials. The work by Hamp-Lyons and Heasley (727) contains some process-oriented activities and the widely used Jordan (750), which follows a product approach, has been revised along process lines.

However, EAP students have clear targets or products in mind. They must, at some stage, produce texts which conform to certain specifications, often quite rigorous specifications in terms of the sequencing — and perhaps the actual wording — of points and layout. Thus, in addition to process-oriented activities, the EAP writing class must include some study of models or final products. (See the debate between Horowitz (733) and Hamp-Lyons (723) and Liebman-Kleine (758).)

This implies some study of written texts. Thus, while reading may not necessarily be aided by writing practice, writing is certainly aided by extensive reading. Only if they have had exposure to their target-level texts, thus internalising the model or target, will students have a proper idea of what they should write. So Davies (702) argues, although she also points out that the texts that students have to read as part of their course (for example, textbooks, journal articles) may be different from what they should read to help them with writing (examination answers, essays, dissertations). (See also Cooper (699).)

As with other areas of EAP, textbooks may be common core in terms of topics and tasks, or more specific. Examples of the former are given by Glendinning and Mantell (717), Hamp-Lyons and Heasley (727), Johnson (749), Jordan (750) and Oshima and Hogue (778), (779). Specific-purpose writing courses include Dudley-Evans (706) on report writing and Weissberg and Buker (808) on experimental research report writing. The writing of examination answers is considered by several people: in articles by Dudley-Evans (707), Hamp-Lyons (724) and Horowitz (732), and in a textbook by Howe (735).

Listening in EAP: what is involved?

Listening in EAP involves listening to lectures, and listening and interacting in seminars and tutorials (see the discussion on speaking in EAP below). Problems with lecture comprehension may derive from features of the language as such, for example the use of informal language by the lecturer (see Johns and Dudley-Evans (582, p. 17)). Several researchers have noted the importance of the lecturer's use of discourse markers as an aid to comprehension (Chaudron and Richards (696), Lebauer (757), Tyler *et al.* (802)). Other problems may derive from the students' lack of previous exposure to the spoken realisation of forms which they already know from reading, and from the particular accent of English used by a lecturer. A major difficulty for students may be the taking of notes at speed. Several practical suggestions about listening comprehension are made by Richards (786), and Benson (687) provides a detailed case study of one student's strategies for lecture listening.

Published materials take several forms. Adkins and McKean (681) and K. James *et al.* (739) use complete but specially written audio-texts, gradually increasing in length, with various kinds of controlled note-taking exercises. The Cassell EAP series (for example Yates (813)) uses a similar approach in the listening and note-taking part of each unit. T. Lynch (761) and McDonough (764) use extracts from authentic lectures, with a variety of types of exploitation. Ruetten (789) uses complete authentic lectures, of varying length and complexity. The materials so far mentioned all consist of a textbook and audiotapes, but what is obviously needed is video-recorded material, so that the contribution of body language, blackboard work and other visual aids can be considered. In addition, students need exposure to lengthy examples of listening, in preparation for the normal fifty-minute-long (or more) lectures of real life. Such exposure, however, is perhaps best obtained live.

Speaking in EAP: a matter of language proficiency or knowledge of subject matter and community?

Speaking in EAP is a relatively neglected area. In needs analyses it normally emerges as the least needed skill, although Christison and Krahnke (697) suggest that this finding does not represent reality. If not a need, speaking is often a want, since in many students' opinions oral proficiency is the best indicator of mastery of a language. EAP speaking involves participation in tutorials and seminars, asking questions in lectures (see McKenna (768)), oral presentations (see page 51), and social interaction with other students.

There are few published materials for practising EAP speaking. K. James (738) and Lynch and Anderson (762) both consider seminars and oral presentations; Morrow and Johnson (774), (775) deal with social English. Practical suggestions are made by Jordan (752), referring to pyramid discussions.

Empirically, EAP speaking has been an under-researched area. Many suggestions about how students should best be helped have been based on introspection and observation of students in the language classroom, not the specialist classroom or lecture theatre. Earlier suggestions have focused on the linguistic realisation of language functions thought to be important in seminars and lectures, for example interrupting, questioning and challenging (Cawood (694), Johns and Johns (746), C. Johns (745), Lynes and Woods (763), Price (781)). More recently, and especially in the USA, research has been more ethnographically oriented, looking at the nature of the 'discourse communities' (see pages 25–7 and McKenna (768)), in which students and lecturers interact, and considering the social relationships, the imperatives and constraints, which are set up therein. Research into seminar participation by both native-English-speaking and non-native students by Furneaux *et al.* (715) suggests that what is important for success is not linguistic control of appropriate discourse functions but knowledge of the subject matter under discussion. Clearly, linguistic proficiency can help the non-native, especially for confidence-boosting, but what is indicated is a need not so much for language but for information about the academic situation.

Study skills: what is involved?

All the activities discussed above may be considered elements of study skills. Alternatively, we could adopt a narrower approach and reserve the term *study skills* for the more mechanical aspects of the academic world, for example reference skills and the use of the library, the layout of theses and dissertations (footnotes, the bibliography), note-taking. All these skills need to be taught to the native speaker of English as well as the non-native (see, for example, Casey (693)). Some published textbooks focus on these 'mechanical skills', for example O'Brien and Jordan (777), Salimbene (790) and Wallace (806). Hamp-Lyons and Courter (725) additionally offer help with the writing of research papers. Other textbooks combine elements of these study skills with practice in reading, writing or listening, for example Adkins and McKean (681), Floyd (712), Montgomery (773), Glendinning and Holmstrom (716), Yates (812), (813) and the *Skills for Learning* series (795). Some textbooks give practice in several skills, including study skills, aiming particularly at examination practice, for example McEldowney (766) and Williams (810).

One study task which can help to integrate all the language skills and to practise some of the more mechanical study skills is 'doing a project', in which students conduct research and produce a project (or term paper). See the discussion of this on pages 50−1.

EAP: conclusions

EAP is a continuously developing area. It is linked to the concerns of ESP in general, contributing for example to the debate on authenticity. In fact, much of the development of ESP has taken place through work in EAP situations. At the same time, EAP takes ideas from ELT, for example work in the process approach to writing. The current concern is with 'studying in context', that is, with identifying the social as well as academic requirements of a particular situation and equipping students to cope. This implies some study, of an ethnographic type, preferably by the students themselves. A further implication is that generalisations cannot be made, although A.M. Johns (744) expresses an interest in discovering what is generalisable from community to community. More research is clearly needed and, while more textbooks for EAP would be welcome (for example in the area of speaking), at the same time the current trend seems to be for more local, context-specific in-house materials.

Bibliography

(A) General

Books and articles

(1) Aupelf/Goethe Institut/British Council (1981) *English for Specific Purposes*, Triangle 1, Montreal: Aupelf.

(2) Bickley, V. (ed.) (1989) *Language Teaching and Learning Styles within and across Cultures*, Hong Kong: Institute of Language in Education, Education Department.

(3) British Council (1978) *English for Specific Purposes*, ELT Documents special, London: The British Council.

(4) British Council (1980) *Projects in Materials Design*, ELT Documents special, London: The British Council.

(5) Brumfit, C.J. (ed.) (1983) *Language Teaching Projects for the Third World*, ELT Document 116, Oxford: Pergamon Press in association with the British Council.

(6) Chamberlain, D. and Baumgardner, R.J. (eds) (1988) *ESP in the Classroom: Practice and evaluation*, ELT Document 128, Modern English Publications in association with the British Council.

(7) Coffey, B. (1984) 'ESP: English for specific purposes' [state of the art article], *Language Teaching*, vol. 17, 1, pp. 2−16.

(8) Cornu, A.-M., Vanparijs, J., Delahaye, M. and Baten, L. (eds) (1986) *Beads or Bracelet: How shall we approach LSP?*, selected papers from the 5th European Symposium on LSP, Leuven, Belgium, 26−30 August 1985, Leuven: Oxford University Press.

(9) Freudenstein, R., Beneke, J. and Ponische, H. (eds) (1981) *Language Incorporated: Teaching foreign languages in industry*, Oxford: Pergamon Press and Munich: Max Hueber Verlag.

(10) Harper, D.P.L. (ed.) (1979) *English for Specific Purposes*, papers from the 2nd Latin American Regional Conference, Cocoyoc, Mexico, 25−30 March 1979, Mexico: The British Council.

(11) Harper, D.P.L. (ed.) (1986) *ESP for the University*, ELT Document 123, Oxford: Pergamon Press in association with the British Council.

(12) Hoedt, J., Lundquist, L., Picht, H. and Qvistgaard, J. (eds) (1982) *Pragmatics and LSP*, Proceedings of the 3rd European Symposium on LSP, Copenhagen, August 1981, Copenhagen: Copenhagen School of Economics.

(13)   Hoedt, J. and Turner, R. (eds) (1981) *New Bearings in LSP*, Copenhagen: Copenhagen School of Economics.

(14)   Holden, S. (ed.) (1977) *English for Specific Purposes*, Modern English Publications.

(15)   Hutchinson, T. and Waters, A. (1987) *English for Specific Purposes: A learning-centred approach*, Cambridge: Cambridge University Press.

(16)   James, G. (ed.) (1984) *The ESP Classroom: Methodology, materials, expectations*, papers from the 4th biennial Selmous conference, Exeter, March 1983, Exeter Linguistic Studies, vol. 7, Exeter: University of Exeter.

(17)   Johns, A.M. (1990) 'ESP in the USA: State of the art', talk given at the 2nd Latin American ESP Colloquium, Santiago de Chile, November 1990.

(18)   Johns, A.M. (1991) 'English for specific purposes (ESP): Its history, contributions and future', in Celce-Murcia, M. (ed.) *Teaching English as a Second/Foreign Language* (2nd edition), New York: Newbury House.

(19)   Kennedy, C. and Bolitho, R. (1984) *English for Specific Purposes*, Basingstoke: Macmillan.

(20)   Lauren, C. and Nordman, M. (eds) (1989) *From Office to School: Special language and internationalisation*, selected papers from the 6th European Symposium on LSP, Vaasa, Finland, 3–7 August 1987, Clevedon, Avon: Multilingual Matters.

(21)   Lauren, C. and Nordman, M. (eds) (1989) *Special Language: From humans thinking to thinking machines*, selected papers from the 6th European Symposium on LSP, Vaasa, Finland, 3–7 August 1987, Clevedon, Avon: Multilingual Matters.

(22)   McDonough, J. (1984) *ESP in Perspective*, London: Collins.

(23)   Mackay, R. and Mountford, A. (eds) (1978) *English for Specific Purposes*, London: Longman.

(24)   Mackay, R. and Palmer, J.D. (eds) (1981) *Languages for Specific Purposes: Program design and evaluation*, Rowley, MA: Newbury House.

(25)   Pugh, A.K. and Ulijn, J. (eds) (1984) *Reading for Professional Purposes: Studies and practices in native and foreign languages*, London: Heinemann.

(26)   Richards, K. (1989) 'Pride and prejudice: The relationship between ESP and training', *English for Specific Purposes*, vol. 8, 3, pp. 207–22.

(27)   Robinson, P.C. (1980) *ESP (English for Specific Purposes): The present position*, Oxford: Pergamon Press.

(28)   Robinson, P.C. (1989) 'An overview of English for Specific Purposes', in Coleman (117), pp. 395–427.

(29)   Selinker, L., Tarone, E. and Hanzeli, V. (eds) (1981) *English for Academic and Technical Purposes: Studies in honor of Louis Trimble*, Rowley, MA: Newbury House.

(30)   Strevens, P. (1980) '"Functional Englishes" (ESP)', in *Teaching English as an International Language: From practice to principle*, Oxford: Pergamon Press, pp. 105–21.

(31)   Swales, J. (1985) 'ESP: The heart of the matter or the end of the affair?', in Quirk, R. and Widdowson, H.G. (eds) *English in the World: Teaching and learning the language and literatures*, Cambridge: Cambridge University Press in association with the British Council, pp. 212–23.

(32)   Swales, J. (1985) *Episodes in ESP*, Hemel Hempstead: Prentice Hall.

(33)   Swales, J. and Mustafa, H. (eds) (1984) *English for Specific Purposes in the Arab World*, papers from the Summer Institute on ESP in the Arab World, University of Aston in Birmingham, August 1983, Birmingham: Language Studies Unit, University of Aston.

(34) Tickoo, M.L. (ed.) (1986) *Language across the Curriculum*, selected papers from the RELC seminar on 'Language across the curriculum', Singapore, 22–26 April 1985, Anthology Series 15, Singapore: SEAMEO Regional English Language Centre.

(35) Tickoo, M.L. (ed.) (1988) *ESP: State of the art*, Anthology Series 21, Singapore: SEAMEO Regional English Language Centre.

(36) Todd Trimble, M., Trimble, L. and Drobnic, K. (eds) (1978) *English for Specific Purposes: Science and technology*, Corvallis, OR: English Language Institute, Oregon State University.

(37) Ulijn, J.M. and Pugh, A.K. (eds) (1985) *Reading for Professional Purposes: Methods and materials in teaching languages*, Leuven, Belgium: Acco (Academic Publishing Corporation).

(38) Waters, A. (ed.) (1983) *Issues in ESP*, Lancaster Practical Papers in English Language Education, no. 5, 1982, Oxford: Pergamon Press.

(39) Widdowson, H.G. (1981) 'TESOL and English for special purposes: The curse of Caliban', in Fisher, J.C., Clarke, M.A. and Schachter, J. (eds) *On TESOL '80: Building bridges: Research and practice in teaching English as a second language*, Washington, DC: TESOL, pp. 50–60.

(40) Widdowson, H.G. (1983) *Learning Purpose and Language Use*, Oxford: Oxford University Press.

(41) Williams, R., Swales, J. and Kirkman, J. (eds) (1984) *Common Ground: Shared interests in ESP and communication studies*, ELT Document 117, Oxford: Pergamon Press in association with the British Council.

Journals

(42) *Al-Manakh*, twice a year: English Language Unit, Faculty of Science, University of Kuwait, PO Box 5969, Safat, 13060 Kuwait.

(43) *EMP Newsletter: English for Medical and Paramedical Purposes*, yearly: English Language and Medical Study Skills Units, Health Sciences Centre, University of Kuwait, PO Box 24923, Safat, 13110 Kuwait.

(44) *English for Specific Purposes*, three times a year (formerly twice yearly and entitled *ESP Journal* from vol. 1, 1 until vol. 4, 2), New York: Pergamon Press/The American University. Editorial offices: ELI, University of Michigan, 2001 N. University Building, Ann Arbor, MI 48109, USA, and Academic Skills Center, San Diego State University, San Diego, CA 92182, USA.

(45) *English for Specific Purposes*, newsletter: English Language Institute, University of Oregon, numbers 1–72. Ceased publication.

(46) *The ESPecialist*, twice a year: Sao Paulo, Brazil. Address for correspondence: the ESPecialist, a/c de Maria Lucia dos Reis, CEPRIL, Rua Monte Alegre, 984, CEP: 05014 — Sao Paulo, SP, Brazil.

(47) *ESPMENA Bulletin: English for special purposes in the Middle East and North Africa*, twice a year: English Language Servicing Unit, Post Box 32, Faculty of Arts, University of Khartoum, Sudan.

(48) *INTER EST*, International network for teaching and research in English for science and technology, information exchange, twice a year: % Magnar Brekke, Department of English, University of Bergen, Sydnesplass 9, N-5007 Bergen, Norway.

(49) *Language Testing Update*, yearly: Centre for Research in Language Education, University of Lancaster, UK.

(50) *Language Training*, quarterly: Language Training Services, 5 Belvedere, Lansdown

Road, Bath, Avon BA1 5ED, UK.

(51) *Pharos: An ESP Newsletter*, twice a year: ESP Centre, Alexandria University, P.O. Box 314, Ibrahimiya, Alexandria, Egypt.

(52) *Tunisia ESP Newsletter*, yearly: Institut Bourguiba Des Langues Vivantes, 47 Avenue de la Liberté, Tunis 1002, Belvedere, Tunisia.

(53) *Unesco ALSED-LSP Newsletter*, twice a year: The LSP Centre, The Copenhagen School of Economics, Dalgas Have 15, DK-2000 Copenhagen F, Denmark.

(B) Needs analysis

(54) Andrews, S. (1984) 'The effect of Arabicization on the role of service English', in Swales and Mustafa (33), pp. 172–83.

(55) Berwick, R. (1989) 'Needs assessment in language programming: From theory to practice', in Johnson (297), pp. 48–62.

(56) Brindley, G.P. (1984) *Needs Analysis and Objective Setting in the Adult Migrant Education Programme*, Sydney, NSW: Adult Migrant Education Service. (Revised edition: 1991, Sydney, New South Wales: National Centre for English Language Teaching and Research, Macquarie University.)

(57) Brindley, G.P. (1989) 'The role of needs analysis in adult ESL programme design', in Johnson (297), pp. 63–78.

(58) Carrier, M. (1983) 'Computer assisted needs analysis', *Language Training*, vol. 4, 4.

(59) Chambers, F. (1980) 'A re-evaluation of needs analysis', *ESP Journal*, vol. 1, 1, pp. 25–33.

(60) Coleman, H. (1988) 'Analysing language needs in large organisations', *English for Specific Purposes*, vol. 7, 3, pp. 155–69.

(61) Cumaranatunge, L.K. (1988) 'An EOP case study: domestic aides in West Asia', in Chamberlain and Baumgardner (6), pp. 127–33.

(62) Cunningsworth, A. (1983) 'Needs analysis: A review of the state of the art', *System*, vol. 11, 2, pp. 149–55.

(63) Davies, A. (1981) Review of Munby's *Communicative syllabus design*, *TESOL Quarterly*, vol. 15, 3, pp. 332–6.

(64) Drobnic, K. (1978) 'Mistakes and modifications in course design', in Todd Trimble *et al.* (36), pp. 313–21.

(65) Early, P.B. (1981) 'Designer's needs versus learner's needs: Conversation in the L2 classroom', in Aupelf/Goethe Institut/British Council (1), pp. 132–47.

(66) Fanselow, J. (1980) '"It's too damn tight" — Media in ESL classrooms: Structural features in technical/subtechnical English', *TESOL Quarterly*, vol. 14, 2, pp. 141–55.

(67) Hawkey, R. (1980) 'Syllabus design for specific purposes', in the British Council (4), pp. 82–133.

(68) Hawkey, R. (1983) 'Programme development for learners of English for vocational purposes', in Richterich (86), pp. 79–87.

(69) Holliday, A. (1984) 'Research into classroom culture as necessary input into syllabus design', in Swales and Mustafa (33), pp. 29–51.

(70) Holliday, A. and Cooke, T. (1983) 'An ecological approach to ESP', in Waters (38), pp. 123–43.

(71) Horowitz, D.M. (1986) 'What professors actually require: Academic tasks for the ESL classroom', *TESOL Quarterly*, vol. 20, 3, pp. 445–62.

(72) Jacobson, W.H. (1986) 'An assessment of the communication needs of non-native speakers of English in an undergraduate physics lab', *English for Specific Purposes*, vol. 5, 2, pp. 173–87.

(73) Johns, A.M. (1981) 'Necessary English: A faculty survey', *TESOL Quarterly*, vol. 15, 1, pp. 51–7.

(74) Knight, D. (1981) 'Needs definition and course design in "one-off" contexts', in Aupelf/Goethe Institut/British Council (1), pp. 89–98.

(75) Lawson, K.H. (1979) *Philosophical Concepts and Values in Adult Education*, Milton Keynes: Open University Press.

(76) Lonnfors, P. (1987) 'Needs analysis project for the lay person', paper given at the 6th European Symposium on LSP, University of Vaasa, Finland.

(77) Mackay, R. (1978) 'Identifying the nature of the learner's needs', in Mackay and Mountford (23), pp. 21–37.

(78) Mackay, R. and Bosquet, M. (1981) 'LSP curriculum development — from policy to practice', in Mackay and Palmer (24), pp. 1–28.

(79) Markee, N. (1986) 'The relevance of sociopolitical factors to communicative course design', *English for Specific Purposes*, vol. 5, 1, pp. 3–16.

(80) Martin, C. (1981) 'Languages for specific purposes: learners' needs and teaching developments', in ECHE and NATFHE: *Modern Languages for Industry*, pp. 19–28.

(81) Mountford, A. (1981) 'The what, the why and the way', in Aupelf/Goethe Institut/British Council (1), pp. 19–34.

(82) Munby, J. (1978) *Communicative Syllabus Design*, Cambridge: Cambridge University Press.

(83) Munby, J. (1984) 'Communicative syllabus design: Principles and problems', in Read, J.A.S. (ed.) *Trends in Language Syllabus Design*, Anthology Series 13, Singapore: SEAMEO Regional English Language Centre, pp. 55–67.

(84) Pilbeam, A. (1979) 'The language audit', *Language Training*, vol. 1, 2.

(85) Ramani, E., Chacko, T., Singh, S.J. and Glendinning, E. (1988) 'An ethnographic approach to syllabus design: A case study of the Indian Institute of Science, Bangalore', *English for Specific Purposes*, vol. 7, 2, pp. 81–90.

(86) Richterich, R. (ed.) (1983) *Case Studies in Identifying Language Needs*, Oxford: Pergamon Press.

(87) Richterich, R. and Chancerel, J.L. (1980) *Identifying the Needs of Adults Learning a Foreign Language*, Oxford: Pergamon Press.

(88) Robinson, P.C. (1986) 'Needs analysis: From product to process', in Cornu, Vanparijs, Delahaye and Baten (8), pp. 32–44.

(89) Scharer, R. (1983) 'Identification of learners' needs at Eurocentres', in Richterich (86), pp. 106–16.

(90) Schmidt, M. (1981) 'Needs assessment in English for specific purposes: The case study', in Selinker, Tarone and Hanzeli (29), pp. 199–210.

(91) Schroder, K. (1981) 'Methods of exploring language needs in industry', in Freudenstein *et al.* (9), pp. 43–54.

(92) Schutz, N.W. and Derwing, B.L. (1981) 'The problem of needs assessment in English for specific purposes: Some theoretical and practical considerations', in Mackay and Palmer (24), pp. 29–44.

(93) Shaw, P. (1982) 'Ad hoc needs analysis', *Modern English Teacher*, vol. 10, 1, pp. 10−15.

(94) Svendsen, C. and Krebs, K. (1984) 'Identifying English for the job: Examples from health care occupations', *ESP Journal*, vol. 3, 2, pp. 153−64.

(95) Tarantino, M. (1988) 'Italian in-field EST users self-assess their macro- and micro-level needs: A case study', *English for Specific Purposes*, vol. 7, 1, pp. 33−53.

(96) Weir, C.J. (1983) 'Identifying the language needs of overseas students in tertiary education in the United Kingdom', unpublished PhD thesis, University of London.

(C) The analysis of language for ESP

(97) Alber-DeWolf, R. (1984) 'Term-formation processes in English, German, French and Russian', in Pugh and Ulijn (25), pp. 166−73.

(98) Alderson, J.C. and Alvarez, G. (1980) 'The development of strategies for the assignment of semantic information to unknown lexemes in text', *ESPecialist*, no. 1, pp. 7−14.

(99) Arnon, R. (1989) 'Technical English: The linguistic analyses of some registers', in Lauren and Nordman (20), pp. 49−58.

(100) Baker, M. (1988) 'Sub-technical vocabulary and the ESP teacher: An analysis of some rhetorical items in medical journal articles', *Reading in a Foreign Language*, vol. 4, 2, pp. 91−105.

(101) Barber, C.L. (1962) 'Some measurable characteristics of modern scientific prose', in *Contributions to English Syntax and Phonology*, Gothenburg Studies in Linguistics 14, Stockholm: Almquist and Wiksell. Reprinted in Swales (32), pp. 1−14.

(102) Bazerman, C. (1989) *Shaping Written Knowledge*, Madison, WI: The University of Wisconsin Press.

(103) de Beaugrande, R. (1987) 'Special purpose language and linguistic theory', *Unesco ALSED-LSP Newsletter*, vol. 10, 2 (25), pp. 2−11.

(104) de Beaugrande, R. (1989) 'Special purpose language as a complex system: The case of linguistics', in Lauren and Nordman (21), pp. 3−29.

(105) Bhatia, V.K. (1987) 'Language of the law' [State of the art article], *Language Teaching*, vol. 20, 4, pp. 227−34.

(106) Biber, D. (1988) *Variation across Speech and Writing*, Cambridge: Cambridge University Press.

(107) Bloor, M. and Bloor, T. (1986) 'Languages for specific purposes: Practice and theory', CLCS Occasional Paper No. 19, Dublin: Centre for Language and Communication Studies, Trinity College.

(108) Bramki, D. and Williams, R. (1984) 'Lexical familiarization in economics text, and its pedagogic implications in reading comprehension', *Reading in a Foreign Language*, vol. 2, 1, pp. 169−81.

(109) Bruce, N. (1984) 'Rhetorial constraints and information structure in medical research report writing', *English for Medical and Paramedical Purposes Newsletter*, vol. 1, 1, pp. 5−18.

(110) Carter, R. and McCarthy, M. (1988) *Vocabulary and Language Teaching*, Harlow: Longman.

(111) Chiu, R. (1973) 'Register constraints on the choice of the English verb', *RELC Journal*, vol. 4, 1, pp. 33−47.

(112) Coleman, H. (1985) 'Talking shop: an overview of language and work', in Coleman (116), pp. 105–29.

(113) Coleman, H. (1989) Introduction to Coleman (117), pp. 1–23.

(114) Coleman, H. (1989) 'The present and future of work', in Coleman (117), pp. 109–27.

(115) Coleman, H. (ed.) (1984) *Language and Work 1: Law, industry, education* (Special issue, *International Journal of the Sociology of Language* 49), Berlin: Mouton.

(116) Coleman, H. (ed.) (1985) *Language and work 2: The health professions* (Special issue: *International Journal of the Sociology of Language* 51), Berlin: Mouton.

(117) Coleman, H. (ed.) *Working with Language: A multidisciplinary consideration of language use in work contexts*, Contributions to the Sociology of Language 52, Berlin: Mouton de Gruyter.

(118) Connor, U. and Kaplan, R.B. (eds) (1987) *Writing across Languages: Analysis of L2 text*, Reading, MA: Addison-Wesley.

(119) Cooper, C. (1985) 'Aspects of article introductions in IEEE publications', unpublished M.Sc. TESP dissertation, University of Aston in Birmingham.

(120) Crookes, G. (1986) 'Towards a validated analysis of scientific text structure', *Applied Linguistics*, vol. 7, 1, pp. 57–70.

(121) Di Pietro, R.J. (ed.) (1982) *Linguistics and the Professions*, Proceedings of the 2nd Annual Delaware Symposium on Language Studies, Norwood, NJ: Ablex.

(122) Draskau, J. (1986) 'A valency-type analysis of four mono-lexical verbs and two polylexical verbs in English LSP texts from two subject fields, marine engineering and veterinary science', *Unesco ALSED-LSP Newsletter*, vol. 9, 2 (23), pp. 25–42.

(123) Dubois, B.L. (1982) 'The construction of noun phrases in biomedical journal articles', in Hoedt *et al.* (12), pp. 49–67.

(124) Dubois, B.L. (1988) 'Citation in biomedical journal articles', *English for Specific Purposes*, vol. 7, 3, pp. 181–93.

(125) Dudley-Evans, T. (1986) 'Genre analysis: An investigation of the introduction and discussion sections of M.Sc. dissertations', in Coulthard, M. (ed.) *Talking about Text*, Discourse Analysis Monograph no. 13, Birmingham: English Language Research, University of Birmingham, pp. 128–45.

(126) Dudley-Evans, T. (1987) Introduction to Dudley-Evans (128), pp. 1–9.

(127) Dudley-Evans, T. (1989) 'An outline of the value of genre analysis in LSP work', in Lauren and Nordman (21), pp. 72–9.

(128) Dudley-Evans, T. (ed.) (1987) *Genre Analysis and ESP*, ELR Journal, no. 1, Birmingham: English Language Research, University of Birmingham.

(129) Dudley-Evans, T. and Henderson, W. (eds) (1990) *The Language of Economics: The analysis of economics discourse*, ELT Document 134, Modern English Publications in association with the British Council.

(130) Ewer, J.R. (1978) 'Factors facilitating comprehension and prediction in formal oral and scientific English (preliminary report)', unpublished report, Santiago, Chile: Department of English, University of Chile.

(131) Ewer, J.R. (1979) 'The modals in formal scientific discourse: Function, meaning and use', unpublished report, Santiago, Chile: Department of English, University of Chile.

(132) Ewer, J.R. (1981) 'Formal written and oral scientific English: Main microacts (functions/notions) and their indicators (principal exponents)', unpublished report, Santiago, Chile: Department of English, University of Chile.

(133) Ewer, J.R. and Latorre, G. (1967) 'Preparing an English course for students of science', *ELT Journal*, vol. 21, 3, pp. 221–9.

(134)   Farrington, O. (1981) 'The first five seconds: The ESP teacher and "out-of-the-blue" language', in British Council (550), pp. 65−70.

(135)   Flick, W.C. and Anderson, J.I. (1980) 'Rhetorical difficulty in scientific English: A study in reading comprehension', *TESOL Quarterly*, vol. 14, 3, pp. 345−51.

(136)   Fox, J. (1981) 'Specifying the lexis for computer-assisted learning courses', in Aupelf/ British Council/Goethe Institut (1), pp. 113−21.

(137)   Godman, A. and Payne, E.M.F. (1979) *Longman Dictionary of Scientific Usage*, Harlow and London: Longman.

(138)   Gorm Hansen, I. (1981) 'LSP — Aspects of teaching methods at the university level', in Hoedt and Turner (13), pp. 151−60.

(139)   Grabarczyk, Z. (1989) 'Scientific discourse against the background of standard language', in Lauren and Nordman (21), pp. 180−9.

(140)   Grabe, W. (1987) 'Contrastive rhetoric and text-type research', in Connor and Kaplan (118), pp. 115−37.

(141)   Grabe, W. (1988) 'English, information access, and technology transfer: A rationale for English as an international language', *World Englishes*, vol. 7, 1, pp. 63−72.

(142)   Gregory, M. (1967) 'Aspects of varieties differentiation', *Journal of Linguistics*, vol. 3, pp. 177−98.

(143)   Gustaffson, M. (1975) *Some Syntactic Properties of English Law Language*, Finland: University of Turku.

(144)   Halliday, M.A.K. (1961) 'Categories of the theory of grammar', *Word*, 17, pp. 241−92.

(145)   Halliday, M.A.K. (1978) *Language as Social Semiotic*, London: Edward Arnold.

(146)   Halliday, M.A.K., McIntosh, A. and Strevens, P. (1964) *The Linguistic Sciences and Language Teaching*, London: Longman.

(147)   Hoey, M. (1983) *On the Surface of Discourse*, London: Allen & Unwin.

(148)   Hoffman, L. (1981) 'The linguistic analysis and teaching of LSP in the German Democratic Republic', in Hoedt and Turner (13), pp. 107−30.

(149)   Hoffman, L. (1986) 'Material design in function of defined objectives', in Cornu *et al.* (8), pp. 45−60.

(150)   Hopkins, A. and Dudley-Evans, T. (1988) 'A genre-based investigation of the discussion sections in articles and dissertations', *English for Specific Purposes*, vol. 7, 2, pp. 113−21.

(151)   Houghton, D. and Wallace, R.G. (1978) *An Accounting Vocabulary and Guide to Basic Accounting Terms*, Birmingham: English Language Research, University of Birmingham.

(152)   Huckin, T.N. and Olsen, L.A. (1984) 'On the use of informants in LSP discourse analysis', in Pugh and Ulijn (25), pp. 120−9.

(153)   Huddleston, R.D., Hudson, R.A., Winter, E.O. and Henrici, A. (1968) *Sentence and Clause in Scientific English*, mimeo, London: Communication Research Centre, Department of General Linguistics, University College.

(154)   Hüllen, W. (1981) 'Movements on earth and in the air', *ESP Journal*, vol. 1, 2, pp. 141−53.

(155)   Hüllen, W. (1981) 'The teaching of English for specific purposes: A linguistic view', in Freudenstein *et al.* (9), pp. 57−71.

(156)   Hutchinson, T. and Waters, A. (1980) 'Communication in the technical classroom: "You just shove this little chappie in here like that"', in British Council (4), pp. 7−36.

(157)   Inman, M. (1978) 'Lexical analysis of scientific and technical prose', in Todd Trimble *et al.* (36), pp. 242−56.

(158) Irgl, V. (1986) 'The metaphor in the language of commerce', in Cornu *et al.* (8), pp. 258—63.

(159) Irgl, V. (1989) 'Synonymy in the language of business and economics', in Lauren and Nordman (21), pp. 275—82.

(160) Jupp, T.C. and Hodlin, S. (1976) *Industrial English*, London: Heinemann.

(161) Kaplan, R. (ed.) (1987) *Annual Review of Applied Linguistics*, vol. 7, 1986, Cambridge: Cambridge University Press.

(162) Kennedy, G.C. (1987) 'Expressing temporal frequency in academic English', *TESOL Quarterly*, vol. 21, 1, pp. 69—86.

(163) King, P. (1989) ' The uncommon core: Some discourse features of student writing', *System*, vol. 17, 1, pp. 13—20.

(164) Krashen, S. (1981) *Second Language Acquisition and Learning*, Oxford: Pergamon Press.

(165) Lackstrom, J., Selinker, L. and Trimble, L. (1973) 'Technical rhetorical principles and grammatical choice', *TESOL Quarterly*, vol. 7, 2, pp. 127—36.

(166) Laufer, B. (1986) 'A case for vocabulary in EAP reading comprehension materials', in Cornu *et al.* (8), pp. 284—91.

(167) Laufer, B. (1989) 'What percentage of text-lexis is essential for comprehension?', in Lauren and Nordman (21), pp. 316—23.

(168) Lauren, C. and Nordman, M. (1986) 'Two dimensions of technolects — and their didactic implications', in Cornu *et al.* (8), pp. 61—9.

(169) Lauren, C. and Nordman, M. (1989) Introduction to Lauren and Nordman (21), pp. ix—xi.

(170) Lenz, F. (1989) 'Discourse analysis in occupational settings: "Technical meetings"', in Lauren and Nordman (21), pp. 161—70.

(171) Leow Kam Foong (1983) 'Identification of the structures of law reports, with the view of helping students read cases more efficiently', unpublished MAAL project, Department of Linguistic Science, University of Reading.

(172) Longe, V.U. (1985) 'Aspects of textual features of officialese — the register of public administration', *IRAL*, vol. 23, 4, pp. 301—14.

(173) Loots, M. (1986) 'Compiling a list of academically relevant words', in Cornu *et al.* (8), pp. 264—73.

(174) Maher, J. (1986) 'The development of English as an international language of medicine', *Applied Linguistics*, vol. 7, 2, pp. 206—18.

(175) Maher, J. (1986) 'English for medical purposes' [State of the art article], *Language Teaching*, vol. 19, 2, pp. 112—45.

(176) Malcolm, L. (1987) 'What rules govern tense usage in scientific articles?', *English for Specific Purposes*, vol. 6, 1, pp. 31—43.

(177) Martin, A.V. (1976) 'Teaching academic vocabulary to foreign graduate students', *TESOL Quarterly*, vol. 10, 1, pp. 91—9.

(178) Master, P. (1987) 'Generic *the* in *Scientific American*', *English for Specific Purposes*, vol. 6, 3, pp. 165—86.

(179) Miller, C.R. and Selzer, J. (1985) 'Special topics of argument in engineering reports', in Odell, L. and Goswami, D. (eds) *Writing in Nonacademic Settings*, New York: Guilford Press, pp. 309—41.

(180) Murray, D.E. (1988) 'Computer-mediated communication: Implications for ESP', *English for Specific Purposes*, vol. 7, 1, pp. 3—18.

(181) Myers, G. (1988) 'The social construction of science and the teaching of English: An

example of research', in Robinson (787), pp. 143—50.

(182)   van Naerssen, M. and Kaplan, R.B. (1987) 'Language and science', in Kaplan (161), pp. 86—104.

(183)   Olsen, L.A. (1981) 'Noun compounding in EST', mimeo, University of Michigan.

(184)   Ostyn, P., Vandecasteele, M., Deville, G., Kelly, P. (1986) 'Towards an optimal programme of FL vocabulary acquisition', in Cornu *et al.* (8), pp. 292—305.

(185)   Pettinari, C. (1983) 'The function of a grammatical alternation in 14 surgical reports', *Applied Linguistics*, vol. 4, 1, pp. 55—76.

(186)   Pettinari, C. (1985) 'A comparison of the production of surgical reports by native and non-native speaking surgeons', in Benson, J.D. and Greaves, W.S. (eds) *Systemic Perspectives on Discourse*, vol. 2, Norwood, NJ: Ablex, pp. 187—203.

(187)   Phillips, M.K. (1985) *Aspects of Text Structure: An investigation of the lexical organisation of text*, Amsterdam: North-Holland.

(188)   Phillips, M.K. (1989) *Lexical Structure of Text*, Discourse Analysis Monograph no. 12, Birmingham: English Language Research, University of Birmingham.

(189)   Porter, D. (1976) 'Scientific English: An oversight in stylistics?' *Studia Anglica Posnaniensa*, no. 8, Poznan, Poland.

(190)   Quirk, R., Greenbaum, G., Leech, G. and Svartvik, J. (1972) *A Grammar of Contemporary English*, London: Longman.

(191)   Renouf, A. (1987) 'Corpus development', in Sinclair, J.M. (ed.) *Looking Up: An account of the COBUILD project in lexical computing*, London: Collins Cobuild, Collins ELT, pp. 1—40.

(192)   Roberts, R.P. (1984) 'Contextual dictionaries for Languages for Special Purposes', in Pugh and Ulijn (25), pp. 154—65.

(193)   Ross, C.J. (1988) 'British term bank project — the Heriot-Watt experience', *Unesco ALSED-LSP Newsletter*, vol. 11, 1 (26), pp. 10—22.

(194)   Rounds, P.L. (1987) 'Characterizing successful classroom discourse for NNS teaching assistant training', *TESOL Quarterly*, vol. 21, 4, pp. 643—71.

(195)   Rounds, P.L. (1987) 'Multifunctional personal pronoun use in an educational setting', *English for Specific Purposes*, vol. 6, 1, pp. 13—29.

(196)   Rudzka-Ostyn, B. (1986) 'Vocabulary teaching: A cognitive approach', in Cornu *et al.* (8), pp. 241—55.

(197)   Sager, J.C. (1981) 'Approaches to terminology and the teaching of terminology', *Fachsprache*, vol. 3, 3, pp. 98—106.

(198)   Sager, J.C., Dungworth, D. and McDonald, P.F. (1980) *English Special Languages: Principles and practice in science and technology*, Wiesbaden: Oscar Brandtstetter Verlag.

(199)   Salager, F. (1983) 'The lexis of fundamental medical English: Classificatory framework and rhetorical function (a statistical approach)', *Reading in a Foreign Language*, vol. 1, 1, pp. 54—64.

(200)   Salager, F. (1984) 'Compound nominal phrases in scientific-technical literature: Proportion and rationale', in Pugh and Ulijn (25), pp. 136—45.

(201)   Salager, F., Defives, G. and de Filipis, M. (1986) 'Grammar and English written communication: A principal component analysis', in Cornu *et al.* (8), pp. 127—41.

(202)   Salager-Meyer, F., Defives, G., Jensen, C. and de Filipis, M. (1989) 'Communicative function and grammatical variations in medical English scholarly papers: A genre analysis study', in Lauren and Nordman (21), pp. 151—60.

(203)   Salager-Meyer, F., Defives, G., Jensen, C. and de Filipis, M. (1989) 'Principal

component analysis and medical English discourse: An investigation into genre analysis', *System*, vol. 17, 1, pp. 21—34.

(204) Salmi-Tolonen, T. (1989) 'On some syntactic features of European Community Law English', in Lauren and Nordman (20), pp. 39—48.

(205) Selinker, L. (1979) 'On the use of informants in discourse analysis and "Language for specialized purposes"', *IRAL*, vol. XVII, 3, pp. 189—215.

(206) Selinker, L. (1986) 'LSP and interlanguage: Interlanguage and LSP', *ESPMENA Bulletin*, no. 22, pp. 1—13.

(207) Selinker, L. (1986) 'Understanding interlanguage within academic discourse domains', in Tickoo (34), pp. 23—46.

(208) Selinker, L. and Douglas, D. (1985) 'Wrestling with "context" in interlanguage theory', *Applied Linguistics*, vol. 6, 2, pp. 190—204.

(209) Selinker, L. and Douglas, D. (1986) 'Comparing episodes in discourse domains in LSP and interlanguage studies', in Cornu *et al.* (8), pp. 366—78.

(210) Selinker, L. and Douglas, D. (1987) 'LSP and interlanguage: Some empirical studies', introduction to *English for Specific Purposes*, vol. 6, 2, pp. 75—85.

(211) Selinker, L. and Douglas, D. (eds) (1987) *Interlanguage*: special issue of *English for Specific Purposes*, vol. 6, 2.

(212) Selinker, L., Lackstrom, J. and Trimble, L. (1970) 'Grammar and technical English', in Lugton, R.C. (ed.) *English as a Second Language: Current issues*, Center for Curriculum Development, Chilton. Reprinted in *English Teaching Forum*, September—October 1972, pp. 3—14.

(213) Selinker, L., Todd Trimble, M. and Trimble, L. (1976) 'Presuppositional information in EST discourse', *TESOL Quarterly*, vol. 10, 3, pp. 281—90.

(214) Selinker, L., Todd Trimble, M. and Trimble, L. (1978) 'Rhetorical function-shifts in EST discourse', *TESOL Quarterly*, vol. 12, 3, pp. 311—20.

(215) Selinker, L. and Trimble, L. (1974) 'Formal written communication and ESL', *Journal of Technical Writing and Communication*, vol. 4, 2, pp. 81—91.

(216) Selinker, L., Trimble, L. and Vroman, R. (1974) 'Presupposition and technical rhetoric', *ELT Journal*, vol. XXIX, 1, pp. 59—65.

(217) Siliakus, H. (1989) '25 years on — another look at the frequency criterion', in Lauren and Nordman (20), pp. 78—84.

(218) Sinclair, J.M. (1966) 'Beginning the study of lexis', in Bazell, C.E., Catford, J.C., Halliday, M.A.K. and Robins, R.H. (eds) *In Memory of J.R. Firth*, London: Longman, pp. 410—30.

(219) Spencer, A. (1975) 'Semantic combinations in economics and law — a case for special treatment', *ESPMENA Bulletin*, no. 3, pp. 30—3.

(220) Spencer, A. (1975/9) *Noun—Verb Expressions in Legal English*, University of Khartoum, 1975; University of Aston, 1979.

(221) Swales, J. (1976) 'Verb frequencies in scientific English', *ESPMENA Bulletin*, no. 4, pp. 28—31.

(222) Swales, J. (1981) *Aspects of Article Introductions*, Aston ESP Research Reports 1, Birmingham: Language Studies Unit, University of Aston.

(223) Swales, J. (1981) 'The function of one type of particle in a chemistry textbook', in Selinker, Tarone and Hanzeli (29), pp. 40—52.

(224) Swales, J. (1983) 'Vocabulary work in LSP: A case of neglect?', *Bulletin CILA*, no. 37, pp. 21—34.

(225) Swales, J. (1984) 'ESP comes of age?': 21 years after "Some measurable characteristics

of modern scientific prose"', *Unesco ALSED-LSP Newsletter*, vol. 7, 2 (19), pp. 9–20.

(226)   Swales, J. (1985) 'English as the international language of research', *RELC Journal*, vol. 16, 1, pp. 1–8.

(227)   Swales, J. (1986) 'Citation analysis and discourse analysis', *Applied Linguistics*, vol. 7, 1, pp. 39–56.

(228)   Swales, J. (1986) 'ESP in the big world of reprint requests', in Discussions and Notes, *English for Specific Purposes*, vol. 5, 1, pp. 81–5.

(229)   Swales, J. (1986) 'A genre-based approach to language across the curriculum', in Tickoo (34), pp. 10–22.

(230)   Swales, J. (1988) 'Discourse communities, genres and English as an international language', *World Englishes*, vol. 7, 2, pp. 211–20.

(231)   Swales, J. (1990) *Genre Analysis*, Cambridge: Cambridge University Press.

(232)   Tadros, A.A. (1981) 'Linguistic prediction in economics texts', unpublished PhD thesis, University of Birmingham.

(233)   Tadros, A.A. (1985) *Prediction in Text*, Discourse Analysis Monograph no. 10, Birmingham: English Language Research, University of Birmingham.

(234)   Tadros, A.A. (1989) 'Predictive categories in university textbooks', *English for Specific Purposes*, vol. 8, 1, pp. 17–31.

(235)   Tarone, E., Dwyer, S., Gillette, S. and Icke, V. (1981) 'On the use of the passive in two astrophysics journal papers', *ESP Journal*, vol. 1, 2, pp. 123–40. Reprinted in Swales (32).

(236)   Thakur, D. (1969) 'A stylistic description of four restricted uses of English in science', unpublished PhD thesis, University of Reading.

(237)   Thomas, P. (1988) 'Analysis of an English and French LSP: Some comparisons with English general text corpora', *Unesco ALSED-LSP Newsletter*, vol. 11, 1 (26), pp. 2–10.

(238)   Tinberg, R.J. (1988) 'The pH of a volatile genre', *English for Specific Purposes*, vol. 7, 3, pp. 205–12.

(239)   Todd, M. (1981) 'An analysis of training manuals', unpublished MA thesis, University of Birmingham.

(240)   Todd Trimble, M. and Trimble, L. (1982) 'Rhetorical-grammatical features of scientific and technical texts as a major factor in written ESP communication', in Hoedt *et al.* (12), pp. 199–216.

(241)   Trimble, L. (1985) *English for Science and Technology: A discourse approach*, Cambridge: Cambridge University Press.

(242)   Turner, R. (1981) 'A note on "special languages" and "specific purposes"', in Hoedt and Turner (13), pp. 1–23.

(243)   Varantola, K. (1984) 'On noun phrase structure in Engineering English', *Annales Universitatis Turkuensis*, Turku, Finland.

(244)   Varantola, K. (1986) 'Special language and general language: Linguistic and didactic aspects', *Unesco ALSED-LSP Newsletter*, vol. 9, 2 (23), pp. 10–20.

(245)   Varantola, K. (1987) 'Popularization strategies and text functional shifts in scientific/technical writing', *Unesco ALSED-LSP Newsletter*, vol. 10, 2 (25), pp. 33–52.

(246)   Voracek, J. (1987) 'ESP: Superstructure and microlanguage', in Discussions and research notes, *English for Specific Purposes*, vol. 6, 1, pp. 53–6.

(247)   Voracek, J. (1989) 'Terminology across the social systems', in Lauren and Nordman (20), pp. 13–20.

(248) Weissberg, R.C. (1984) 'Given and new: Paragraph development models from scientific English', *TESOL Quarterly*, vol. 18, 3, pp. 485–99.

(249) West, G.K. (1980) 'That-nominal constructions in traditional rhetorical divisions of scientific research papers', *TESOL Quarterly*, vol. 14, 4, pp. 483–9.

(250) Wickrama, D.U.W. (1982) 'An approach to legal vocabulary: Element analysis', *English for Specific Purposes* (newsletter), no. 68 Special Issue: Legal English II, pp. 11–12.

(251) Widdowson, H.G. (1978) *Teaching Language as Communication*, Oxford: Oxford University Press.

(252) Widdowson, H.G. (1979) 'The description of scientific language', in Widdowson, H.G. *Explorations in Applied Linguistics*, Oxford: Oxford University Press, pp. 51–61.

(253) Williams, R. (1984) 'A cognitive approach to English nominal compounds', in Pugh and Ulijn (25), pp. 146–53.

(254) Zuck, L.V. and Zuck, J. (1984) 'The main idea: Specialist and non-specialist judgments', in Pugh and Ulijn (25), pp. 130–5.

(255) Zumrawi, F. (1984) 'Using the specialized educational informant: Some implications for course design and content', *ESPMENA Bulletin*, no. 18, pp. 7–14.

(D) Syllabus and course design for ESP

(256) Allen, J.P.B. (1984) 'Functional-analytic course design and the variable focus curriculum', in Brumfit, C.J. (ed.) *The Practice of Communicative Teaching*, ELT Document 124, Oxford: Pergamon Press in association with the British Council, pp. 3–24.

(257) Allen, J.P.B. and Widdowson, H.G. (1978) 'Teaching the communicative use of English', in Mackay and Mountford (23), pp. 56–77.

(258) Allen, J.P.B. and Widdowson, H.G. (eds) *English in Focus* series, Oxford: Oxford University Press.

(259) Arnold, E. (1989) 'Tasks as organising schema in EVP', *Tunisia ESP Newsletter*, no. 5, pp. 4–9.

(260) Auerbach, E.A. and Burgess, D. (1985) 'The hidden curriculum of survival ESL', *TESOL Quarterly*, vol. 19, 3, pp. 475–95.

(261) Auerbach, E.A. and Wallerstein, N. (1987) *ESL for Action: Problem-posing at work*, Reading, MA: Addison-Wesley.

(262) Bates, M. (1978) 'Writing *Nucleus*', in Mackay and Mountford (23), pp. 78–98.

(263) Bates, M. and Dudley-Evans, T. (eds) *Nucleus — English for Science and Technology* series, London: Longman.

(264) Bell, R.T. (1981) 'Notional syllabuses: to grade or not to grade?', in Richards, D. (ed.) *Communicative Course Design*, papers from a colloquium held at the Regional English Language Centre, February 1980, Occasional Papers 17, Singapore: SEAMEO Regional English Language Centre, pp. 14–25.

(265) Bhatia, V.K. (1986) 'Specialist-discipline and the ESP curriculum', in Tickoo (34), pp. 47–63.

(266) Bloor, M. (1984) 'Identifying the components of a language syllabus: A problem for the designers of courses in ESP or Communication Studies', in Williams *et al.* (41), pp. 15–25.

(267) Board, K. (1986) 'Report back on a 1985 case study', in *Appropriate Technology*, Dunford House Seminar Report, London: British Council, pp. 11–15.

(268)   Bowers, R. (1980) 'War stories and romances: Exchanging experience in ELT', in British Council (4), pp. 71–81.

(269)   Breen, M.P. (1984) 'Process syllabuses for the language classroom', in Brumfit, C.J. (ed.) *General English Syllabus Design*, ELT Document 118, Oxford: Pergamon Press in association with the British Council, pp. 47–60.

(270)   Breen, M.P. (1987) 'Contemporary paradigms in syllabus design', Parts I and II [State of the art articles], *Language Teaching*, vol. 20, 2, pp. 81–92; vol. 20, 3, pp. 157–74.

(271)   Brinton, D.M., Snow, M.A. and Wesche, M.B. (1989) *Content-based Second Language Instruction*, New York: Newbury House.

(272)   Brumfit, C.J. (1984) 'Key issues in curriculum and syllabus design for ELT', in *Curriculum and Syllabus Design in ELT*, Dunford House Seminar Report, London: British Council, pp. 7–12.

(273)   Clark, M.A. and Silberstein, S. (1988) 'Problems, prescriptions, and paradoxes in second anguage teaching', *TESOL Quarterly*, vol. 22, 4, pp. 685–700.

(274)   Clyne, E. (1984) 'Industrial language training in the Arab world: A task description of course design', in Swales and Mustafa (33), pp. 151–69.

(275)   Coleman, H. (1987) 'Teaching spectacles and learning festivals', *ELT Journal*, vol. 41, 2, pp. 97–103.

(276)   Courtney, M. (1988) 'Some initial considerations for course design', *English for Specific Purposes*, vol. 7, 3, pp. 195–203.

(277)   Crocker, A. (1982) 'LSP and methodology: Some implications for course design and implementation in EALP', *English for Specific Purposes*, no. 67, pp. 6–7.

(278)   Crocker, A. (1984) 'Method as input and product of LSP course design', in Swales and Mustafa (33), pp. 129–50.

(279)   Crombie, W. (1988) 'ESP: fact or fiction?', summary of a paper given at the IATEFL–TESOL Conference, Edinburgh, April 1988, in *TESOL Scotland Conference Newsletter/IATEFL Newsletter*, no. 100, p. 10.

(280)   Ewer, J.R. and Hughes-Davies, E. (1971, 1972) 'Further notes on developing an ELT programme for students of science and technology', *ELT Journal*, vol. 26, 1, pp. 65–70; vol. 26, 3, pp. 269–73. Reprinted in Swales (32).

(281)   Ewer, J.R. and Latorre, G. (1969) *A Course in Basic Scientific English*, London: Longman.

(282)   Fanning, P. (1988) 'Skill-based syllabuses: Some issues', *English for Specific Purposes*, vol. 7, 2, pp. 103–12.

(283)   Flowerdew, J. (1986) 'Cognitive style and specific-purpose course design', *English for Specific Purposes*, vol. 5, 2, pp. 121–9.

(284)   Graham, J.C. and Beardsley, R.S. (1986) 'English for specific purposes: Content, language and communication in a pharmacy course model', *TESOL Quarterly*, vol. 20, 2, pp. 227–45.

(285)   Green, D.Z. and Lapkin, S. (1984) 'Communicative language test development', in Allen, P. and Swain, M. (eds) *Language Issues and Education Policies: Exploring Canada's multilingual resources*, ELT Document 119, Oxford: Pergamon Press in association with the British Council, pp. 129–48.

(286)   Herbert, A.J. (1965) *The Structure of Technical English*, London: Longman.

(287)   Heyneman, J., Berwick, R. and Baird, D. (1983) 'In-house language training in a Japanese company', *Language Training*, vol. 4, 2.

(288) Hirayama-Grant, G. and Sedgwick, M. (1978) 'ESP syllabus design processes in retrospect', in Todd Trimble *et al.* (36), pp. 322–36.

(289) Horey, P. (ed.) (1984) *ELC Occasional Papers 2*, Jeddah: King Abdulaziz University, College of Engineering, Saudi Arabia.

(290) Huckin, T. and Olsen, L.A. (1984) 'The need for professionally oriented ESL instruction in the United States', *TESOL Quarterly*, vol. 18, 2, pp. 273–94.

(291) Huerta, T., Ibanez, I. and Kaulen, A. (1987) 'Balancing institutional and motivational factors in ESP syllabus design', *English for Specific Purposes*, vol. 5, 2, pp. 189–95.

(292) Hutchinson, T. (1978) 'The practical demonstration', in *Practical Papers in English Language Education*, vol. 1, Lancaster: Institute for English Language Education, pp. 1–42.

(293) Hutchinson, T. and Waters, A. (1980) 'ESP at the crossroads', *English for Specific Purposes*, no. 36, pp. 1–6. Reprinted in Swales (32), pp. 174–85.

(294) Hutchinson, T. and Waters, A. (1981) 'Performance and competence in English for Specific Purposes', *Applied Linguistics*, vol. 2, 1, pp. 56–69.

(295) Hutchinson, T. and Waters, A. (1984) *Interface: English for technical communication*, Harlow: Longman.

(296) Hutchinson, T. and Waters, A. (1985) 'Topics, tasks and language', *EFL Gazette*, January.

(297) Johnson, R.K. (ed.) (1989) *The Second Language Curriculum*, Cambridge: Cambridge University Press.

(298) Kachru, B.B. (1988) 'ESP and non-native varieties of English: Towards a shift in paradigm', in Chamberlain and Baumgardner (6), pp. 9–28.

(299) Kennedy, C.J. (1986) 'Language planning, channel management, and ESP', in *Language in Education in Africa*, Seminar proceedings 26, Edinburgh, Centre of African Studies, University of Edinburgh, pp. 69–99.

(300) Kennedy, C.J. 'Costs, benefits and motivation in ESP', *ESPMENA Bulletin*, no. 26, pp. 1–9.

(301) Koh, M.Y. (1988) 'ESP for engineers: A reassessment', *ELT Journal*, vol. 42, 2, pp. 102–8.

(302) Koh, M.Y. and Cheung, D. (1986) 'Communication skills for engineering undergraduates: A discipline-language integrated approach', in Tickoo (34), pp. 64–75.

(303) Litwack, D.M. (1979) 'Procedure: The key to developing an ESP curriculum', *TESOL Quarterly*, vol. 13, 3, pp. 383–91.

(304) McAlpin, J. and Wilson, J. (eds) (1984) *ELC Occasional Papers 3*, Jeddah: King Abdulaziz University, College of Engineering, Saudi Arabia.

(305) McConnell, J. (1981) 'Technicians and language', *Language Training*, vol. 2, 4.

(306) Mackay, R. (1981) 'Developing a reading curriculum for ESP', in Selinker *et al.* (29), pp. 134–45.

(307) Mackay, R. (1986) 'The dimensions of LSP courses: A Canadian perspective', in Cornu *et al.* (8), pp. 4–31.

(308) Markee, N. (1989) 'ESP within a new descriptive framework', *World Englishes*, vol. 8, 2, pp. 133–46.

(309) Mohan, B. (1986) *Language and Content*, Reading, MA: Newbury House.

(310) Mullen, N.D. and Brown, P.C. (1984) *English for Computer Science*, Oxford: Oxford University Press.

(311)   Nolasco, R. and Arthur, L. (1988) *Large Classes*, London and Basingstoke: Macmillan.

(312)   Nunan, D. (1989) 'Hidden agendas: The role of the learner in programme implementation', in Johnson (297), pp. 176–86.

(313)   O'Keeffe, L. (1983) 'Unique and recurrent elements in syllabuses for ESP', in Brumfit (5), pp. 151–60.

(314)   Parkinson, L. and O'Sullivan, K. (1991) 'Negotiating the learner-centred curriculum', in Brindley, G. (ed.) *The Second Language Curriculum in Action*, Sydney, NSW: National Centre for English Language Teaching and Research, pp. 112–27.

(315)   Phillips, M.K. (1981) 'Toward a theory of LSP methodology', in Mackay and Palmer (24), pp. 92–105.

(316)   Phillips, M.K. (1982) 'Study skills training and the notion of task', in Kennedy, C. (ed.) *English Language Research Journal*, no. 3, English Language Research, University of Birmingham, pp. 1–8.

(317)   Pilbeam, A. (1983) 'Some thoughts on short intensive courses', *Language training*, vol. 4, 1.

(318)   Prabhu, N.S. (1987) *Second Language Pedagogy: A perspective*, Oxford: Oxford University Press.

(319)   Robinson, P.C. (1988) 'The management of language training' [State of the art article], *Language Teaching*, vol. 21, 3, pp. 146–57.

(320)   Saunders, G.P. (1984) 'Flexibility: A critical aspect of ESP course design and methodology', in McAlpin and Wilson (304), pp. 33–42.

(321)   Scott, H. and Scott, J. (1984) 'ESP and Rubik's cube: Three dimensions in course design and materials writing', in McAlpin and Wilson (304), pp. 13–22.

(322)   Swales, J.M. (1989) 'Service English programme design and opportunity cost', in Johnson (297), pp. 79–90.

(323)   Swan, M. (1985) 'A critical look at the communicative approach 2', *ELT Journal*, vol. 39, 2, pp. 76–87.

(324)   Tollefson, J.W. (1990) *Planning Language, Planning Equality*, London: Longman.

(325)   White, R.V. (1988) *The ELT Curriculum: Design, innovation and management*, Oxford: Basil Blackwell.

(326)   Widdowson, H.G. (1981) 'English for specific purposes: Criteria for course design', in Selinker *et al.* (29), pp. 1–11.

(327)   Wilkins, D.A. (1976) *Notional Syllabuses*, Oxford: Oxford University Press.

(328)   Willing, K. (forthcoming): *Problem-solving Communication in the Professional Workplace*, Sydney, NSW: National Centre for English Language Teaching and Research.

(329)   Wilson, J. (1986) 'General principles', in Harper (11), pp. 7–26.

(330)   Xavier, L., Ramani, P.N. and Joseph, M.V. (eds) (1986) *Innovations in ELT: The Loyola experience*, Madras: Department of English, Loyola College.

(E)   Methodology for ESP

(331)   Allwright, J. and Allwright, R. (1977) 'An approach to the teaching of medical English', in Holden (14), pp. 58–62.

(332)   Bloor, M. and St John, M.J. (1988) 'Project writing: The marriage of process and product', in Robinson (787), pp. 85–94.

(333) Brammer, M. and Sawyer-Lauçanno, C. (1990) 'Business and industry: Specific purpose language training', in Crookall and Oxford (342), ch. 12, pp. 143–50.

(334) Candlin, C.N. (1987) 'Towards task-based language learning', in Candlin and Murphy (335), pp. 5–22.

(335) Candlin, C.N. and Murphy, D.F. (eds) (1987) *Language Learning Tasks*, Lancaster Practical Papers in English Language Education, vol. 7, Hemel Hempstead: Prentice Hall.

(336) Chamberlain, D. and Baumgardner, R.J. (1988) Introduction to Chamberlain and Baumgardner (6), pp. 1–3.

(337) Charles, D. (1984) 'The use of case studies in business English', in James (16), pp. 24–33.

(338) Chirnside, A. (1986) 'Talking for specific purposes', in Harper (11), pp. 141–8.

(339) Coleman, H. (1987) '"Little tasks make large return": Task-based language learning in large crowds', in Candlin and Murphy (335), pp. 121–45.

(340) Crookall, D. (1984) 'The use of non-ELT simulations', *ELT Journal*, vol. 38, 4, pp. 262–73.

(341) Crookall, D. (1990) 'International relations: Specific purpose language training', in Crookall and Oxford (342), ch. 13, pp. 151–8.

(342) Crookall, D. and Oxford, R.L. (eds) (1990) *Simulation, Gaming and Language Learning*, New York: Newbury House.

(343) Dorrity, T. (1983) 'Using logical problems in ESP', *ELT Journal*, vol. 37, 2, pp. 145–9.

(344) Dubin, F. (1985) 'The use of simulation in courses for language teachers', *System*, vol. 13, 3, pp. 231–6.

(345) Dubois, B.L. (1986) 'Needed: EST public communication for non-native speakers of English', *English for Specific Purposes*, vol. 5, 1, pp. 73–9.

(346) Everett, C. (1981) 'Science activities in the language classroom', unpublished MAAL project, Department of Linguistic Science, University of Reading.

(347) Flowerdew, J. (1984) 'Group work based on rhetorical functions: Some applications in the field of English for science and technology (EST)', *World Language English*, vol. 4, 1, pp. 62–6.

(348) Fried-Booth, D. (1982) 'Project work with advanced classes', *ELT Journal*, vol. 36, 2, pp. 98–103.

(349) Fried-Booth, D. (1986) *Project Work*, Oxford: Oxford University Press.

(350) Heath Robinson, W. (1981) *Inventions*, London: Duckworth.

(351) Herbolich, J. (1979) 'Box kites', *English for Specific Purposes*, no. 29, Reprinted in Swales (32), pp. 130–4.

(352) Huckin, T.N. (1988) 'Achieving professional communicative relevance in a "generalized" ESP classroom', in Chamberlain and Baumgardner (6), pp. 62–70.

(353) Hutchinson, T. (1988) 'Making materials work in the ESP classroom', in Chamberlain and Baumgardner (6), pp. 71–5.

(354) Hutchinson, T. and Sawyer-Lauçanno, C. (1990) 'Science and technology: Specific purpose language training', in Crookall and Oxford (342) ch. 11, pp. 135–41.

(355) Jones, K. (1982) *Simulations in Language Teaching*, Cambridge: Cambridge University Press.

(356) Littlejohn, A. and Hicks, D. (1987) 'Task-centred writing activities', in Candlin and Murphy (335), pp. 69–91.

(357) Long, M.H. (1975) 'Group work and communicative competence in the ESOL

classroom', in Burt, M.K. and Dulay, H.C. (eds) *On TESOL '75: New directions in language learning, teaching and bilingual education*, selected papers from the 9th annual TESOL convention, Los Angeles, Washington, DC: TESOL, pp. 211–23.

(358)   McGinley, K. (1985) 'ESP syllabus change and simulation', *System*, vol. 13, 3, pp. 269–71.

(359)   Markee, N. (1984) 'The methodological component in ESP operations', *ESP Journal*, vol. 3, 1, pp. 3–24.

(360)   Mountford, A. (1988) 'Factors influencing ESP materials production and use', in Chamberlain and Baumgardner (6), pp. 76–84.

(361)   Nesi, H. and Skelton, J. (1987) 'The structure of oral presentations', *ESPMENA Bulletin*, 24, pp. 6–13.

(362)   Nolasco, R.H. (1980) 'Science activity and the language teacher', *Forum*, vol. XVIII, 1, pp. 12–14.

(363)   *North Sea Challenge*, London: BP Educational Service.

(364)   Nunan, D. (1989) *Designing Tasks for the Communicative Classroom*, Cambridge: Cambridge University Press.

(365)   Peretz, A.S. (1988) 'Student-centred learning through content-based instruction: Use of oral report projects in the advanced EFL reading class', *Reading in a Foreign Language*, vol. 5, 1, pp. 181–91.

(366)   Phillips, M.K. and Shettlesworth, C. (1976) 'Questions in the design and use of courses in English for specialized purposes', in Nickel, G. (ed.) *Proceedings of the 4th International Congress of Applied Linguistics*, Stuttgart: AILA and HochschulVerlag, pp. 249–64.

(367)   Piotrowski, M.V. (1982) 'Business as usual: Using the case method to teach ESL to executives', *TESOL Quarterly*, vol. 16, 2, pp. 229–38.

(368)   Robinson, P.C. (1978) 'Projects', in British Council (690), pp. 75–8.

(369)   Sawyer, M. (1989) 'Language learning by the case method', in Bickley (2), pp. 138–43.

(370)   Schofield, J. (1988) 'Presentation skills and the language learner', *Language Training*, vol. 9, 3.

(371)   Scott, M.R. (1984) 'Self-access in ESP', in *TEAM (Teachers of English: Arab Monthly*, Journal of the English Language Centre, University of Petroleum and Minerals, Dhahran, Saudi Arabia), no. 49, pp. 14–21.

(372)   Souillard, A. and Kerr, A. (1987) 'Practicing presentations with science and technology students', *Forum*, vol. XXV, 3, pp. 29–31.

(373)   Sturtridge, G. (1977) 'Using simulations in teaching English for specific purposes', in Holden (14), pp. 32–4.

(374)   Sturtridge, G. (1981) 'Role play and simulations', in Johnson, K. and Morow, K. (eds) *Communication in the Classroom*, Harlow: Longman, pp. 126–30.

(375)   Swales, J. (1988) 'Communicative language teaching in ESP contexts', in Brumfit, C.J. (ed.) *Annual Review of Applied Linguistics*, vol. 8, Cambridge: Cambridge University Press, pp. 48–57.

(376)   Thompson, P. (1989) 'Oral presentations in an academic context: Nature, teaching and assessment', unpublished MATEFL dissertation, University of Reading.

(377)   Tudor, I. (1987) 'Using translation in ESP', *ELT Journal*, vol. 41, 4, pp. 268–73.

(378)   Waters, A. (1988) 'ESP: Back to the future!', *ESPecialist*, vol. 9, 1–2, pp. 27–43.

(379)   Wright, D.W. (1980) 'TEFL and ESP in French higher education: The case study and role play approach', *System*, vol. 8, 2, pp. 103–11.

(380)   Zawadzki, J. and Saunders, P. (1990) 'Presentation skills: Learning lessons from native speakers', *Language Training*, vol. 10, 4.

(F) Materials for ESP

(381) Alderson, J.C. (1979) 'Materials evaluation', in Harper (10), pp. 145–55.

(382) Alderson, J.C. (1986) 'Computers in language testing', in Leech, G. and Candlin, C.N. (eds) *Computers in English Language Teaching and Research*, Harlow: Longman, pp. 99–110.

(383) Allwright, R.L. (1979) 'ESP and classroom management: The role of teaching materials', in Harper (10), pp. 91–107.

(384) Allwright, R.L. (1981) 'What do we want teaching materials for?', *ELT Journal*, vol. 36, 1, pp. 5–18.

(385) Atlan, J. (1989) 'Creating courseware for teaching LSP on a multimedia training system', in Lauren and Nordman (21), pp. 374–83.

(386) Baten, L., Cornu, A.-M. and Engels, L.V. (1989) 'The use of concordances in vocabulary acquisition', in Lauren and Nordman (21), pp. 452–67.

(387) Bates, M. (1979) 'Some uses of transfer and inference in *Nucleus* exercises', in Harper (10), pp. 57–68.

(388) Baumgardner, R.J., Chamberlain, D., Dharmapriya, A.T. and Staley, B.W. (1986) 'ESP for engineers: Two approaches', in Tickoo (34), pp. 93–104.

(389) Bevan, V. (1982) 'The self-instruction video module: A solution in ESP', in Geddes and Sturtridge (412), pp. 134–60.

(390) Bhatia, V.K. (1983) 'Simplification v. easification: The case of legal texts', *Applied Linguistics*, vol. 4, 1, pp. 42–54.

(391) Bonamy, D. (1981) 'Using video to teach technical English: A description of a materials production experiment', in *Practical Papers in English Language Education*, vol. 4, Lancaster: Institute for English Language Education, University of Lancaster, pp. 135–68.

(392) Botha, J.J. (1982) 'Computer-based education and the teaching of English for special purposes: Report of a project in progress', *System*, vol. 10, 3, pp. 277–84.

(393) Breen, M.P. and Candlin, C.N. (1987) 'Which materials?: A consumer's and designer's guide', in Sheldon (448), pp. 13–28.

(394) Candlin, C.N., Bruton, C.J. and Leather, J.H. (1976) 'Doctors in casualty: Applying communicative competence to components of specialist course design', *IRAL*, vol. 14, 3, pp. 245–72.

(395) Candlin, C.N., Bruton, C.J., Leather, J.H. and Woods, E.G. (1981) 'Designing modular materials for communicative language learning; an example: Doctor–patient communication skills', in Selinker *et al.* (29), pp. 105–33.

(396) Candlin, J., Charles, D. and Willis, J. (1982) 'Making a programme: A case study observed', in Candlin, J., Charles, D., Willis, J., *Video in English Language Teaching*, Language Studies Research Report, Birmingham: Language Studies Unit, University of Aston in Birmingham, pp. 122–34.

(397) Chaplen, E.F. (n.d.) 'Advantages and disadvantages of the team approach to developing and teaching an ESP programme', mimeo, ESP Reference Collection, Language Studies Unit, University of Aston in Birmingham.

(398) Charles, D. (1984) 'Video content and techniques in ELT', *Language Centre News*, vol. 2, University of Jyvaskyla, Finland, pp. 9–18.

(399) Chitravelu, N. (1980) 'Introduction: English for Special Purposes Project', in British Council, *The University of Malaya English for Special Purposes Project*, ELT Document 107, London: The British Council, pp. v–xvi.

(400) Chitravelu, N. (1980) 'The revised version of the UMESPP materials: A résumé', in British Council (as for (399)), pp. 116−21.

(401) Clarke, D.F. (1989) 'Communicative theory and its influence on materials production' [State of the art article], *Language Teaching*, vol. 22, 2, pp. 73−86.

(402) Cousin, W.D. (1984) 'Specification for a clozentropy computer programme to handle cloze passages and open-ended self-assessment questions', in James (16), pp. 34−9.

(403) Crocker, A. and Swales, J. (1984) 'Exploiting video in LSP: Towards an art of the improbable', in Swales and Mustafa (33), pp. 262−70.

(404) Danchik, D. (1984) 'Starting small with computers', in McAlpin and Wilson (304), pp. 8−12.

(405) Davies, F. (1985) 'Toward a classroom based methodology for identifying information structures in text', in Ulijn and Pugh (37), pp. 103−22.

(406) Davies, G. (1986) 'Using the computer in task-oriented language-learning activities', in Aupelf/The British Council/Goethe-Institut, *New Technology and Foreign Language Learning*, Triangle 5, Paris: Didier Erudition, pp. 96−105.

(407) Dudley-Evans, A. (1981) 'A communicative approach to the teaching of writing', in Richards, D. (ed.) *Communicative Course Design*, papers from a colloqium held at RELC, Singapore, February 1980, Occasional Papers 17, Singapore: SEAMEO Regional English Language Centre, pp. 26−43.

(408) Dudley-Evans, A. (1984) 'The use of an ESP textbook in Egyptian secondary schools', in Swales and Mustafa (33), pp. 292−8.

(409) Dudley-Evans, A. and Bates, M. (1987) 'The evaluation of an ESP textbook', in Sheldon, L.E. (448), pp. 99−109.

(410) Ewer, J.R. and Boys, O. (1981) 'The EST textbook situation: An enquiry', *ESP Journal*, vol. 1, 2, pp. 87−105.

(411) Geddes, M. (1982) '"Talking heads" and study skills programmes', in Geddes and Sturtridge (412), pp. 62−8.

(412) Geddes, M. and Sturtridge, G. (eds) (1982) *Video in the Language Classroom*, London: Heinemann.

(413) Gimenez, T. (1987) 'Check-list for materials production in the context of ESP', *ESPecialist*, no. 17, pp. 87−94.

(414) Greenhalgh, J.S. (1984) 'Authenticity in technical English', paper presented at the symposium on English for Specific Purposes, March 1984, Alexandria.

(415) Hahn, W.V. (1989) 'LSP and computer application: New fields of activity for LSP research and development', in Lauren and Nordman (21), pp. 479−92.

(416) Hollis, J. (1989) 'ESP for airline reservation agents', *Language Training*, vol. 10, 3.

(417) Johns, T.F. (1981) 'The uses of an analytic generator: The computer as teacher of English for specific purposes', in British Council (550), pp. 95−105.

(418) Jones, G.M. (1990) 'ESP textbooks: Do they really exist?', *English for Specific Purposes*, vol. 9, 1, pp. 89−93.

(419) Jordan, R.R. (1978) 'Language practice material for economists', in Mackay and Mountford (23), pp. 179−89.

(420) Jordan, R.R. (ed.) (1983) *Case Studies in ELT*, London and Glasgow: Collins ELT.

(421) Kalinyazgan, J. (1985) 'Using pictures in groups for teaching technical English', *Forum*, vol. XXIII, 1, pp. 41−2.

(422) Kay, N. (1990) 'Business English, computers and orienteering', report of a workshop given at the 24th IATEFL Conference, Dublin, 27−30 March 1990, *IATEFL Newsletter*, 108, pp. 4−5.

(423) Kennedy, C. (1983) 'Video in English for specific purposes', in McGovern, J. (ed.) *Video Applications in Language Teaching*, ELT Document 114, Oxford: Pergamon Press in association with the British Council, pp. 95–102.

(424) Kerridge, D. (1982) 'The use of video films', in Geddes and Sturtridge (412), pp. 107–21.

(425) Kitto, M. (1987) 'The pragmatic purchaser', in Sheldon (448), pp. 76–81.

(426) Leckey, J. (1987) 'Curriculum cobbling, or how companies can take over and effectively use commercial materials', in Sheldon (448), pp. 109–18.

(427) Lynch, T. (1983) 'Television as a source of "simplified readers"', paper presented at the TESOL Scotland inaugural conference, Edinburgh, 15 October 1983.

(428) McDonough, J. (1983) 'Steps in the design of academic listening materials', in Jordan (420), pp. 179–87.

(429) MacWilliam, I. (1986) 'Video and language comprehension', *ELT Journal*, vol. 40, 2, pp. 131–5.

(430) Moore, J.D. (1977) 'The preparation of rhetorically focussed materials for service courses in English', in British Council, *English for Specific Purposes: An international seminar*, Proceedings of the seminar held at Paipa, Colombia, 17–22 April 1977, Colombia: The British Council, pp. 41–51.

(431) Morrison, J. (1978) 'Designing a course in advanced listening comprehension', in Mackay and Mountford (23), pp. 161–78.

(432) Morrow, K. (1977) 'Authentic texts and ESP', in Holden (14), pp. 13–15.

(433) Nyns, R. (1988) 'Using the computer to teach reading comprehension skills', *ELT Journal*, vol. 42, 4, pp. 253–61.

(434) O'Neill, R. (1982) 'Why use textbooks?', *ELT Journal*, vol. 36, 2, pp. 104–11.

(435) Phillips, M.K. (1982–3) 'The microcomputer and ESP: Purposes, programs and priorities', *ESPMENA Bulletin*, vol. 16, pp. 27–35.

(436) Phillips, M.K. (1985) 'Logical possibilities and classroom scenarios for the development of CALL', in Brumfit, C.J., Phillips, M.K. and Skehan, P. (eds) *Computers in English Language Teaching: A view from the classroom*, ELT Document 122, Oxford: Pergamon Press in association with the British Council, pp. 25–46.

(437) Phillips, M.K. and Shettlesworth, C.C. (1978) 'How to ARM your students: A consideration of two approaches to providing materials for ESP', in British Council (690), pp. 23–35. Reprinted in Swales (32), pp. 102–14.

(438) Pilbeam, A. (1987) 'Can published materials be widely used for ESP courses?', in Sheldon (448), pp. 119–24.

(439) Robinson, B. (1978) '. . . by the bike pump', *ESPMENA Bulletin*, vol. 11, pp. 21–4.

(440) St John, M.J. (1989) 'Questions at the interface of writing, word-processing and ESP', in Lauren and Nordman (20), pp. 121–7.

(441) Sampson, K. (1989) 'The Camel pack: A self access system for computer assisted medical English learning', *EMP Newsletter*, vol. 6, 1, pp. 22–3.

(442) Scarbrough, D. (1988) 'Software for English language teaching', Survey review, *ELT Journal*, vol. 42, 4, pp. 301–14.

(443) Scott, H. (1984) 'Rubik's cube in action: Applying the theory in materials design', in McAlpin and Wilson (304), pp. 23–9.

(444) Scott, M. and McAlpin, J. (1979) 'Towards a wider repertoire of exercise types', in Harper (10), pp. 45–56.

(445) Sheerin, S. (1982) 'Exploiting television videos with particular reference to teaching ESP', in Geddes and Sturtridge (412), pp. 122–33.

(446)   Sheldon, L.E. (1987) 'Introduction', Sheldon (448), pp. 1–10.
(447)   Sheldon, L.E. (1988) 'Evaluating ELT textbooks and materials', *ELT Journal*, vol. 42, 4, pp. 237–46.
(448)   Sheldon, L.E. (ed.) (1987) *ELT Textbooks and Materials: Problems in evaluation and development*, ELT Document 126, Modern English Publications in association with the British Council.
(449)   Skehan, P. (1981) 'ESP teachers, computers and research', in British Council (550), pp. 106–25.
(450)   Souillard, A. (1989) 'Visuals for practising oral and aural skills with science and technology students', *Forum*, vol. XXVII, 23, pp. 24–7.
(451)   Sturtridge, G., McAlpin, J. and Harper, D. (1977) 'The British Council and the English language problems of overseas students: English for academic purposes materials development', in Cowie and Heaton (700), pp. 108–20.
(452)   Swales, J. (1978) 'Writing *Writing Scientific English*', in Mackay and Mountford (23), pp. 43–55.
(453)   Swales, J. (1980) 'ESP: The textbook problem', *ESP Journal*, vol. 1, 1, pp. 11–23.
(454)   Swales, J. (1983) 'Developing materials for writing scholarly introductions', in Jordan (420), pp. 188–200.
(455)   Todd Trimble, R.M. and Trimble, L. (1977) 'The development of EFL materials for occupational English', in British Council (as for (430)), pp. 52–70.
(456)   Tomalin, B. and Stempleski, S. (1990) *Video in Action: Recipes for using video in EFL/ESL*, Hemel Hempstead: Prentice Hall.
(457)   Tudor, I. (1986) 'Frameworks for the exploitation of video in the language classroom', *British Journal of Language Teaching*, vol. 24, 1, pp. 19–22.
(458)   Widdowson, H.G. (1979) 'The authenticity of language data', in Widdowson, H.G. *Explorations in Applied Linguistics*, Oxford: Oxford University Press, pp. 163–72.
(459)   Widdowson, H.G. (1979) 'The simplification of use', in Widdowson, H.G. *Explorations in Applied Linguistics*, Oxford: Oxford University Press, pp. 185–91.
(460)   Williams, R. (1981) 'A procedure for ESP textbook analysis and evaluation on teacher education courses', *ESP Journal*, vol. 1, 2, pp. 155–62.
(461)   Williams, R. (1983–4) 'Using video to develop strategies in listening comprehension and examination answer writing', *English Language Research Journal*, no. 4, English Language Research, University of Birmingham.
(462)   Willis, J.D. (1979) 'Exploiting authentic audio-visual material in an English course for technicians', in Ziahosseiny, S.M. and Mountford, A. (eds) *English for Special Purposes*, selected papers from the 2nd regional ESP conference, Isfahan University, November 1977, Association of Professors of English in Iran, pp. 105–21.
(463)   Wilson, J. (1986) 'Task-based language learning', in Harper (11), pp. 27–64.
(464)   Wood, A.S. (1982) 'An examination of the rhetorical structure of authentic chemistry texts', *Applied Linguistics*, vol. III, 2, pp. 121–43.

(G)   Evaluation and testing in ESP

(465)   Alderson, J.C. (1985) 'Is there life after the course?', in Alderson (468), pp. 129–50.
(466)   Alderson, J.C. (1988) 'Testing English for specific purposes: How specific can we get?', in Hughes (498), pp. 16–28.

(467) Alderson, J.C. (1988) 'Testing and its administration in ESP', in Chamberlain and Baumgardner (6), pp. 87−97.

(468) Alderson, J.C. (ed.) (1985) *Evaluation*, Lancaster Practical Papers in English Language Education, vol. 6, Oxford: Pergamon Press.

(469) Alderson, J.C. and Beretta, A. (eds) (1991) *Evaluating Second Language Education*, Cambridge: Cambridge University Press.

(470) Alderson, J.C., Candlin, C.N., Clapham, C.M., Martin, D.J. and Weir, C.J. (1986) 'Language proficiency testing for migrant professionals: New directions for the occupational English test', report submitted to the Council on Overseas Professional Qualifications by the Testing and Evaluation Consultancy, Lancaster: Institute for English Language Education, University of Lancaster.

(471) Alderson, J.C. and North, B. (eds) (1991) *Language Testing in the 1990's, Review of English Language Teaching*, vol. 1, 1, Basingstoke: Modern English Publications in association with the British Council.

(472) Alderson, J.C. and Urquhart, A.H. (1983) 'The effect of student background discipline on comprehension: A pilot study', in Hughes, A. and Porter, D. (eds) *Current Developments in Language Testing*, London: Academic Press, pp. 121−7.

(473) Alderson, J.C. and Urquhart, A.H. (1985) 'The effect of students' academic discipline on their performance on ESP reading tests', *Language Testing*, vol. 2, 2, pp. 192−204.

(474) Alderson, J.C. and Waters, A. (1983) 'A course in testing and evaluation for ESP teachers or "How bad were my tests?"', in Waters (38), pp. 39−61.

(475) Allison, D. and Webber, L. (1984) 'What place for performative tests?', *ELT Journal*, vol. 38, 3, pp. 199−203.

(476) Bachman, L. (1981) 'Formative evaluation in specific purpose program development', in Mackay and Palmer (24), pp. 106−16.

(477) Bachman, L. (1989) 'The development and use of criterion-referenced tests of language ability in language program evaluation', in Johnson (297), pp. 242−58.

(478) Beauchamp, P. (1989) *Review of English for Specific Purposes Course Models*, New South Wales: Surveys and Evaluative Studies Division, Multicultural Education Unit, New South Wales Department of Technical and Further Education.

(479) Bell, M. (1982) *Guidelines for the Evaluation of TAFE Programs*, Technical and Further Education Services, Australia.

(480) Beretta, A. (1986) 'A case for field-experimentation in program evaluation', *Language Learning*, vol. 36, 3, pp. 295−309.

(481) Beretta, A. (1986) 'Program-fair language teaching evaluation', *TESOL Quarterly*, vol. 20, 3, pp. 431−44.

(482) Brindley, G. (1989) *Assessing Achievement in the Learner-centred Curriculum*, Sydney: National Centre for English Language Teaching and Research, Macquarie University.

(483) British Council, English Teaching Information Centre (1990) 'International English Language Testing System (IELTS)', *Language Testing Update*, issue 8, pp. 8−9.

(484) Brown, J.D. (1989) 'Language program evaluation: a synthesis of existing possibilities', in Johnson (297), pp. 222−58.

(485) Celani, M.A.A. (1988) 'A participatory evaluation', *ESPecialist*, vol. 9, 1−2, pp. 9−25.

(486) Celani, M.A.A., Holmes, J.L., Ramos, R.C.G. and Scott, M.R. (eds) (1988) *The Brazilian ESP Project: An evaluation*, Sao Paulo: Educ-Editora Da Puc-Sp.

(487) Clapham, C. (1990) 'Is ESP testing justified?', unpublished paper given at the 12th

Language Testing Research Colloquium, San Francisco, CA.

(488)   Coleman, H. (1980) 'Evaluating the communicative proficiency of overseas dentists', *Practical Papers in English Language Education*, vol. 3, Lancaster: Institute for English Language Education, University of Lancaster, pp. 1–18.

(489)   Coleman, H. (1989) 'Testing "appropriate behaviour" in an academic context', in Bickley (2), pp. 361–72.

(490)   Corbett, P. (1986) 'Testing oral interaction between bands three and five', in Harper (11), pp. 171–5.

(491)   Douglas, D. (1990) 'The MATHSPEAK Pilot Project: A field-specific versus a general test of oral production', *Language Testing Update*, issue 8, p. 7.

(492)   Douglas, D. and Selinker, L. (1985) 'Principles for language tests within the "discourse domains" theory of interlanguage: Research, test construction and interpretation', *Language Testing*, vol. 2, 2, pp. 205–26.

(493)   Elley, W.B. (1989) 'Tailoring the evaluation to fit the context', in Johnson (297), pp. 270–85.

(494)   Graham, J.C. (1987) 'English language proficiency and the prediction of academic success', *TESOL Quarterly*, vol. 21, 3, pp. 505–21.

(495)   Holliday, A. (1988) 'Project work as an evaluation device', *System*, vol. 16, 1, pp. 77–86.

(496)   Horey, P. (ed.) (1984) *Evaluation*, ELC Occasional Papers 4, King Abdulaziz University, College of Engineering, Saudi Arabia.

(497)   Hughes, A. (1988) 'Introducing a needs based test of English for study in an English medium university in Turkey', in Hughes (498), pp. 134–53.

(498)   Hughes, A. (ed.) (1988) *Testing English for University Study*, ELT Document 127, Modern English Publications in association with the British Council.

(499)   Kennedy, C. (1985) 'Formative evaluation as an indicator of students' wants and attitudes', *ESP Journal* vol. 4, 2, pp. 93–9.

(500)   Lackstrom, J.E. (1990) 'Review of *The Brazilian ESP Project: An evaluation* by Celani *et al.* (486)', *English for Specific Purposes*, vol. 9, 1, pp. 95–8.

(501)   Land, G. (1983) 'A made-to-measure ESP course for banking staff', *ESP Journal*, vol. 2, 2, pp. 161–71.

(502)   Language Training Services and Carroll, B.J. (1987) *The Business English Test*, Bath, Avon: Language Training Services.

(503)   Lee, Y.P., Fok, A.C.Y.Y., Lord, R. and Low, G. (eds) (1985) *New Directions in Language Testing*, Oxford: Pergamon Press.

(504)   Lewkowicz, J. and Moon, J. (1985) 'Evaluation: a way of involving the learner', in Alderson (468), pp. 45–80.

(505)   Light, R.L., Ming Xu and Mossop, J. (1987) 'English proficiency and the academic performance of international students', *TESOL Quarterly*, vol. 21, 2, pp. 251–61.

(506)   London Chamber of Commerce and Industry, English for Business tests, Sidcup, Kent: London Chamber of Commerce and Industry.

(507)   Long, M.H. (1984) 'Process and product in ESL program evaluation', *TESOL Quarterly*, vol. 18, 3, pp. 409–25.

(508)   Low, G. (1982) 'The direct testing of academic writing in a second language', *System*, vol. 10, 3, pp. 247–57.

(509)   Low, G. (1985) 'Validity and the problem of direct language proficiency tests', in Alderson (468), pp. 151–68.

(510) Low, G. and Lee, Y.P. (1985) 'How shall a test be referenced?', in Lee *et al.* (503), pp. 119−26.

(511) Lynch, B.K. (1990) 'A context-adaptive model for program evaluation', *TESOL Quarterly*, vol. 24, 1, pp. 23−42.

(512) McCormick, R., Bynner, J., Clift, P., James, M. and Brown, C.M. (eds) (1982) *Calling Education to Account*, Oxford: Heinemann, and Milton Keynes: Open University Press.

(513) McGinley, K. (1984) 'Some notes on evaluation in ESP', in James (16), pp. 89−96.

(514) McGinley, K. (1986) 'Coming to terms with evaluation', *System*, vol. 14, 3, pp. 335−41.

(515) Mackay, R. (1981) 'Accountability in ESP programmes', *ESP Journal*, vol. 1, 2, pp. 107−21.

(516) Moody, H.L.B. (1979) 'Some introductory thoughts on evaluation in teaching ESP', in Harper (10), pp. 139−44.

(517) Morrison, D.M. and Lee, N. (1985) 'Simulating an academic tutorial: A test validation study', in Lee *et al.* (503), pp. 85−92.

(518) Murphy, D.F. (1985) 'Evaluation in language teaching: Assessment, accountability and awareness', in Alderson (468), pp. 1−17.

(519) Murphy-O'Dwyer, L. (1985) 'Diary studies as a method for evaluating teacher training', in Alderson (468), pp. 97−128.

(520) Nunan, D. (1989) *Understanding Language Classrooms: A guide for teacher-initiated action*, Hemel Hempstead: Prentice Hall.

(521) Pearson, I. (1988) 'Tests as levers for change', in Chamberlain and Baumgardner (6), pp. 98−107.

(522) Potts, P.J. (1985) 'The role of evaluation in a communicative curriculum, and some consequences for materials design', in Alderson (468), pp. 19−44.

(523) Rea, P.M. (1983) 'Evaluation of educational projects, with special reference to English language education', in Brumfit (5), pp. 85−98.

(524) Rea, P.M. (1984) 'Language tests as indicators of academic achievement', in Culhane, T., Klein Braley, C. and Stevenson, D.K. (eds) *Practice and Problems in Language Testing*, Occasional Papers no. 29, Colchester: Department of Language and Linguistics, University of Essex, pp. 140−58.

(525) Robinson, P.C. (1988) Unpublished report on a British Council/ODA sponsored evaluation of an EST textbook in use, West Bengal, India, January 1988.

(526) St John, M.J. (1990) 'UET(O) to UETESOL: The revised JMB examination in English for academic purposes', *Language Testing Update*, issue 8, pp. 10−14.

(527) Skehan, P. (1984) 'Issues in the testing of English for specific purposes', *Language Testing*, vol. 1, 2, pp. 202−20.

(528) Skehan, P. (1988) 'Language testing', Part I [State of the art article], *Language Teaching*, vol. 21, 4, pp. 211−21.

(529) Smith, S. (1989) 'On using questionnaires for in-company course evaluation', *Language Training*, vol. 10, 2.

(530) Swan, J. (1986) 'ESP course evaluation: what can we learn from our "masters"?', unpublished paper given at the CULI International Conference on Trends in Language Programme Evaluation, Bangkok, Thailand, December 1986.

(531) Waters, A. (1987) 'Participatory course evaluation in ESP', *English for Specific Purposes*, vol. 6, 1, pp. 3−12.

(532) Weir, C.J. (1988) 'The specification, realization and validation of an English language proficiency test', in Hughes (498), pp. 45–110.

(533) Weir, C.J. (1990) *Communicative Language Testing*, Hemel Hempstead: Prentice Hall.

(534) Wesche, M. (1987) 'Second language performance testing: The Ontario Test of ESL as an example', *Language Testing*, vol. 4, 2, pp. 28–47.

(535) Westaway, G. (1987) 'English Language Testing Service Revision Project (ELTSREV) progress report: January 1988', *Language Testing Update*, issue 3, pp. 2–5.

(536) Williams, K.L. (1990) 'Three new tests for overseas students entering postgraduate vocational training courses', *ELT Journal*, vol. 44, 1, pp. 55–65.

(H) The role of the ESP teacher

(537) Abbott, G. (1983) 'Training teachers of EST: Avoiding orthodoxy', *ESP Journal*, vol. 2, 1, pp. 33–6.

(538) Adams Smith, D. (1980) 'Co-operative teaching: Bridging the gap between E and SP', in British Council (549), pp. 76–85.

(539) Adams Smith, D. (1983) 'ESP teacher-training needs in the Middle East', *ESP Journal*, vol. 2, 1, pp. 37–8.

(540) Adams Smith, D. (1984) 'Planning a university language centre in Oman: Problems and proposals', in Swales and Mustafa (33), pp. 197–210.

(541) Akermark, J. (1983) 'Teacher training for ESP in adult education', *ESP Journal*, vol. 2, 1, pp. 39–41.

(542) Arnold, E. (1986) 'Some comments on the science content of ESP', *ESPMENA Bulletin*, no. 21, pp. 1–10.

(543) Arnold, E. (1988) 'Autonomy and the ESP teacher', *Tunisia ESP Newsletter*, no. 4, pp. 3–8.

(544) Barnes, L. and Barnes, B. (1981) 'Science and ESP: Defining some of the problems', *Al Manakh*, vol. 5, 2, pp. 18–55.

(545) Baumgardner, R., Chamberlain, D., Dharmapriya, A.T. and Staley, B.W. (1988) 'Materials case study: National Diploma in Technology-Engineering', in Chamberlain and Baumgardner (6), pp. 145–62.

(546) Beech, J.G. (1982) 'Teacher selection: A written approach', *Language Training*, vol. 3, 3.

(547) Blue, G. (1981) 'Self-directed learning systems and the role of the ESP teacher', in British Council (550), pp. 58–64.

(548) Brennan, M. and van Naerssen, M. (1989) 'Language and content in ESP', *ELT Journal*, vol. 43, 3, pp. 196–205.

(549) British Council (1980) *Team Teaching in ESP*, ELT Document 106, London: British Council English Teaching Information Centre.

(550) British Council (1981) *The ESP Teacher: Role, development and prospects*, ELT Document 112, London: British Council English Teaching Information Centre.

(551) Burkart, E.I. (1980) 'The check procedure in a technical English training course', *Forum*, vol. XVIII, 2, pp. 29–32.

(552) Calderbank, M. and Holliday, A. (1989) 'An ESP approach to teacher training', *Pharos*, no. 2, pp. 2–4.

(553) Campany, N. (1989) 'The management connection', *Language Training*, vol. 10, 3.

(554) Chamberlain, R. (1980) 'The SP of the E', in British Council (549), pp. 97–108.

(555) Chambers, F. and McDonough, J. (1981) 'How many people? Opposing views on the function and preparation of the ESP teacher', in British Council (550), pp. 71–80.

(556) Cortese, G. (1986) 'An experiment in minimal teacher-training for ESP', *ESP Journal*, vol. 4, 2, pp. 77–92.

(557) Crofts, J.N. (1981) 'Subjects and objects in ESP teaching materials', in Selinker, Tarone and Hanzeli (29), pp. 146–53.

(558) Deyes, A.F. (1980) 'The role of the teacher and the role of the student in ESP courses', paper given at the 2nd national seminar of the Brazilian National ESP Project.

(559) Dudley-Evans, T. (1983) 'An experiment in the team teaching of English for occupational purposes', in Dudley-Evans (560), pp. 35–41.

(560) Dudley-Evans, T. (1983) *Papers on Team Teaching and Syllabus Design*, Occasional Papers 27, Singapore: SEAMEO Regional English Language Centre.

(561) Dudley-Evans, T. (1983) 'Towards team teaching: A description of cooperation between language and subject teachers at Ngee Ann College', in Dudley-Evans (560), pp. 22–34.

(562) Dudley-Evans, T. (1984) 'The team teaching of writing skills', in Williams *et al.* (41), pp. 127–34.

(563) Early, P. (1981) 'The ESP teacher's role: Implications for the "knower-client" relationship', in British Council (550), pp. 42–52.

(564) de Escorcia, B.A. (1984) 'Team-teaching for students of economics: A Colombian experience', in Williams *et al.* (41), pp. 135–44.

(565) de Escorcia, B.A. (1985) 'ESP and beyond: A quest for relevance', in Quirk, R. and Widdowson, H.G. (eds) *English in the World: Teaching and learning the language and literatures*, Cambridge: Cambridge University Press in association with the British Council, pp. 228–37.

(566) Ewer, J.R. (1983) 'Teacher training for EST: Problems and methods', *ESP Journal*, vol. 2, 1, pp. 9–31.

(567) Franco, A.L. (1985) 'Beyond the classroom: Monitoring at industry', *ESP Journal*, vol. 4, 2, pp. 153–60.

(568) Gee, S., Huxley, M. and Johnson, D. (1984) 'Teaching communication skills and English for academic purposes: A case study of a problem shared', in Williams *et al.* (41), pp. 115–26.

(569) Greenall, G. (1981) 'The EST teacher: A negative view', in British Council (550), pp. 23–7.

(570) Guezguez, S. (1986) 'Team teaching: One way of motivating EFL students', in *English Teaching Forum*, vol. 24, 2, pp. 42–3.

(571) Hansen, A.G. and van Hammen, D.L. (1980) 'The English teacher and the camera: Team teaching for special purposes', in British Council (549), pp. 92–6.

(572) Harmer, J. (1979) 'A non-specific approach to the training of teachers for purpose language teaching', in Harper (10), pp. 159–66.

(573) Henderson, W. and Skehan, P. (1980) 'The team teaching of introductory economics to overseas students', in British Council (549), pp. 34–47.

(574) Holmes, J. (1979) 'The CESC scientific and technical project', in Lexden Centre (Oxford) Ltd (589), pp. 57–68.

(575) Holmes, J. (1979) 'Perceiving aims', in Lexden Centre (Oxford) Ltd (589), pp. 43–9.

(576) Houghton, D. (1980) 'A collaborative approach to the teaching of vocabulary for accounting students', in British Council (549), pp. 24–33.

(577) Ivanic, R. (1980) 'Moving towards subject–language integration for a college of FE',

in British Council (549), pp. 48—69.

(578)   Jackson, M. and Price, J. (1981) 'A way forward: A fusion of two cultures', in British Council (550), pp. 33—41.

(579)   Johns, A.M. (1983) 'Teacher training in the People's Republic of China', *ESP Journal*, vol. 2, 1, pp. 49—50.

(580)   Johns, A.M. (1988) 'ESP and the future: Less innocence abroad', in Tickoo (35), pp. 21—6.

(581)   Johns, T.F. (1981) 'Some problems of a world-wide profession', in British Council (550), pp. 16—22.

(582)   Johns, T.F. and Dudley-Evans, T. (1980) 'An experiment in team-teaching of overseas postgraduate students of transportation and plant biology', in British Council (549), pp. 6—23. Reprinted in Swales (32), pp. 137—55.

(583)   Johnson, C. (1986) 'The problems of intensive courses', *Language Training*, vol. 7, 2.

(584)   Kennedy, C. (1979) 'The training of teachers for ESP', in Holden (14), pp. 41—7.

(585)   Kennedy, C. (1983) 'An ESP approach to EFL/ESL teacher training', *ESP Journal*, vol. 2, 1, pp. 73—85.

(586)   Kennedy, C. (1983) 'How specific is ESP teacher training?' *ESP Journal*, vol. 2, 1, pp. 51—2.

(587)   Kennedy, C. (1985) 'Teacher as researcher and evaluator: One suggested solution to some recurrent problems in ELT and ESP', *ESPecialist*, no. 12, pp. 3—15.

(588)   Lavery, M. (1985) 'The industrial language trainer', *Language Training*, vol. 6, 1.

(589)   Lexden Centre (Oxford) Ltd (1979) *Lexden Papers 1*, essays on teaching English for specific purposes by the staff of the Colchester English Study Centre, Colchester: Lexden Centre (Oxford) Ltd.

(590)   Lexden Centre (Oxford) Ltd (1981) *Lexden Papers 2*, essays on teaching English for specific purposes by the staff of the Colchester and Bedford English Study Centres, Colchester: Lexden Centre (Oxford) Ltd.

(591)   Lilley, A. (1987) 'Banking on English', *Language Training*, vol. 8, 4.

(592)   Lilley, A.D. (1984) 'The establishment of an independent, inter-faculty ESP centre', in Swales and Mustafa (33), pp. 184—96.

(593)   McDonough, J. (1988) 'ESP: Teaching the teachers', *Language Training*, vol. 9, 3.

(594)   Mackay, R. (1983) 'The need for close integration of components in ESP programs', *ESP Journal*, vol. 2, 1, pp. 58—9.

(595)   Morray, M.K. (1980) 'INELEC: Teamwork in an EST program', in British Council (549), pp. 86—91.

(596)   Pilbeam, A. (1982) 'Teacher selection and the ELT consultant', *Language Training*, vol. 3, 3.

(597)   Pilbeam, A. (1986) 'Recent trends in company language training', *Language Training*, vol. 7, 4.

(598)   Reed, B. (1983) 'An ESP case study: Teaching English to technical instructors', *Language Training*, vol. 4, 3.

(599)   Rivers, W. (1983) 'Designing teacher training to meet local needs', *ESP Journal*, vol. 2, 1, pp. 66—7.

(600)   Robinson, B. (1981) 'The helpful ESP teacher', in British Council (550), pp. 28—32.

(601)   Robinson, B.J. (1988) 'Washing machine makers soak in English!', *Language Training*, vol. 9, 4.

(602)   Scott-Barrett, F. (1989) 'How technical can you get?', *Language Training*, vol. 10,1.

(603)   Sheerin, S. (1981) 'Some difficulties, real and imagined, in conducting medical case

conferences in the teaching of doctor/doctor language', in Lexden Centre (Oxford) Ltd (590), pp. 34–44.

(604) Shih, M. (1986) 'Content-based approaches to teaching academic writing', *TESOL Quarterly*, vol. 20, 4, pp. 617–48.

(605) Skehan, P. (1980) 'Team teaching and the role of the ESP teacher', in British Council (691), pp. 23–37.

(606) Skeldon, P. and Swales, J. (1983) 'Working with service English timetables', *ELT Journal*, vol. 37, 2, pp. 138–44.

(607) Snow, M.A. and Brinton, D.M. (1988) 'Content-based language instruction: Investigating the effectiveness of the adjunct model', *TESOL Quarterly*, vol. 22, 4, pp. 553–74.

(608) Strevens, P. (1988) 'The learner and teacher of ESP', in Chamberlain and Baumgardner (6), pp. 39–44.

(609) Swales, J. (1984) 'Thoughts on, in and outside the classroom', in James (16), pp. 7–16.

(610) Swales, J. and L'Estrange, H. (1983) 'ESP administration and ESP teacher training', *ESP Journal*, vol. 2, 1, pp. 87–100.

(611) Tarone, E. (1983) 'Teacher training at the University of Minnesota compared to the Ewer model', *ESP Journal*, vol. 2, 1, pp. 68–70.

(612) Webb, J. (1981) Foreword to Lexden Centre (Oxford) Ltd (590).

(613) White, G. (1981) 'The subject specialist and the ESP teacher', in Lexden Centre (Oxford) Ltd (590), pp. 9–14.

(614) Williams, R. (1981) 'The potential benefits to the ESP profession from greater awareness of developments and practices in L1 Communication Skills learning', in British Council (550), pp. 90–5.

(I) Business English

(615) Ardo, Z. (1988) *English for Practical Management*, Oxford: Oxford University Press.

(616) Arthur, L. (1983) 'Survey review: Business English materials', *ELT Journal*, vol. 37, 2, pp. 166–75.

(617) Badger, I. (1989) 'Learning business English through self-instruction', unpublished MATEFL dissertation, University of Reading.

(618) Beresford, C. (1984) *Business Communication: Practical written English for the business world*, London: BBC English.

(619) Brieger, N. and Comfort, J. (1985) *Business Issues*, Hemel Hempstead: Prentice Hall.

(620) Brieger, N., Comfort, J., Hughes, S. and West, C. (1987) *Business Contacts*, Hemel Hempstead: Prentice Hall.

(621) Brieger, N. and Cornish, A. (1989) *Secretarial Contacts: Communication skills for secretaries and personal assistants*, Hemel Hempstead: Prentice Hall.

(622) Bruce, K. (1987) *Telephoning*, Harlow: Longman.

(623) Carrier, M. (1985) *Business Reading Skills*, Walton-on-Thames: Nelson.

(624) Casler, K. and Palmer, D. (1989) *Business Assignments*, Oxford: Oxford University Press.

(625) Comfort, J., Revell, R. and Stott, C. (1984) *Business Reports in English*, Cambridge: Cambridge University Press.

(626) Cotton, D. (1980) *International Business Topics*, London: Evans Brothers.

(627) Cotton, D. (1988) *Keys to Management*, Walton-on-Thames: Nelson.

(628)　Cotton, D. and McGrath, A. (1985) *Terms of Trade*, London: Edward Arnold.

(629)　Cotton, D. and Owen, R. (1980) *Agenda Casebook*, London: Harrap.

(630)　Coulton, T. and Rossiter, P. (1988) *Good Terms: Everyday English for professional people*, Filmscan Lingual House.

(631)　Cowcher, L. (1987) 'Cross-cultural sensitization: Some perspectives for business English courses', unpublished M.Sc. TESP dissertation, University of Aston in Birmingham.

(632)　Davies, S. *et al.* (1989) Bilingual handbooks of business correspondence and communication: English—French, English—German, English—Italian, English—Spanish, Hemel Hempstead: Prentice Hall.

(633)　Doherty, M., Knapp, L. and Swift, S. (1987) *Write for Business*, Harlow: Longman.

(634)　Ellis, M. and O'Driscoll, N. (1987) *Socializing*, Longman Business English Skills series, Harlow: Longman.

(635)　Ellis, M., O'Driscoll, N. and Pilbeam, A. (1984) *Professional English*, Harlow: Longman.

(636)　Goodale, M. (1987) *The Language of Meetings*, Hove, Sussex: Language Teaching Publications.

(637)　Goodale, M. (1987) *Meetings: Ten simulations on international topics*, Hove, Sussex: Language Teaching Publications.

(638)　Gowdridge, C. (1989) Unpublished MATEFL assignment on ESP, University of Reading.

(639)　Hanks, P. and Corbett, J. (1986) *Business Listening Tasks*, Cambridge: Cambridge University Press.

(640)　Hollett, V., Carter, R., Lyon, L. and Tanner, E. (1989) *In at the Deep End: Speaking activities for professional people*, Oxford: Oxford University Press.

(641)　Howe, B. (1987) *Portfolio*, Harlow: Longman.

(642)　Hughes, G., Pilbeam, A. and West, C. (1982) *Business Talk*, Harlow: Longman.

(643)　Jenkins, S. and Hinds, J. (1987) 'Business letter writing: English, French and Japanese'. *TESOL Quarterly*, vol. 21, 2, pp. 327—49.

(644)　Johns, A.M. (1980) 'Cohesion in written business discourse: Some contrasts', *ESP Journal*, vol. 1, 1, pp. 35—44.

(645)　Johns, A.M. (1987) 'The language of business', in Kaplan (161), pp. 3—17.

(646)　Jones, L. and Alexander, R. (1989) *International Business English*, Cambridge: Cambridge University Press.

(647)　Kerridge, D. (1988) *Presenting Facts and Figures*, Longman Business English Skills Series, Harlow: Longman.

(648)　Kitto, M. (1984) 'Understanding telex messages', *Reading in a Foreign Language*, vol. 2, 1, pp. 182—7.

(649)　Knowles, P.L. and Bailey, F. (1987) *Functioning in Business*, Harlow: Longman.

(650)　Lampi, M. (1986) 'Linguistic components of strategy in business negotiations', unpublished licentiate thesis, University of Jyvaskyla, Finland.

(651)　Land, G. (1986) *Business Reading*, Harlow: Longman.

(652)　Lees, G: (1983) *Negotiate in English*, London: Harrap.

(653)　Lees, G. (1984) 'The businessman and the language teacher', *World Language English*, vol. 3, 2, pp. 133—7.

(654)　Littlejohn, A. (1988) *Company to Company*, Cambridge: Cambridge University Press.

(655)　McGovern, J. and McGovern, J. (1984) *Bank on Your English: An elementary course in communication for bank employees*, Oxford: Pergamon.

(656)　Matthews, C. (1987) *Business Interactions*, Hemel Hempstead: Prentice Hall.

(657) Methold, K. and Tadman, J. (1982) *Office to Office: Practical business communication*, Harlow: Longman.

(658) Micheau, C. and Billmyer, K. (1987) 'Discourse strategies for foreign business students: Preliminary research findings', *English for Specific Purposes*, vol. 6, 2, pp. 87–97.

(659) Naterop, B.J. and Revell, R. (1987) *Telephoning in English*, Cambridge: Cambridge University Press.

(660) Neu, J. (1986) 'American-English business negotiations: Training for non-native speakers', *English for Specific Purposes*, vol. 5, 1, pp. 41–57.

(661) O'Driscoll, N. and Pilbeam, A. (1987) *Meetings and Discussions*, Longman Business English Skills Series, Harlow: Longman.

(662) Palstra, R. (1987) *Telephone English*, Hemel Hempstead: Prentice Hall.

(663) Palstra, R. (1988) *Telex English*, Hemel Hempstead: Prentice Hall.

(664) Pickett, D. (1989) 'The sleeping giant: Investigations in business English', *Language International*, vol. 1, 1, pp. 5–11.

(665) Poon, W. (1989) 'Language ability, motivation and learning habits of business students', in Bickley (2), pp. 100–11.

(666) Pote, M., Wright, D., Esnol, A., Lees, G. and Soulieux, R. (1985) *A Case for Business English*, Hemel Hempstead: Prentice Hall.

(667) Radice, F. (1981) *English for International Trade*, London: Evans Brothers.

(668) Radice, F. (1985) *Language for Banking*, London: Collins ELT.

(669) Rowlands, K.E. (1983) *Management Assignment*, London: Hodder & Stoughton.

(670) Sawyer-Lauçanno, C. (1987) *Case Studies in International Management*, Hemel Hempstead: Prentice Hall.

(671) Schleppegrell, M. and Royster, L. (1990) 'Business English: An international survey', *English for Specific Purposes*, vol. 9, 1, pp. 3–16.

(672) Scullion, M. (1987) *Managing People: An intermediate course in English for management*, London: Edward Arnold.

(673) Spiro, G. (1985) *Business Information*, London: Edward Arnold.

(674) Trickey, D. (1990) 'Management skills', a review of Casler and Palmer (624), *EFL Gazette*, March 1990, p. 23.

(675) White, G. and Khidhayir, M. (1983) *In Business*, London: Harrap.

(676) Williams, M. (1988) 'Language taught for meetings and language used in meetings: Is there anything in common?', *Applied Linguistics*, vol. 9, 1, pp. 45–58.

(677) Wilson, D. (1988) 'Business sense', a review of Littlejohn (654) and of Coulton and Rossiter (630), *EFL Gazette*, December 1988, p. 18.

(678) Wilson, M. (1987) *Writing for Business*, Walton-on-Thames: Nelson.

(679) Zak, H. and Dudley-Evans, T. (1986) 'Features of word-omission and abbreviation in telexes', *English for Specific Purposes*, vol. 5, 1, pp. 59–71.

(J) EAP (English for Academic Purposes)

(680) Adams Smith, D.E. (1981) 'Levels of questioning: Teaching creative thinking through ESP', *Forum*, vol. 19, 1, pp. 15–21.

(681) Adkins, A. and McKean, I. (1983) *Text to Note*, London: Edward Arnold.

(682) Alderson, J.C. and Lukmani, Y. (1989) 'Cognition and reading: Cognitive levels as embodied in test questions', *Reading in a Foreign Language*, vol. 5, 2, pp. 253–70.

(683) Anderson, P.L. (1986) 'English for academic listening: Teaching the skills associated

with listening to extended discourse', *Foreign Language Annals*, vol. 19, 5, pp. 391–7.

(684)   Armanet, C.M. and Obese-jecty, K. (1981) 'Towards student autonomy in the learning of English as a second language at university level', *ELT Journal*, vol. 36, 1, pp. 24–8.

(685)   Bachman, L. (1986) *Reading English Discourse: Business, economics, law and political science*, Englewood Cliffs, NJ: Prentice Hall.

(686)   Baltra, A. (1983) 'Learning how to cope with reading in English for academic purposes in 26 hours', *Reading in a Foreign Language*, vol. 1, 1, pp. 20–34.

(687)   Benson, M.J. (1989) 'The academic listening task: A case study', *TESOL Quarterly*, vol. 23, 3, pp. 421–45.

(688)   Blue, G. (1988) 'Individualising academic writing tuition', in Robinson (787), pp. 95–9.

(689)   Braine, G. (1988) 'A reader reacts . . .', *TESOL Quarterly*, vol. 22, 4, pp. 700–2.

(690)   British Council (1978) *Presessional Courses for Overseas Students*, ETIC Occasional Paper, London: The British Council.

(691)   British Council (1980) *Study Modes and Academic Development of Overseas Students*, ELT Document 109, London: The British Council.

(692)   Bruce, N.J. (1989) 'The roles of analysis and the conceptual matrix in a process approach to teaching academic study and communication skills', in Bickley (2), pp. 236–60.

(693)   Casey, F. (1985) *How to Study: A practical guide*, Basingstoke: Macmillan.

(694)   Cawood, G. (1978) 'Seminar strategies: Asking for repetition or clarification', in British Council (690), pp. 64–6.

(695)   Celia, M.H.C. (1984) 'Reading comprehension exercises: How to design process and product-oriented tasks', *ESPecialist*, no. 10, pp. 53–69.

(696)   Chaudron, C. and Richards, J.C. (1986) 'The effect of discourse markers on the comprehension of lectures', *Applied Linguistics*, vol. 7, 2, pp. 113–27.

(697)   Christison, M.A. and Krahnke, K.J. (1986) 'Student perceptions of academic language study', *TESOL Quarterly*, vol. 20, 1, pp. 61–81.

(698)   Collier, V.P. (1987) 'Age and rate of acquisition of second language for academic purposes', *TESOL Quarterly*, vol. 21, 4, 617–41.

(699)   Cooper, M. (1981) 'Aspects of the structure of written academic discourse and implications for the design of reading programmes', in Aupelf/Goethe Institut/British Council (1), pp. 47–65.

(700)   Cowie, A.P. and Heaton, J.B. (eds) (1977) *English for Academic Purposes*, University of Reading: BAAL/SELMOUS.

(701)   Currie, P. and Cray, E. (1987) *Strictly Academic: A reading and writing text*, New York: Newbury House.

(702)   Davies, F. (1988) 'Designing a writing syllabus in English for academic purposes: Process and product', in Robinson (787), pp. 130–42.

(703)   DeCarrico, J. and Nattinger, J.R. (1988) 'Lexical phrases for the comprehension of academic lectures', *English for Specific Purposes*, vol. 7, 2, pp. 91–102.

(704)   Deyes, T. (1987) 'Towards a minimum discourse grammar for ESP reading courses', *Reading in a Foreign Language*, vol. 3, 2, pp. 417–28.

(705)   Doushaq, M.H. (1986) 'An investigation into stylistic errors of Arab students learning English for academic purposes', *English for Specific Purposes*, vol. 5, 1, pp. 27–39.

(706)   Dudley-Evans, T. (1985) *Writing Laboratory Reports*, Melbourne, Australia: Nelson Wadsworth.

(707)   Dudley-Evans, T. (1988) 'A consideration of the meaning of "discuss" in examination

answers', in Robinson (787), pp. 47–52.

(708) Dunkel, P. (1988) 'The content of L1 and L2 students' lecture notes and its relation to test performance', *TESOL Quarterly*, vol. 22, 2, pp. 259–81.

(709) Dunkel, P., Mishra, S. and Berliner, D. (1989) 'Effects of note taking, memory, and language proficiency on lecture learning for native and nonnative speakers of English', *TESOL Quarterly*, vol. 23, 3, pp. 543–9.

(710) Edge, J. (1983) 'Reading to take notes and to summarize: A classroom procedure', *Reading in a Foreign Language*, vol. 1, 2, pp. 93–8.

(711) Evans, E.E. (1988) '"Advanced" ESL reading: Language competence revisited', *System*, vol. 16, 3, pp. 337–46.

(712) Floyd, J. (1984) *Study Skills for Higher Education*, Harlow: Longman.

(713) Foster, P. (1986) 'Negotiating the ELTS obstacle', *ESPMENA Bulletin*, 22, pp. 13–20.

(714) Frydenberg, G. (1982) 'Designing an ESP reading skills course', *ELT Journal*, vol. 36, 3, pp. 156–63.

(715) Furneaux, C., Locke, C., Robinson, P.C. and Tonkyn, A.P. (1991) 'Talking heads and shifting bottoms: The ethnography of seminars', in Adams, P., Heaton, J.B. and Howarth, P. (eds) *Socio-cultural Issues in English for Academic Purposes*, *Review of English Language Teaching*, vol. 1, 2, Basingstoke: Modern English Publications in association with the British Council, pp. 75–87.

(716) Glendinning, E. and Holmstrom, B. (1990) *Study Reading*, Cambridge: Cambridge University Press.

(717) Glendinning, E. and Mantell, H. (1983) *Write Ideas*, Harlow: Longman.

(718) Haarman, L., Leech, P. and Murray, J. (1988) *Reading Skills for the Social Sciences*, Oxford: Oxford University Press.

(719) Hall, D., Hawkey, R., Kenny, B. and Storer, G. (1986) 'Patterns of thought in scientific writing: A course in information structuring for engineering students', *English for Specific Purposes*, vol. 5, 2, pp. 147–60.

(720) Hall, D. and Kenny, B. (1988) 'An approach to a truly communicative methodology: The AIT pre-sessional course', *English for Specific Purposes*, vol. 7, 1, pp. 19–32.

(721) Hamp-Lyons, E. (1982) Review of EAP reading textbooks, *TESOL Quarterly*, vol. 16, 2, pp. 253–62.

(722) Hamp-Lyons, L. (1985) 'Two approaches to teaching reading: A classroom based study', *Reading in a Foreign Language*, vol. 3, 1, pp. 363–73.

(723) Hamp-Lyons, L. (1986) 'No new lamps for old yet, please', *TESOL Quarterly*, vol. 20, 4, pp. 790–6.

(724) Hamp-Lyons, L. (1988) 'The product before: Task-related influences on the writer', in Robinson (787), pp. 35–46.

(725) Hamp-Lyons, L. and Courter, K.B. (1984) *Research Matters*, Rowley, MA: Newbury House.

(726) Hamp-Lyons, L. and Heasley, B. (1984) 'Textbooks for teaching writing at the upper levels', *ELT Journal*, vol. 38, 3, pp. 209–15.

(727) Hamp-Lyons, L. and Heasley, B. (1987) *Study Writing*, Cambridge: Cambridge University Press.

(728) Hill, J.K. (1981) 'Effective reading in a foreign language: An experimental reading course in English for overseas students', *ELT Journal*, vol. 35, 3, pp. 270–81.

(729) Hill, S., Soppelsa, B. and West, G. (1982) 'Teaching ESL students to read and write experimental-research papers', *TESOL Quarterly*, vol. 16, 3, pp. 333–47.

(730) Holliday, A., Kary, A. and Zikri, M. (1990) 'Putting "constraints" first: Distance

learning adapted to a reading and writing course in difficult classroom conditions',
Occasional Papers in the Development of English Language Education, Cairo: Centre
for Developing English Language Teaching, Ain Shams University.

(731)   Holliday, A.R. and Zikri, M. (1988) 'Distance learning in large classes', *Appropriate
Methodology*, Proceedings of the 7th National Symposium on English Teaching in
Egypt, Cairo: Centre for Developing English Language Teaching, Ain Shams
University.

(732)   Horowitz, D. (1986) 'Essay examination prompts and the teaching of academic writing',
English for Specific Purposes, vol. 5, 2, pp. 107−20.

(733)   Horowitz, D. (1986) 'Process, not product: Less than meets the eye', *TESOL Quarterly*,
vol. 20, 1, pp. 141−4.

(734)   Horowitz, D. (1989) 'The undergraduate research paper: Where research and writing
meet', *System*, vol. 17, 3, pp. 347−57.

(735)   Howe, P.M. (1983) *Answering Examination Questions*, Glasgow: Collins ELT.

(736)   Huaiyuan, Y. (1988) 'Using seminar techniques to improve oral English: The Chinese
experience', *System*, vol. 16, 2, pp. 201−6.

(737)   James, D.V. (1989) *Medicine*, EAP series, London: Cassell.

(738)   James, K. (1984) *Speak to Learn: Oral English for academic purposes*, London and
Glasgow: Collins ELT.

(739)   James, K., Jordan, R.R. and Matthews, A. (1979) *Listening Comprehension and Note-
taking Course*, Glasgow: Collins ELT.

(740)   Johns, A.M. (1985) 'Summary protocols of "underprepared" and "adept" university
students: Replications and distortions of the original', *Language Learning*, vol. 35,
4, pp. 495−517.

(741)   Johns, A.M. (1986) 'Coherence and academic writing: Some definitions and suggestions
for teaching', *TESOL Quarterly*, vol. 20, 2, pp. 247−65.

(742)   Johns, A.M. (1988) 'Another reader reacts ...' *TESOL Quarterly*, vol. 22, 4,
pp. 705−7.

(743)   Johns, A.M. (1988) 'Reading for summarizing: An approach to text orientation and
processing', *Reading in a Foreign Language*, vol. 4, 2, pp. 79−90.

(744)   Johns, A.M. (1988) 'The discourse communities dilemma: Identifying transferable skills
for the academic milieu', *English for Specific Purposes*, vol. 7, 1, pp. 55−9.

(745)   Johns, C. (1978) 'Seminar discussion strategies', in British Council (690), pp. 60−3.

(746)   Johns, C. and Johns, T. (1977) 'Seminar discussion strategies', in Cowie and Heaton
(700), pp. 99−107.

(747)   Johns, T. and Davies, F. (1983) 'Text as a vehicle for information: The classroom
use of written texts in teaching reading in a foreign language', *Reading in a Foreign
Language*, vol. 1, 1, pp. 1−19.

(748)   Johnson, C.M. and Johnson, D. (1988) *General Engineering*, London: Cassell.

(749)   Johnson, K. (1981) *Communicate in Writing*, Harlow: Longman.

(750)   Jordan, R.R. (1980, 1990) *Academic Writing Course*, London: Collins.

(751)   Jordan, R.R. (1989) 'Engish for academic purposes (EAP)' [State of the art article],
Language Teaching, vol. 22, 3, pp. 150−64.

(752)   Jordan, R.R. (1990) 'Pyramid discussions', *ELT Journal*, vol. 44, 1, pp. 46−54.

(753)   Jordan, R.R. and Nixson, F.I. (1986) *Language for Economics*, Glasgow: Collins.

(754)   Kaplan, R.B. and Shaw, P. (1983) *Exploring Academic Discourse*, Rowley, MA:
Newbury House.

(755)   Kharma, N.N. (1981) 'An attempt to individualise the reading skill at Kuwait

University', *ELT Journal*, vol. 35, 4, pp. 398–404.

(756) Koh, M.Y. (1985) 'The role of prior knowledge in reading comprehension', *Reading in a Foreign Language*, vol. 3, 1, pp. 375–80.

(757) Lebauer, R. (1984) 'Using lecture transcripts in EAP lecture comprehension courses', *TESOL Quarterly*, vol. 18, 1, pp. 41–54.

(758) Liebman-Kleine, J. (1986) 'In defense of teaching process in ESL composition', *TESOL Quarterly*, vol. 20, 4, pp. 783–8.

(759) Long, M.H., Allen, W., Cyr, A., Pomeroy, C., Ricard, E., Spada, N. and Vogel, P. (1980) *Reading English for Academic Study*, Rowley, MA: Newbury House.

(760) Lynch, E.S. (1988) *Reading for Academic Success: Selections from across the curriculum*, New York: Collier Macmillan.

(761) Lynch, T. (1983) *Study Listening*, Cambridge: Cambridge University Press.

(762) Lynch, T. and Anderson, B. (1991) *Study Speaking*, Cambridge: Cambridge University Press.

(763) Lynes, C. and Woods, L. (1984) 'Teaching seminar skills', *The British Journal of Language Teaching*, vol. 22, 3, pp. 157–9.

(764) McDonough, J. (1978) *Listening to Lectures* (Computing, Sociology, Biology, Government), Oxford: Oxford University Press.

(765) McDonough, J. (1986) 'English for academic purposes: A research base?', *English for Specific Purposes*, vol. 5, 1, pp. 17–25.

(766) McEldowney, P. (1982) *English in Context*, Walton-on-Thames: Nelson.

(767) McGinley, K. (1985) 'Finding and using books: Using the library in ESP courses', *Forum*, vol. XXIII, 2, pp. 44–6.

(768) McKenna, E. (1987) 'Preparing foreign students to enter discourse communities in the US', *English for Specific Purposes*, vol. 6, 3, pp. 187–202.

(769) Mead, R. (1980) 'Expectations and sources of motivation in ESP', *English Language Research Journal*, no. 1, English Language Research, University of Birmingham, pp. 14–28.

(770) Mead, R. (1985) *English for Economics*, Harlow: Longman.

(771) Mohammed, M. and Swales, J. (1984) 'Factors affecting the successful reading of technical instructions', *Reading in a Foreign Language*, vol. 2, 2, pp. 206–17.

(772) Mohan, B.A. and Lo, W.A.-Y. (1985) 'Academic writing and Chinese students: transfer and development factors', *TESOL Quarterly*, vol. 19, 3, pp. 515–34.

(773) Montgomery, M. (1982) *Study Skills for Colleges and Universities in Africa*, Harlow: Longman.

(774) Morrow, K. and Johnson, K. (1979) *Communicate 1*, Cambridge: Cambridge University Press.

(775) Morrow, K. and Johnson, K. (1980) *Communicate 2*, Cambridge: Cambridge University Press.

(776) Nunes, M.B.C. (1988) 'Teaching reading and designing materials in mixed ability classes', *ESPecialist*, vol. 9, 1–2, pp. 299–320.

(777) O'Brien, T. and Jordan, R.R. (1985) *Developing Reference Skills*, London: Collins.

(778) Oshima, A. and Hogue, A. (1983) *Writing Academic English: A writing and sentence structure workbook for international students*, Reading, MA: Addison-Wesley.

(779) Oshima, A. and Hogue, A. (1988) *Introduction to Academic Writing*, Reading, MA: Addison-Wesley.

(780) Pearson, C.R. (1981) 'Advanced academic skills in the low-level ESL class', *TESOL Quarterly*, vol. 15, 4, pp. 413–23.

(781)   Price, J. (1978) 'Seminar strategies: Agreement and disagreement', in British Council (690), pp. 67–70.

(782)   Raimes, A. (1987) 'Language proficiency, writing ability, and composing strategies: A study of ESL college student writers', *Language Learning*, vol. 37, 3, pp. 439–68.

(783)   Ramani, E. (1988) 'Developing a course in research writing for advanced ESP learners', in Chamberlain and Baumgardner (6), pp. 45–53.

(784)   *Reading and Thinking in English* (1979, 1980), Oxford: Oxford University Press.

(785)   Reid, J.M. (1987) 'The learning style preferences of ESL students', *TESOL Quarterly*, vol. 21, 1, pp. 87–111.

(786)   Richards, J.C. (1983) 'Listening comprehension: Approach, design, procedure', *TESOL Quarterly*, vol. 17, 2, pp. 219–40.

(787)   Robinson, P.C. (ed.) (1988) *Academic Writing: Process and product*, ELT Document 129, Modern English Publications in association with the British Council.

(788)   Rornstedt, K. and McGory, J.T. (1988) *Reading Strategies for University Students*, New York: Collier-Macmillan.

(789)   Ruetten, M.K. (1986) *Comprehending Academic Lectures*, New York: Macmillan.

(790)   Salimbene, S. (1985) *Strengthen Your Study Skills!*, Rowley, MA: Newbury House.

(791)   Santos, T. (1988) 'Professors' reactions to the academic writing of nonnative-speaking students', *TESOL Quarterly*, vol. 22, 1, pp. 69–90.

(792)   Scott, M., Carioni, L., Zanatta, M., Bayer, E. and Quintanilha, T. (1984) 'Using a "standard exercise" in teaching reading comprehension', *ELT Journal*, vol. 18, 2, pp. 114–20.

(793)   Selinker, L. (1987) 'A note on research in an EAP writing clinic', *ESPMENA Bulletin*, no. 24, pp. 1–6.

(794)   Sinderman, G. and Horsella, M. (1989) 'Strategy markers in writing', *Applied Linguistics*, vol. 10, 4, pp. 438–46.

(795)   *Skills for Learning* (1980, 1981), Walton-on-Thames: Nelson, and University of Malaya Press.

(796)   Smithies, M. (1981) 'Formal style in an oral culture: Problems at the university level', *ELT Journal*, vol. 35, 4, pp. 369–72.

(797)   Smithies, M. (1983) 'Reading habits at a third-world technological university', *Reading in a Foreign Language*, vol. 1, 2, pp. 111–18.

(798)   Spack, R. (1988) 'Initiating ESL students into the academic discourse community: How far should we go?', *TESOL Quarterly*, vol. 22, 1, pp. 29–51.

(799)   Stevenson, J.L. and Sprachman, S. (1981) *Reading the Social Sciences in English*, London: Longman.

(800)   Swales, J. (1987) 'Using the literatures in teaching the research paper', *TESOL Quarterly*, vol. 21, 1, pp. 41–68.

(801)   Tredick, D.J. (1990) 'ESL writing assessment: Subject-matter knowledge and its impact on performance', *English for Specific Purposes*, vol. 9, 2, pp. 123–43.

(802)   Tyler, A.E., Jefferies, A.A. and Davies, C.E. (1988) 'The effect of discourse structuring devices on listener perceptions of coherence in non-native university teacher's spoken discourse', *World Englishes*, vol. 7, 2, pp. 100–10.

(803)   Ulijn, J.M. (1984) 'Reading for professional purposes: Psycholinguistic evidence in a cross-linguistic perspective', in Pugh and Ulijn (25), pp. 66–81.

(804)   Ulijn, J.M. 'A present state of LSP reading research as reflected by a recent symposium', in Ulijn and Pugh (37), pp. 12–24.

(805) Walker, C. (1987) 'Individualising reading', *ELT Journal*, vol. 41, 1, pp. 46–9.

(806) Wallace, M. (1980) *Study Skills in English*, Cambridge: Cambridge University Press.

(807) Weckert, C.W. (1989) 'The cultural and contextual constraints impinging upon overseas students studying at an Australian tertiary institution', in Bickley (2), pp. 60–9.

(808) Weissberg, R. and Buker, S. (1989) *Writing Up Research: Experimental research report writing for students of ESL/EFL*, Hemel Hempstead: Prentice Hall.

(809) Willes, M. (1989) 'Learning to study in English: Students' and university teachers' perceptions of the process', in Bickley (2), pp. 112–16.

(810) Williams, R. (1982) *Panorama*, Harlow: Longman.

(811) Williams, R. (1983) 'Teaching the recognition of cohesive ties in reading a foreign language', *Reading in a Foreign Language*, vol. 1, 1, pp. 35–53.

(812) Yates, C. St J. (1988) *Earth Sciences*, EAP series, London: Cassell.

(813) Yates, C. St J. (1989) *Agriculture*, EAP series, London: Cassell.

Index